Employment in America

Employment
in
America

Congressional Quarterly Inc.
1414 22nd Street N.W., Washington, D.C. 20037

Congressional Quarterly Inc.

Congressional Quarterly Inc., an editorial research service and publishing company, serves clients in the fields of news, education, business and government. It combines specific coverage of Congress, government and politics by Congressional Quarterly with the more general subject range of an affiliated service, Editorial Research Reports.

Congressional Quarterly publishes the *Congressional Quarterly Weekly Report* and a variety of books, including college political science textbooks under the CQ Press imprint and public affairs paperbacks designed as timely reports to keep journalists, scholars and the public abreast of developing issues and events. CQ also publishes information directories and reference books on the federal government, national elections and politics, including the *Guide to Congress*, the *Guide to the U.S. Supreme Court*, the *Guide to U.S. Elections* and *Politics in America*. The *CQ Almanac*, a compendium of legislation for one session of Congress, is published each year. *Congress and the Nation*, a record of government for a presidential term, is published every four years.

CQ publishes *The Congressional Monitor*, a daily report on current and future activities of congressional committees, and several newsletters including *Congressional Insight*, a weekly analysis of congressional action, and *Campaign Practices Reports*, a semimonthly update on campaign laws.

CQ conducts seminars and conferences on Congress, the legislative process, the federal budget, national elections and politics, and other current issues. CQ Direct Research is a consulting service that performs contract research and maintains a reference library and query desk for clients.

Library of Congress Cataloging in Publication Data

Main entry under title:

Employment in America.

    Bibliography: p.
    Includes index.
    1. Labor and laboring classes — United States — 1970- . I. Congressional Quarterly, inc.
HD8072.5.E46   1983   331.12'0973   83-10131
ISBN 0-87187-272-2

Editor: Nancy Lammers
Contributors: Tom Arrandale, Robert Benenson, Nancy A. Blanpied, Mary H. Cooper, Alan Ehrenhalt, Pamela Fessler, Hoyt Gimlin, Kathy Goodwin, Martha V. Gottron, Diane Granat, Richard Kipling, Marc Leepson, Mary L. McNeil, Michael R. Meyer, John L. Moore, Alan Murray, Andy Plattner, Jean Rosenblatt, Sandra Stencel, William Sweet, William V. Thomas, Roger Thompson, Elizabeth Wehr, Richard Worsnop
Designer: Mary L. McNeil
Cover: Richard A. Pottern
Graphics: Robert Redding
Photo Credits: American Petroleum Institute (cover), Uniphoto (cover), *St. Petersburg Times*, General Motors Corp., American Iron and Steel Institute, *The Washington Post*, Black Star/Ravi Arya, Department of Energy
Indexer: Elizabeth Furbush

Congressional Quarterly Inc.

Eugene Patterson *Editor and President*
Wayne P. Kelley *Publisher*
Peter A. Harkness *Deputy Publisher and Executive Editor*
Robert E. Cuthriell *Director, Research and Development*
Robert C. Hur *General Manager*
I. D. Fuller *Production Manager*
Maceo Mayo *Assistant Production Manager*
Sydney E. Garriss *Computer Services Manager*

Book Department

David R. Tarr *Director*
Joanne D. Daniels *Director, CQ Press*
John L. Moore *Assistant Director*
Michael D. Wormser *Associate Editor*
Martha V. Gottron *Associate Editor*
Barbara R. de Boinville *Senior Editor, CQ Press*
Nancy Lammers *Senior Editor*
Susan D. Sullivan *Developmental Editor, CQ Press*
Margaret C. Thompson *Senior Writer*
Carolyn Goldinger *Project Editor*
Janet E. Hoffman *Project Editor*
Mary L. McNeil *Project Editor*
Robert S. Mudge *Project Editor*
Patricia M. Russotto *Editorial Assistant*
Esther D. Wyss *Editorial Assistant*
Mary Ames Booker *Editorial Assistant*
Judith Aldock *Editorial Assistant*
Elizabeth H. Summers *Editorial Assistant*
Nancy A. Blanpied *Indexer*
Barbara March *Secretary*
Patricia Ann O'Connor *Contributing Editor*
Elder Witt *Contributing Editor*

Table of Contents

Tables, Charts and Graphs

PREFACE

With U.S unemployment levels reaching post-Depression highs in late 1982 and early 1983, political leaders, economists, business executives and journalists turned increasing attention to what was widely regarded as the nation's No. 1 problem: putting millions of Americans back to work.

The United States had experienced four recessions since the end of the boom period of the 1950s and 1960s. The last of the four appeared to be waning by the end of April 1983, with unemployment, which usually peaks toward the end of a recession, falling slightly to 10.2 percent from its 10.8 percent high in December 1982 and January 1983. Other factors signaled a recovery, and by the end of 1983's first quarter Martin S. Feldstein, chairman of President Ronald Reagan's Council of Economic Advisers, announced updated and rosier economic predictions for growth in the U.S. economy.

Regardless of the recovery's strength, experts were predicting that some people never would get their jobs back. History supported this view; after each of the more serious recessions unemployment settled to a level higher than it was before the downturn.

This phenomenon was attributed, at least in part, to the problem of "structural" unemployment. The U.S. economy was experiencing a slow but fundamental restructuring, changing from one based on factories and machines to one based on services and high-technology industries. As traditional smokestack industries struggled to compete with foreign competition, thousands of new companies — supported by venture capital — surged ahead, marketing state-of-the-art computer-related products.

Few analysts were willing to predict whether, in the end, all these changes would result in a net loss or gain of jobs. Most equivocated about whether the laid-off steel and auto workers would ever be retrained and finally rehired in unrelated, high-tech jobs. Certain areas of the country — most notably the industrial heartlands of the Midwest and Northeast — were straining to revamp their local economies to survive. Others, especially those in the Sun Belt, enjoyed the new affluence, at the same time trying to accommodate the influx of those who had deserted their homes elsewhere in the hopes of finding something better.

As the more than 500 members of Congress watched these developments, they tried to protect their jobless constituents and to anticipate their districts' or states' future needs. Bills were introduced to promote domestic industry, to create jobs, to avoid mortgage foreclosures, to retrain workers, to feed, clothe and house the unemployed, and more. President Reagan initially resisted these remedies, preferring instead to rely on the trickle-down effects from a healthy private industry. But finally, with high unemployment and a serious recession persisting, he yielded and signed some of the less drastic relief bills.

Employment in America examines these issues in detail, providing an overview of where the nation's economy was headed and how job opportunities were changing to meet these challenges. Drawing upon Congressional Quarterly's coverage of Capitol Hill, the book focuses on how Congress was dealing with the shift in employment trends.

The first chapter provides an overall picture of the nation's employment outlook, highlighting the growth and changes in the labor force as well as in the labor market. Chapter 2 focuses on the computer's development and the use of the microprocessor in automated manufacturing and robotics. The effects of foreign competition on U.S. industry, especially traditional industries such as automobiles and steel but also others such as textiles and agriculture, are covered in Chapter 3. The next chapter chronicles the history of U.S. jobs programs, concentrating on the discussions and legislative actions during the Reagan administration. The day-to-day problems of the unemployed — paying bills, feeding families, maintaining health insurance, and staying warm — and how Congress was attempting to help are the fifth chapter's subjects. The book's final chapter provides sketches of the country's various regions and describes how each was faring during the recession.

Nancy Lammers
May 1983

Employment in America

Computer operator mounts a magnetic tape that stores information on a text-processing system.

Chapter 1

THE U.S. EMPLOYMENT OUTLOOK

In a sober speech assessing the state of the union on Jan. 25, 1983, President Ronald Reagan confronted the nation's serious economic troubles. "Right now we need both realism and idealism," Reagan said as he acknowledged that curing the nation's economic problems had "taken more time, and a higher toll, than any of us wanted." Referring to the unemployment rate, which had reached post-World War II highs during his administration, the president continued, "Unemployment is far too high .... No domestic challenge is more crucial than providing stable, permanent jobs for all Americans who want to work."

Late in 1982 the American economy sank into its deepest recession since the Great Depression of the 1930s. The unemployment rate reached 10.8 percent in December 1982 before improving slightly in the early months of 1983. According to seasonally adjusted figures for February 1983, 11.5 million Americans who were looking for work were unable to find it. The numbers increased dramatically when one factored in those working part time who wanted full-time work and those who had become so discouraged that they had quit looking for work. At the end of February, 6.5 million individuals fit into the first category; the latest figures available for discouraged workers from the Bureau of Labor Statistics, as of December 1982, placed that number at 1.8 million workers.

Certain segments of the population were hit particularly hard. Black unemployment in February 1983 was 19.7 percent, black teenage unemployment 45.4 percent, and Hispanic joblessness 15.8 percent. Unemployment in the goods-producing sector — including construction, agriculture and manufacturing — also reached double digits. The impact was harshest in the industrial Great Lakes and Midwest states and in the timber-reliant Northwest. The deep slump in the auto industry by 1983

1

had put Michigan — with 699,000 people, or 16.5 percent of its work force, unable to find jobs — on a near-depression footing.

The problem of unemployment, or related economic ills, seemed to permeate the country. According to a September 1982 Gallup Poll, unemployment had become Americans' greatest worry. Of those surveyed, nearly half — 48 percent — singled out unemployment as the country's greatest problem, followed by the high cost of living at 23 percent. Eighty-five percent of the respondents to a similar survey conducted by Gallup in April 1982 said they would take a 10 percent pay cut to avoid a layoff and 77 percent said they would be unlikely to find a comparable job if they were laid off. For the first time in generations, a large majority of Americans appeared pessimistic about financial and career growth, for themselves and for the work force at large.

Recent history fostered the pessimism. Americans had watched the beginnings and ends of three recessions since the waning of the 1960s' economic boom and were in the midst of the fourth and worst. After each one, except for the relatively brief downturn during 1979 and 1980, the unemployment rate settled at a higher plateau. Basic industries such as automobile and steel had been battered and shrunken by foreign competition, high interest rates and burdensome costs. Depressed economic conditions had cut into airline traffic while operating costs spiraled upward. Two big international airlines — British-based Laker and Braniff International — went belly up in 1982 alone. International Harvester was teetering on the brink of bankruptcy throughout 1982. And the much-vaunted yet largely unknown technological explosion of computers and robots threatened thousands of workers lacking new skills.

Analysts spent much of 1982 revising their projections of economic recovery, pushing the expected date further and further into the future. Yet two hopeful signs that year were interest rates and inflation. The prime lending rate, which hovered around 16 percent for the first half of 1982, dropped in December to 11.5 percent. The Consumer Price Index also declined dramatically, rising only 3.9 percent in 1982, compared with 8.9 percent in 1981.

Aside from the high unemployment rate, the early months of 1983 brought additional hope for recovery. Surges in the leading economic indicators portended greater business activity. The expected economic recovery, if combined with reduced interest rates, was expected to release a pent-up demand for housing, cars and other durable goods.

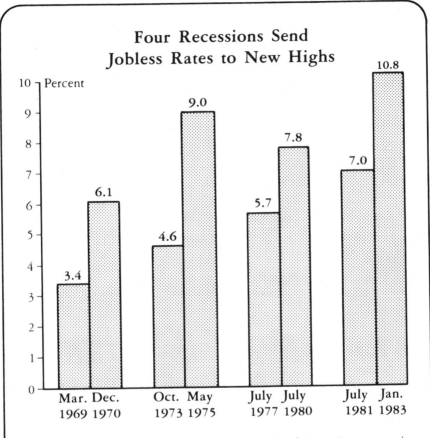

Four Recessions Send
Jobless Rates to New Highs

There have been four recessions since the end of the 1960s economic boom: 1969-70, 1974-75, 1979-80 and 1981-83. Except for the relatively brief 1979-80 economic downturn, each recession has sent unemployment to new highs. The months selected for this graph represent the pre-recession lows in unemployment and the recession highs.

Source: U.S. Department of Labor, Bureau of Labor Statistics

Employment levels in the basic industries were not likely to return to pre-recession levels, but a growing number of experts held that the economy was experiencing a fundamental change, which eventually would result in a net gain of jobs in the high-technology and service industries. President Reagan appeared to place increasing confidence in this view, heralding in his 1983 State of the Union address the country's pioneer spirit that was "opening up another vast frontier of opportunity — the frontier of high technology."

U.S. Labor Market Evolves

Changes in the size and composition of the labor force occurred at a rapid pace since the Great Depression. According to the BLS, about 112 million Americans were employed or actively sought work in February 1983, a figure larger than the entire U.S. population in 1920. The civilian labor force was more than twice that of 1940 (52.7 million) and was up from 82.7 million in 1970. The labor force of the 1980s was composed not only of the traditional working male, but also of about half of the adult women, and an unprecented number of young people, products of the post-World War II baby boom.

Labor Force Grows, Changes

World War II had profound effects on the U.S economy, and on the composition of the labor force. The war effort opened millions of new jobs to women, and female workers entered the labor force as never before. They accounted for 36 percent of the nation's jobholders in 1945, up from 25 percent in 1940. In general, employers' attitudes toward women workers were skeptical, but since women were the only available labor, they were hired.

Then the United States emerged from World War II victorious, its territory unscathed, its international reputation enhanced and, after years of prewar depression, its industries healthy. The country was, in the words of President Harry S Truman's 1949 State of the Union address, "better able than ever before to meet the needs of the American people and to give them their fair chance in the pursuit of happiness."

For many Americans the pursuit of happiness seemed to entail starting a family. Many of those women who had spent the war years in traditionally male civilian jobs withdrew from the labor force. Whether because of patriotism ("let the vet have the job"), traditional values or prejudice against women in the work force, women left the business world to men — and went home.

High birth rates are a traditional byproduct of a war's aftermath, yet America's postwar baby boom was exceptional in its duration and intensity. Annual births jumped from 2.9 million in 1945 to 3.4 million in

Nuances of the Unemployment Figures

On the first Friday of each month, the Bureau of Labor Statistics (BLS) releases the official national unemployment statistics. The figures are extrapolated from the results of interviews conducted with 60,000 households across the country, with greater attention given to heavily industrialized areas.

The unemployment rate is the percentage of the labor force that is looking for work but cannot find it. The labor force is the sum total of all those people who want to work, whether they are employed or unemployed.

Employed workers are those who have worked at least one hour for pay in the week on which the survey interviews are based. Unemployed workers are defined as persons who have not worked at all in that week, but who have sought work within the previous four weeks. People who have not looked for work within the previous four weeks are called discouraged workers, and they are not counted either as unemployed or as part of the labor force.

For differing reasons, both liberals and conservatives attacked the government's method for calculating unemployment. Labor organizations said the unemployment rate was underestimated, that it should include both discouraged workers and those part-time workers who would take full-time work if it were available to them.

Many conservatives countered that the unemployment rate was exaggerated. They asserted that programs instituted since the Great Depression, such as unemployment insurance, supplemental unemployment benefits and, in some cases, union- or employer-funded benefits, took much of the sting out of unemployment. These benefits, they said, provided many unemployed workers with the leeway of rejecting undesirable employment in favor of waiting for better opportunities.

Others contended that the growing number of two-income families had made rising unemployment less of a disaster. Some conservatives even called for replacement of the unemployment index with a distress index, including only those workers who were in or who were threatened by severe financial distress because of unemployment.

1946, but the peak actually occurred almost 10 years later, in 1957, with 4.3 million births reported.

Much of the economic growth in the postwar era was attributed to the baby boom. The needs of the new generation — housing, schools, services, durable and consumer goods — worked to expand the economy. Many married women with children started back to work to help meet these rising costs. Although the portion of female workers fell to 28 percent right after the war, thousands of housewives soon took full- or part-time jobs to supplement family incomes.

The women's movement, the anti-discriminatory legislation enacted during the 1960s, and the eventual instability of the economy all contributed to the record numbers of women entering the work force in the 1960s and 1970s. By 1966, 40.3 percent of the adult female population was in the work force; by 1976 the percentage had increased to 47.4. The BLS reported that 52.9 percent of the American women were working during February of 1983. Of the 112 million people in the labor force, 48 million — or 43 percent — were women.

In 1982 virtually the entire baby boom population also was in the labor force, with profound effects on society. During the 1970s, the labor force grew by 22 million, compared with 12 million in the 1960s and 7.5 million in the 1950s. While many of the women entering the work force were of the baby-boom generation, older women also sought work, often creating an inter-generational competition for entry-level positions. "Mothers are competing with their kids, because they need a job," said Sar Levitan, an economics professor at George Washington University in Washington, D.C. He also served as chairman of the National Council on Employment Policy, a research organization of labor scholars who study manpower and employment training issues.

Some economists attributed the nation's continued high unemployment rate to the influx of women and people born during the baby boom into the labor force. Even President Reagan, speaking before a group of editors and broadcasters in April 1982, blamed high unemployment rates, in part, on the expansion of the work force. "Part of the unemployment is not as much recession as it is the great increase in the people going into the job market, and, ladies, I'm not picking on anyone, but because of the increase in women who are working today and two-worker families and so forth," Reagan said.

But with many single and divorced women needing to support themselves, and many married women defending their families against

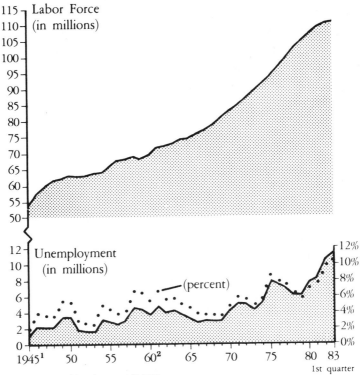

Civilian Labor Force and Unemployment

¹ Persons 14 years old and over, 1945-1959
² Persons 16 years old and over, 1960-1983

The chart illustrates the growth of the civilian labor force against the fluctuations in unemployment figures. Variations between the percentage of unemployment and the actual number of jobless persons are due to the steadily increasing size of the labor force. For example, unemployment figures indicate that nearly two million more people were out of work in 1974 than in 1960, but the percentage of unemployment stood at 5.5 percent for both years because the labor force had grown by 1974.

Source: U.S. Bureau of the Census, *Statistical Abstract of the United States.* Washington, D.C.

inflation and layoffs of male "breadwinners," women were working out of necessity. "The only justification for those who, for political advantage, try to blame our high unemployment rate primarily on the spectacular influx of women into the labor force is that at least they have pinpointed a profound change in the labor force," wrote financial columnist Sylvia Porter. "...Their explanation shrugs off the vital importance of the woman's paycheck to prosperity and to the standard of living of millions of households."

Nevertheless, the economy was strained and there were more people than jobs. Competition for jobs and career advancement was expected to remain intense for those in the 25-to-44 age bracket. Some economists saw reason for optimism in the lower birth rates of the 1960s and 1970s. The labor force, which grew by about 2.5 percent each year in the late 1970s, was expected to expand by only 1.5 percent by the late 1980s. Given a healthy national economy and normal retirement rates by older workers, these economists believed that there should be more jobs to go around and less competition for entry-level positions.

These general statistics meant little to the person who was unemployed or who feared for his or her job in 1983. Many of these people were members of the goods-producing sector of the economy: manufacturing, construction, agriculture. Although the proportion of Americans employed in production jobs had fallen precipitously, from over 80 percent in 1920 to under 33 percent in 1982, many of the jobs in the booming information and service sectors were dependent on the goods-producers.

New Demands on Workers

The manufacturing and construction industries were particularly hard hit by the economic vagaries of the 1970s and 1980s.

Dramatic energy price increases, generous wage-and-benefit packages demanded and received by unionized workers, environmental and safety regulations, and, in some cases, lack of sound management added burdensome costs. Many manufacturers raised prices, making their goods less competitive against cheaper foreign imports. High interest rates resulting from big federal deficits and Carter and Reagan administration attempts to control inflation further crippled demand for big ticket items, such as cars and homes.

In the latest recession, beginning in mid-1981 and continuing in early 1983, adult male blue-collar workers made up the bulk of the

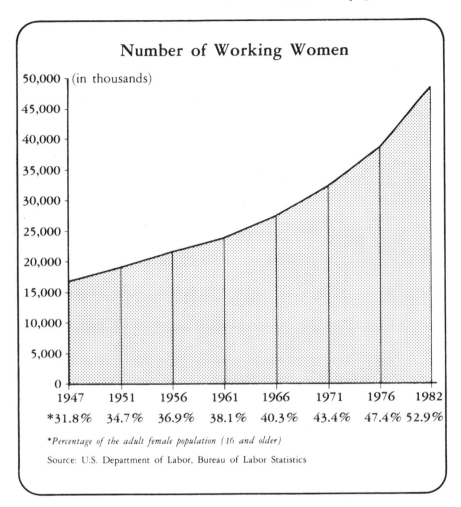

Number of Working Women

50,000 (in thousands)

	1947	1951	1956	1961	1966	1971	1976	1982
*Percentage	31.8%	34.7%	36.9%	38.1%	40.3%	43.4%	47.4%	52.9%

*Percentage of the adult female population (16 and older)

Source: U.S. Department of Labor, Bureau of Labor Statistics

increase in unemployment. While adult males comprised 25.2 percent of the unemployed in 1978, they accounted for 34.5 percent — more than a third — of the jobless in 1982. Their joblessness reflected the recession's severe impact on the nation's industrial base — steel and autos in particular — and its effects on the mainstream of America's work force. In the auto industry alone, over 200,000 jobs were lost between 1978 and 1982. In December 1982, 22 percent of those in construction, 18.1 percent of those in mining, 17.1 percent of those in durable goods manufacturing and 16.5 percent of those in agriculture were out of work. *(Chart on 1982 average unemployment rates by industry, p. 11)*

The general perception among labor economists was that prospects for recovery in the construction industry during 1983 were fairly bright if interest rates continued to decline. The nation's housing market, entering the fourth year of its worst slump since World War II, was viewed as being on the brink of a modest recovery in early 1983. Housing industry economists predicted that new home construction would reach 1.36 million units in 1983, as against 1982's estimated total of 1.05 million units.

This was particularly good news because each housing start generated jobs in related fields, such as appliance manufacturing. "The construction industry is very cyclical ... eventually construction will come back in terms of employment and employment growth," said Neal H. Rosenthal, director of the BLS Occupational Outlook Division.

The manufacturing situation was more complicated. Continued foreign competition was expected to hinder a full recovery in the "basic" industries, such as autos, steel and rubber. Industry leaders said that their future competitiveness depended on reducing labor costs and modernizing, in the fashion of the Japanese, and on introducing robots and other computer-controlled equipment into the factories. Labor leaders admitted that there never would be as many jobs in the basic industries as there were prior to 1980. "Even if the auto companies make a complete comeback and exceed the production level of 1973, they would be doing it with fewer people," United Auto Workers President Douglas A. Fraser was quoted as saying in the May 3, 1982, *U.S. News & World Report.*

How many fewer people was the question that frightened blue-collar workers. Already robots had replaced workers, to a very limited degree, particularly in hazardous occupations, such as spray painting, welding, and handling hot or otherwise dangerous materials. But as robots were made more sophisticated and capable of performing complex jobs, many workers feared they would be replaced and relegated to the ranks of the "structurally unemployed." A 1981 study by Carnegie-Mellon University said that by 1990 robots could displace 1 million workers in the automotive, electrical-equipment, machinery and fabricated-metals industries.

Cyclical unemployment is caused by the ups and downs in the economy, but structural unemployment affects workers who are unable to find a job because of individual characteristics, including skill levels, education, or discrimination based on factors such as race, ethnic background or sex. Many blue-collar workers feared their skills would

Unemployment Rate by Industry
1982 Average

Total	8.3
Mining	17.3
Construction	17.5
Manufacturing	10.6
Durable goods	10.9
Non-durable goods	10.2
Transportation, Communications, Public Utilities	6.4
Wholesale and Retail Trade	9.4
Finance, Insurance and Real Estate	4.4
Service Industries	6.2
Public Administration	4.0

Source: U.S. Department of Labor, Bureau of Labor Statistics

not be valuable or needed in the restructured economy envisioned by some economists.

The congressional Joint Economic Committee warned in its 1976 annual report that structural unemployment was not easily remedied:

> Eliminating cyclical unemployment requires recovery of the economy. Dealing with structural unemployment requires not only adequate overall job opportunities, it also means providing workers with remedial education, job training or retraining, psychological assistance, motivation, and placement assistance to help them compete in the job market.

President Reagan's Council of Economic Advisers, in its 1983 economic report to Congress, estimated that even with an eventual recovery, unemployment would hover around 6 or 7 percent. Many jobs, it claimed, would be permanently lost because of structural changes in the economy. Reagan proposed in March 1983 several programs to relieve structural unemployment. *(p. 95)*

There was much apocalyptic talk of "jobs that won't come back," of busy machines and idle hands. Yet many economists and industry experts said the rhetoric was exaggerated. For one thing, robot and computer technology on a large scale remained expensive. Joseph Engleberger, president of the robot-building Unimation Inc., estimated that replacement of just 5 percent of all of the blue-collar jobs in the Western nations would cost $120 billion over the next 40 years. Also, few, if any, industries could afford to plunge quickly into new technologies if they rendered thousands or millions of dollars worth of equipment and factories obsolete.

Some observers believed that the issue was not how many jobs robots would cost, but how many they would save. "... The most cogent response to those concerned with robots threatening jobs is that, without robots, jobs in many industries will disappear altogether," wrote Philip Lynch, the Australian minister for industry and commerce, in *The New York Times* of April 26, 1982. "Without the use of robots, a manufacturer will be unable to compete effectively."

Other economists predicted that demand for workers in the high-technology industries would soar. They pointed out that if there were going to be a lot of robots and computers in factories, workers would be needed to build, maintain and repair them. This has been the historic pattern of American industry: new types of business spring up to replace fading or obsolete ones. "The economy basically will grow over the next decade," said Rosenthal of the BLS. "Some of the workers who are displaced and are unable to get back into the industry they are in will be able to get jobs in other industries."

Levitan of the National Council on Employment Policy agreed. "People are very flexible," he told Congressional Quarterly in the spring of 1982. "You start a new industry, and you may think there will be a [labor] shortage, but when you have the demand, industry can train and can restructure jobs, and the people are absorbed."

However, the transition Levitan described was complicated by the recession. "It's going to be harder and slower and much more painful now, because we don't have a growth economy just sucking people out of declining industries," said Audrey Freedman, senior economist for the Conference Board, a New York-based group that conducts research and publishes studies on business and economics. Economists also pointed

BLOOM COUNTY   by Berke Breathed

out that many workers tend to attach their identities to a certain job or trade and are unwilling to accept the reality that their jobs may be gone forever.

Retraining Workers for 'High-Tech' Jobs

President Reagan caused a flap when he remarked at a news conference early in his administration that the newspapers were full of help-wanted ads, implying that jobs could be had for the asking. Critics countered that most of the jobs available were for highly skilled, highly trained workers such as engineers, technicians and computer experts. For example, career supplements to *The Washington Post* were dominated in 1982 by full- and half-page advertisements for high-technology companies such as Sperry, General Electric, American Satellite Co., MCI Telecommunications, and Planning Research Corporation seeking senior programmers, electronics engineers, microwave path engineers, software engineers and other technical workers.

These jobs, and others like them, demanded specific technical training, training that the average unemployed steelworker lacked. Most observers believed that the United States urgently needed to retrain workers in aging industries for the "high technology" revolution expected to sweep America. "We have to retrain the millions whose current jobs can be kissed goodbye and who will be needed for new work," wrote well-known labor analyst Pat Choate and journalist Noel Epstein, in *The Washington Post* on May 9, 1982.

According to some, the expected industrial changes were likely to be so drastic that industry alone would not be able to handle the training task. Choate and Epstein suggested the establishment of "Individual

13

Training Accounts." Employees and employers would each place $500 a year for six years into a trust fund, to be used for retraining if a worker's job disappeared. The money would be returned to the worker, plus interest, if not used by retirement.

The ruling assumption among many of those who advocated intensive retraining programs was that because the products of high technology were sophisticated and complicated, each of the jobs involved in their production also would be. Levitan rejected this concept. "The idea that the new technologies necessarily require higher skills and that anybody without a Ph.D. becomes obsolescent in the new age is simply exaggerated . . .because the new technologies create a great many jobs that require few skills," he said.

As an example, Levitan described the situation in the health care industry, which had expanded greatly during the 1960s and 1970s. "The health industry obviously created the need for more doctors, more nurses, and some technical people, who are also skilled workers," Levitan said. "But it also created lots of jobs for pan-carriers, people to feed the patients in the hospital and whatever menial jobs there were."

Congress devoted considerable attention to the issue of retraining during the 97th and 98th Congresses. To replace the Comprehensive Employment and Training Act, originally enacted in 1973, Congress and President Reagan agreed finally upon the Job Training Partnership Act to take effect Oct. 1, 1983. The new program authorized by the bill provided training in job skills to the low-income unemployed, with special provisions aimed at workers who had lost their jobs and were unlikely to get them back, for example because of the permanent closing of a factory.

With unemployment reaching new heights in early 1983, President Reagan sent to Congress March 11 a proposal designed to relieve structural unemployment, which included proposals to lower the minimum wage for young workers and to provide a job voucher program for the longer-term unemployed. Reagan stated that the "government can play an important role in assisting three groups of structurally unemployed workers: the long-term unemployed, displaced workers, and youth." *(Proposals, p. 103)*

Where the Jobs Will Be

There was little doubt that those entering the job market were likely to be more successful if they had received technological training. While many college graduates of the early 1980s faced bleak job prospects, engineering graduates, for example, were among the few students being aggressively recruited. *Time* magazine reported in its May 10, 1982, issue that of the 65,000 men and women scheduled to graduate that year with B.S. degrees in engineering, 80 percent would begin work immediately. Average starting salaries reflected the demand, ranging between $21,000 and $30,000.

The 1982-83 *Occupational Outlook Handbook* published by BLS projected faster-than-average growth in almost all engineering fields. Electrical engineering was the largest of the engineering occupations, employing 325,000 people who design and develop electrical and electronic equipment. As demand for computers, communications technology, advanced weaponry and business and consumer goods grew, electrical engineering was expected to boom. The drive for improved production methods was expected to enhance job possibilities for mechanical and industrial engineers. As the defense buildup got under way, aerospace engineering was expected to prosper. The search for additional domestic energy sources was likely to increase demand for petroleum and mining engineers. Other engineering specialties expected to grow included agricultural, biomedical, ceramic, chemical, civil and metallurgical. *(Job prospects box, p. 22)*

A great deal of overlap existed between the engineering and computer industries. Engineers used computers in many capacities, while electrical engineers designed the silicon chips, microprocessors and other components that made today's and tomorrow's computer applications possible. The BLS "Occupational Outlook Quarterly" issued in summer 1981 said that employment of computer and peripheral operators would more than double by 1990. The College Placement Council in Bethlehem, Pa., reported April 27, 1982, that graduating computer science majors were receiving average salary offers of $22,572.

In gross numbers, the greatest demand was likely to be for computer programmers, the people who prepare the coded instructions that tell the computer what to do. There were expected to be 500,000 positions for programmers in 1990, double the 247,000 programming jobs that existed in 1978. Demand also was expected to double for systems analysts, who develop customized plans for data processing and handling. Around 400,000 systems analysts likely will be needed by 1990, up from 182,000 in 1978. The greatest percentage growth in the computer field was projected to be in the area of computer service. With 5 million computer terminals expected to be installed by 1983 alone, the number of service technicians was expected to grow to at least 160,000 by 1990, a 154 percent increase over 1978.

Shortage of Qualified Technical Workers

The need for people trained in scientific and technical subjects was not limited to the engineering and computer fields. For example, as the population got larger and grew older, health care technicians would be in great demand. And as modern weaponry and equipment became more computerized, soldiers would have to be more technologically oriented.

While labor economists projected millions of job openings in technical fields, it did not necessarily follow that there would be enough trained, qualified people to fill them. A great deal of concern existed that the United States was lacking in its abilities to train students and workers in math, science and technical subjects. Some observers foresaw a "knowledge gap," resulting in severe shortages of labor in vital technological fields.

According to an article prepared by the Communications Workers of America for a career supplement to *The Washington Post* published in April 1982, "Top-flight designers, engineers and programmers will be in increasingly short supply as the industry grows." A report prepared for former California Gov. Edmund G. Brown Jr. stated that the electronics industry in that state would have 62,000 openings for electrical and computer scientists by 1987, but that only 14,000 qualified students would graduate from the state's universities during that period.

To an extent, the high-technology fields were victims of their own prosperity. Professors with doctorates in engineering or the computer sciences were lured from the classroom into private industry by big salary offers. Even graduates with bachelor's degrees were being offered salaries commensurate with those of professors who had two to five more years of schooling.

Some observers remarked that technicians, in a way, were eating their own "seed corn." Defections of Ph.D.s and the reluctance of graduates to pursue teaching careers cut down on the size and quality of faculties. At least half of all graduate engineering students were foreigners, many of whom took their skills back to their homelands. At the same time, more undergraduate students wanted technological training, resulting in larger class size and less individual instruction.

George A. Keyworth II, Reagan's White House science adviser, said proposed basic federal research funding included in the 1984 budget proposal would be directed to universities. "University research is important for its ability to push back frontiers of science; but university research is equally important because it directly produces the next generation of research scientists and engineers," he said.

To combat faculty shortages in critical fields, the 1984 budget proposed creating Presidential Young Investigator Awards. These five-year National Science Foundation grants, designed to lure new Ph.D.s away from careers in industry, would provide a new faculty member with up to $100,000 a year for research, with half the money coming from private sources.

Quality of Math and Science Teaching

People also expressed concern that the quality of mathematics and science teaching in the nation's elementary and secondary schools was inferior to that offered in other industrialized countries such as Japan and West Germany. Stanford University Professor Emeritus Paul DeHart Hurd told a National Convocation on Precollege Education in Mathematics and Science, sponsored by the National Academy of Sciences in Washington on May 12, 1982, that only one-third of all high school students took as much as three years of math and that half of all math and science teachers were "unqualified."

Dr. Harry Lustig, dean for science at City College of New York, told *The New York Times* that 12 percent of all math teachers in New York City were not certified to teach that subject in 1981. The problem paralleled what was happening on the college level, since starting salaries for math teachers were $10,000 less than for computer programmers. "Anybody who can master enough math to be a math teacher certainly can master enough to be a computer programmer," Lustig said in the April 6, 1982, issue.

Observers also worried that the decline in math and science skills threatened economic growth and national security. President Reagan, in a written message, told the National Academy of Sciences conference that problems in math and science teaching were "serious enough to compromise the nation's future ability to develop and advance our traditional industrial base to compete in international marketplaces." Many academics and commentators concurred. "I see us becoming industrially a second-rate power," said Dr. Lustig. "I see us losing our lead in health research and basic science, in military science." Itek Corp.

17

Chairman Robert P. Henderson wrote in the March 1982 issue of *Enterprise*: "If this state of affairs is allowed to continue, high technology imports will increase, and the one bright spot in today's U.S. economy will go the way of automobiles, TV sets and shoes."

In the late 1950s, following the Soviet launching of the first space satellite Sputnik, American leaders rushed to bolster the nation's science and math teaching, funding university research and development projects, providing scholarships and otherwise encouraging young people to enter technological careers. Many people in the early 1980s advocated a similar federal investment, but the Reagan administration initially opposed such an effort. "We disagree with those who say that the federal government should be ultimately responsible for this problem," presidential policy adviser Edwin L. Harper told the National Academy of Sciences meeting. Science education funds were slashed in the Reagan administration's first two budgets.

But to reverse what it called a "disturbing decline in the quality of science and math learning in America," the administration said it would propose for fiscal 1984 two new programs to make secondary school teachers more proficient in math and science. A proposed National Science Foundation program would encourage up to 10,000 science and math teachers each year to take additional courses in math, natural sciences and computer science. An Education Department program would provide block grants to local school districts to train additional science and math teachers. Congress also was considering in early 1983 its own, more generous, programs to aid science and math education. On March 2, the House of Representatives authorized $425 million in fiscal 1984 to improve math, science and foreign language education. The Senate had not acted by mid-May.

Private industry was partially responsible for the supposed crisis in science and math education, having coaxed away many present and future instructors with generous pay offers. By 1983 some corporations had started to make amends. For example, the Exxon Foundation donated $15 million to help engineering schools get and keep faculty members, and Motorola gave $1.2 million to Arizona State University's engineering program. "Industry must be willing to invest in long-term educational goals, even if it means leaving some of the best engineering students and faculty in the university," wrote Henry Petroski, a Duke University associate professor of civil and environmental engineering, in a Jan. 21, 1982, *Washington Post* article.

Although many universities were pressed by government aid cutbacks and declining overall enrollments, it was possible that the institutions would act to correct the situation on their own. Noting jokingly that schools might decide that an engineering professor was worth more than an economics professor, Levitan said, "The marketplace can take care of itself."

While much was being said about the problems in science and math instruction, many economists were even more concerned about the overall decline in education. The 18-member National Commission on Educational Excellence, which began work in 1981, warned in its report released in April 1983 of a "tide of mediocrity that threatens our very future as a nation." The blue-ribbon commission of educators estimated some 23 million American adults were functionally illiterate "by the simplest tests of everyday reading, writing, and comprehension." Approximately 13 percent of all high school seniors, and up to 40 percent of minority youths, also were considered functionally illiterate.

Casting its recommendations as a patriotic plea for the country to rescue its battered educational system or risk slipping into scond-place status among industrial nations, the commission called for seven-hour school days, 200- to 220-day school years, much more homework and tougher standards for teachers along with higher pay. Analyst Paul Copperman, who was quoted in the report, predicted: "Each generation of Americans has outstripped its parents in education, in literacy, and in economic attainment. For the first time in the history of our country, the educational skills of one generation will not surpass, will not equal, will not even approach, those of their parents."

At the same time, debt-ridden school systems had cut back on technical and support personnel and programs. The impact of education cutbacks was expected to continue to fall most heavily on those at the bottom of the labor market: minorities and the poor. Many economists were concerned that growing numbers of Americans would be locked out of the job market or locked into low-paying, dead-end jobs.

White-Collar Work Force

Discussions of future employment opportunities centered on the plight of factory workers or the rosy future in high-technology fields. However, the largest single group of workers was made up not of technicians or laborers, but of white-collar workers. Clerical workers alone — secretaries, typists, bookkeepers, clerks and so on — constituted the largest occupational group in the BLS breakdown. Speaking before a 1982 conference on office work and new technology, labor expert Karen Nussman said, "The typical American worker is no longer a man in a hard hat. She is a woman at the typewriter — or, rather, at a keyboard."

In 1980 there were 18.9 million clerical workers in the United States. Although the anticipated percentage growth of 18-27 percent projected for 1990 was not as big as in some other fields, the total number of new clerical jobs, 3.5-5 million, was the largest of any occupation.

The era of technological innovation sweeping the laboratory and the factory was changing the face of the office as well. Electronic word processors were replacing typewriters; whole inventories and filing systems were being placed in easily accessible computer systems; people and businesses were linked with each other and with all sorts of "information banks" by telephone lines; and the advent of personal and home computers had freed some people from the office routine altogether. The word "paperwork" someday could be obsolete, as businesses moved toward the era of the "paperless office."

Many business executives were enthusiastic about advances in office technology. The elimination of reams of paper, smoother work-flow arrangements, and easy accessibility of information led observers to predict greater productivity, profits and growth. Some labor experts also saw computerization as improving the quality of work life at the office. The most tedious tasks, such as typing letters or filing invoices, would be simplified and speeded by the labor-saving capabilities of the computer. The lack of "busy-work" could free clerical workers for more creative assignments.

As in the factory, though, there was a negative view. Labor officials were concerned that growth in information needs and the greater worker-monitoring capacity that computers afforded actually could lead to the creation of more routine and stressful jobs. As workers communicated more with machines and less with people, feelings of isolation could grow. "Think of the alienation of the blue-collar assembly workers, and that's exactly what's being done ... for 20 million Americans who work as clericals," said Karen Nussbaum of the Service Employees International Union, in the Feb. 22, 1982, *U.S. News & World Report*.

There also was concern about the health effects of working with video display terminals (VDT). In the classic study conducted by the National Institute for Occupational Safety and Health during 1979-80, it was found that clerical workers suffered more from the established VDT health hazards — eyestrain, muscle aches, high levels of anxiety, fatigue, and even depression — than VDT users such as reporters and editors did.

A group called 9 to 5, the National Association of Working Women, was becoming increasingly active in advocacy work for clerical employees. Two features under scrutiny by 9 to 5, alleged to increase the stress of clerical workers, were computer monitoring and speedups. Some computers were equipped with features that allowed supervisors to monitor the performance of the employee, including the pace of work reached or the number of errors committed. Speedups were computer-induced increases in the amount of work required of operators, often begun when the workload was heavy.

Many office workers worried about being replaced by computers. Business officials, citing the need for more and different kinds of information and the expansion possibilities inherent in higher productivity, said that automation would not make clerical workers obsolete. According to John J. Connell of the California-based Office Technology Research Group, as quoted in the Nov. 10, 1982, *Washington Post*, "[T]he purpose of technology should no longer be the loss of jobs, but the extension of their capabilities." Pessimists, however, cited several European studies, including one that forecast a 30 percent job loss in France's banking and insurance industries.

There was also the question of whether enough workers would be trained in the office skills of the computer age. "Within a few years, the ability to program and use computers may be as important as being able to read, write, type, drive, or use the telephone," *The Futurist* magazine noted in its August 1981 issue. Rosenthal of the BLS expressed the belief that these predictions might be unfounded. Noting that in his own office secretaries went from standard to electric typewriters to word processors, Rosenthal said: "Their skills are basically learned, at each conversion, in a couple of days. Their basic skills haven't changed, and they're operating fine without any additional types of training."

Some visionaries saw the "office" becoming extinct. The advent of home computers and telecommunications networks, they said, would permit information employees to work at home. Skeptics, though, said that people work better in an office setting. "We egg each other on," said Conference Board economist Freedman. "We transmit a great deal that isn't in the rulebooks or the textbooks. We didn't bring it from school and we don't bring it from the personnel handbook and we don't get it from our bosses, either. We work with each other and interact."

21

What's Hot and What's Not . . .

The following projections were included in the 1982-83 *Occupational Outlook Handbook*, published by the Labor Department's Bureau of Labor Statistics. Written for the general public, the book provides job descriptions, training needs, earnings, working conditions, and expected job prospects through the 1980s for hundreds of careers.

Accountants: Employment was expected to grow faster than average due to pressure on businesses and government agencies to improve budgeting and accounting procedures.

Aerospace engineers: Employment of aerospace engineers was expected to grow faster than average as federal outlays for new military aircraft, missiles and other aerospace systems increased.

Architects: Architects were expected to face competition for jobs through the 1980s. Although employment of architects was expected to rise faster than average, the number of degrees granted in architecture was expected to continue growing as well.

Automobile mechanics: Job opportunities for automobile mechanics were expected to be plentiful. Economic conditions have little effect on the automobile repair business.

Bricklayers: As population and business growth created a need for new homes, factories, offices and other structures, the demand for bricklayers was expected to grow faster than average.

College and university faculty: It seemed likely that enrollments would decline during the 1980s. As a result, job openings would result almost entirely from replacement needs.

Cooks and chefs: The demand for cooks and chefs was projected to increase as the population grew and people dined out more, due to more women working, higher incomes, and more leisure time.

Dentists: Because dental school enrollments had grown in recent years, the supply of new dentists was expected to be in balance with the number needed to fill openings.

Farmers: The trend toward fewer and larger farms was expected to continue, reducing the number of farm owners.

Lawyers: Despite strong growth in the demand for lawyers, the sizable number of law school graduates each year created keen competition for jobs. Competition was likely to remain intense.

Machine tool operators: Employment was expected to increase about as fast as average. Faster and more versatile automatic machine

...In the Job Market

tools and numerically controlled machine tools would result in greater output per worker and limit employment demand.

Pharmacists: The employment outlook for pharmacists was expected to be favorable overall, but geographical considerations would matter.

Police officers: Average growth in the employment of police officers was expected as the nation's population and police protection needs increased. Employment growth would be tempered by increased use of civilian police department employees in traffic control, parking enforcement, and other routine non-hazardous police work.

Programmers: Employment of programmers was expected to grow faster than average as computer usage expands, particularly in firms providing accounting, business management and computer programming services, and in research and development firms.

Retail sales persons: Employment of retail sales persons was expected to grow about as fast as the average for all occupations. The volume of sales was projected to outpace employment increases, however, as self-service is extended to variety and other kinds of stores.

Secondary school teachers: Prospective secondary school teachers would face keen competition for jobs. If past trends continued, the supply of qualified teachers would greatly exceed requirements.

Social workers: Job prospects for social workers varied a great deal. Opportunities depended upon academic credentials, but geographical location was probably the most important consideration.

Systems analysts: Employment of systems analysts was expected to grow much faster than the average as computer capabilities were increased.

Typists: Very good job prospects were expected for typists, even as more typewriters are turned in for word processors.

Veterinarians: Newly qualified vets could expect increased competition in establishing practices, for the number of veterinary school graduates was expected to continue growing.

Writers and editors: Each year, thousands of young people with college degrees in English, journalism, communications and the liberal arts sought writing and editing jobs. Many ended up in other occupations because the supply exceeded the demand, a situation that was expected to continue.

Job Opportunities in the Service Industries

If one were to take a facetious look at the employment scene, big growth would be expected for two kinds of workers: economists, to figure out the nation's economic mess, and psychiatrists, to counsel the confused economists. In fact, fairly rapid growth was predicted in both fields, faster-than-average in economics and as-fast-as-average in psychology. But the number of people seeking these jobs was expected to continue to outrun the number of available positions.

The same was true for many of the professional services. The legal profession provided a glaring example. In 1980, 535,000 lawyers were chasing 416,000 jobs; by 1985, 639,000 lawyers were expected to vie for 500,000 jobs. The gap was expected to widen as the Reagan administration cut back on government litigation and legal services for the poor.

The demand for health care services was expected to continue its growth, creating new positions throughout the industry. Nurses were in especially short supply. However, a geographic imbalance existed, with a glut of workers in big cities with high pay scales and shortages in smaller cities and rural areas where salaries were lower.

Rising incomes and fear of inflation created a great demand in the 1970s for financial services: accounting, tax advising, and investment counseling. These areas were expected to continue their growth in the 1980s. Similarly, affluence and expanded leisure time set off a boom in the personal-consumption services: retail salespersons, hotel and restaurant workers, hairstylists, amusement park and arena workers, exercise instructors, bartenders and many others. Assuming an economic recovery, labor analysts foresaw continued growth in these areas.

A service area not expected to grow was the one most sensitive to population trends: education. The end of the "baby boom" reduced school enrollments and thousands of teachers were laid off. A marginal increase in the birthrate in the early 1980s was expected to boost enrollments, but the severe financial problems of many school systems were expected to hold down employment growth for the time being. Similarly, local fiscal woes were expected to restrain employment in public services in demand, such as police and fire protection and sanitation.

The Uncertainties of Economic Forecasting

Few economists asserted that every single American who desired work would be able to find it. Most economics textbooks stated this was not dangerous, that it was, in fact, necessary, because there had to be a labor pool to replace workers who retired, died, took ill, were fired, or left their jobs for whatever reasons.

As late as 1978, the passage of the Humphrey-Hawkins Act expressed Congress' commitment to a "full employment" jobless rate of 4 percent. Yet most conservative and some liberal economists by 1983 had accepted a target of 6 percent unemployment. No matter what the theoretical level was, the actual level was expected to remain high for some time.

Many economists said this level was too high. "I think that we were much too prompt to accept . . . a full employment level of 6 percent," said Levitan. "I think we could have achieved lower levels of unemployment if we had the proper public policy." To Levitan and other economists like him, proper public policy included the traditional federal weapons against unemployment: job creation and job training. *(Federal Jobs Programs Controversy, p. 95)*

BLS analysts and other economists based their projections of future employment on reams of statistics on population, demographic and employment trends. Nonetheless, their predictions were not fail-safe. The economy and the size of the job market were contingent on many forces — government fiscal policy, balance of trade, OPEC oil pricing decisions, etc. — that were far from predictable.

Looking back to the early 1970s, the United States had low interest rates, little inflation, comparatively low unemployment, a more manageable federal budget deficit , and thriving auto and steel industries. Few, if any, economists in the early 1970s predicted all of the shocks — the enormous oil price increases, the surge of foreign imports, inflation and the decline of basic industries — that contributed to the early 1980s' recessionary economy, high unemployment, high interest rates and a federal deficit projected to go over $200 billion in fiscal 1983.

Economic projections were based on assumptions. It was assumed that a multibillion-dollar defense buildup would create an enormous demand for engineers, computer specialists, skilled factory workers and others in the high-technology fields. However, the size of the projected growth depended on the level of defense spending Congress approved.

Perhaps the most unpredictable element in the employment picture was the length and depth of the recession afflicting the country in early 1983. A recovery was expected, but it was uncertain when it would occur. As long as the economy stagnated, employment was expected to be restrained, and many companies would defer the investment, innovation and research necessary to bring about the projected changes. Signs indicating economic and job growth were cause for optimism, but until the recession ended, all bets were off.

Industrial robot that can "see," being tested by General Motors, will be able to pick up parts and put them in their correct places.

Chapter 2

THE TECHNOLOGICAL REVOLUTION

Electronics advances in the latter half of the 20th century spawned a new generation of sophisticated computers possessing the potential for radically changing virtually every aspect of society. According to the National Academy of Sciences, the impact of this so-called second industrial revolution "could be even greater than that of the original industrial revolution." The first industrial revolution began in England in the mid-18th century and changed the world economy from one based on agriculture to one based on factories and machines.

In his 1983 State of the Union address, President Ronald Reagan reflected: "To many of us now, computers, silicon chips, data processing, cybernetics and all the other innovations of the dawning high-technology age are as mystifying as the workings of the combustion engine must have been when that first Model T rattled down Main Street, U.S.A. But as surely as America's pioneer spirit made us the industrial giant of the 20th Century, the same pioneer spirit today is opening up on another vast front of opportunity, the frontier of high technology."

Advanced factory automation was one part of high technology made possible by the computer. Faced with stiff foreign competition, a declining national productivity rate and an unstable economy, the United States finally was forced to look to factory automation as one way out. Using advanced computer technology, hundreds of companies were experimenting with ways to turn out basic items from automobiles to widgets more efficiently and with higher quality. Others attempted to develop and manufacture the new technology, selling robots or other computer-aided manufacturing systems, instead of traditional machine tools or dies.

Struggle came with these changes, both for the traditional American entrepreneur and for his blue-collar counterpart. Many factories that did not automate, either because they did not see a need or because they could not afford to in the strained economic time, were forced to close their doors. And although the high unemployment plaguing blue-collar workers was not attributed solely to worker displacement due to automation, finding a new job without some retraining was perceived as a problem.

Observers in 1983 were watching just the beginning of the revolution. According to the opening statement of Sen. Lloyd Bentsen, D-Texas, at March hearings by the Joint Economic Committee on robotics and unemployment, sales of robots were expected to rise "at a phenomenal rate of 35 to 50 percent annually. . . . A new generation of robots seems to appear almost monthly now — fruit picking, auto body sanding and painting, welding dirt buckets to bulldozers, drilling bolt holes in F-16 Falcons — the list is growing by leaps and bounds."

Reagan's State of the Union message marked an apparent change in his administration's employment strategy. During the 1980 presidential campaign, Reagan had promised to rebuild older industries and put unemployed workers back on the payroll in the revived steel, auto and other affected plants. But the unyielding unemployment rate, which stood at a little more than 10 percent at the time of his 1983 address, prompted, at least in part, the administration's determination to avoid having job losses blamed on Reagan's policies and instead to attribute them to basic structural changes in the economy resulting from science and technology developments. The Reagan White House began giving strong encouragement to the growth of high-technology industries, at the same time offering hope to the unemployed that new jobs would be created in the developing industries.

Development, History of Computer Industry

The basis for the new industrial revolution was the computer chip, first developed in the early 1960s but perfected only in the 1970s. Chips are tiny silicon wafers, about half the size of a fingernail, that contain the resistors, transistors and diodes serving as the computer's brains. Refinements over time in chip technology allowed the size and price of computers to shrink at the same time that their capacities increased.

The most advanced chips, called microprocessors, contain the entire central processing unit of a computer. Microprocessors can carry out millions of instructions per second and can be reprogrammed to function in different ways. Computer games, digital watches, razor-thin, hand-held calculators and supermarket computer checkout systems all were made possible by advances in microelectronics.

A less visible array of microprocessing technology was being used in a number of ways:

● Two gigantic computers on Capitol Hill contained millions of pieces of information on registered voters, Library of Congress reports and other material. The data was available instantaneously to each member of Congress.

● Office machines in use were able to identify misspelled words in six languages.

● Certain computers were able to edit and analyze the writing quality of technical manuscripts.

● Colleges were using computers to simulate operations for medical students and courtroom situations for law students.

● Computer voice synthesizers were able to translate languages or "read" books aloud.

● Detailed, computerized records of millions of dairy cattle and bulls were used by farmers to get information on feed consumption, breeding patterns, sales and other items.

Scientists the world over were working on even more sophisticated uses of computer technology that, before the year 2000, were expected to alter the lives of millions of people in the industrialized world. Predicting the social and economic significance of these developments was akin "to forecasting the impact of the automobile on society as the first Model T rolled off the assembly line," author-researcher Colin Norman wrote in an October 1980 article for the Worldwatch Institute. But he ventured to say in a later interview that "microelectronic technology will have a pervasive and long-lasting influence on international trade, patterns of employment, communications, industrial productivity, entertainment and social relationships."

Moving from Vacuum Tube to Silicon Chip

The first electronic computer was built in 1946. That landmark machine, the Electronic Numerical Integrator and Calculator — commonly known as ENIAC — was developed at the University of Pennsylvania's Moore School of Engineering. The machine took two-and-a-half years to build. It solved its first problem, an equation involving atomic physics, in two hours. The huge computer filled an entire room, required 18,000 vacuum tubes and needed 140,000 watts of electricity — enough of a drain to dim the lights of west Philadelphia slightly whenever it was switched on. In 1983 a computer with ENIAC's once-revolutionary capabilities would cost less than $100, fit into a pants pocket and run on flashlight batteries.

In 1947, a year after ENIAC went into operation, three scientists at Bell Laboratories in Murray Hill, N.J. — John Bardeen, Walter Brattain and William Shockley — developed the transistor. The three were awarded the Nobel Prize for physics in 1956 for their work on developing the transistor. Author Christopher Evans, in his book *The Mighty Micro*, characterized the transistor as "the most important single invention within the whole complex of inventions which we today call the computer." The transistor is a solid-state, electronic device, composed of semiconductor material, such as germanium or silicon, that controls electric current flow without use of a vacuum. The word derived from *trans*fer re*sistor*, since transistors transfer a current across a resistor. Transistors are less than 1/100th the size of the vacuum tubes they replaced, and they consume much less energy because they are not heat driven. The use of transistors led to the reduction in the size of television sets, radios and computers in the 1950s.

The next big breakthrough in computer technology came in 1959 when scientists at Texas Instruments and Fairchild Camera and Instrument Co. simultaneously developed the integrated circuit, what Colin Norman called "the centerpiece of microelectronic technology." Integrated circuits, used in dozens of types of electronic equipment from computers to digital watches, consist of transistors wired together on individual silicon chips. Integrated circuits were first put into mass production by the semiconductor industry in 1960. Each year thereafter the industry increased the number of transistors that it could place on a single chip and reduced the price at the same time.

By the early 1980s some integrated circuits had up to 100,000 components on a chip only one-fifth of an inch in length. A single chip held more power than ENIAC. Computer scientists were working on developing chips that would hold about 250,000 components; some believed that by the year 1990 there would be an integrated circuit with one million components.

The last big electronics discovery came in 1971 when an American company, Intel, developed the microprocessor, "the most radical advance in electronic componentry in 30 years." The microprocessor is, simply, a

Computer Glossary

CAD/CAM. Computer-aided design and manufacturing.

Chip. Integrated circuit in which all the components are miniaturized and etched on a tiny piece of silicon or like material.

Database. Collection of information in a form that can be manipulated by a computer and retrieved by a user through a terminal.

Diode. Electronic device with only two electrodes used mainly as a rectifier (a device for converting alternating current into direct current).

Hardware. The equipment components of mechanical, magnetic, electrical or electronic devices.

Information retrieval. Process of selecting from a database relevant data using access points, such as subject, name, date.

Integrated circuits. Circuits whose component parts and interconnections are fabricated simultaneously on single silicon chips.

Microcomputers. Computers whose central processing units are microprocessor chips, including personal computers, small business computers, desktop computers and home computers.

Microprocessor. Central processing unit implanted on a chip.

Online. Direct connection to a host computer.

Online distribution service. An organization that offers online access to one or more databases. Also referred to as online vendor, database vendor, online supplier, online retrieval service, search service and timesharing service.

Program. Instructions in a form acceptable to a computer.

Resistor. Electrical or electronic circuit component that has a specified resistance.

Search. Retrieval of information from a database by giving the computer specific commands.

Semiconductor. Material used in transistors having conductance related to temperature.

Software. Generic term for all non-hardware elements in a computer system, including computer programs, data, TV programs, user manuals and documentation.

Terminal. Device for entering data into and/or receiving data from a computer system or a computer network. A typical terminal consists of a keyboard and a printer or video display.

Source: "Glossary of Terms," Link Resources Corporation, 1980.

very advanced type of integrated circuit — a silicon chip that handles the arithmetical and logical functions of the computer's main memory. The microprocessor is programmable; that is, it can carry out a wide range of differing functions.

George H. Heilmeier, vice president for corporate research at Texas Instruments, used a geographical analogy to trace the evolution of the technology that resulted in the microprocessor. "In the mid-1960s," he said in a June 1980 issue of *Newsweek*, "the complexity of a chip was comparable to that of the street network of a small town. Today's microprocessor is comparable to the entire Dallas-Fort Worth area. And the ultimate . . . micro technology will be capable of producing chips whose complexity rivals an urban street network covering the entire North American continent."

Evolution of the Semiconductor Industry

Large contracts from the federal government — primarily from the Department of Defense and the National Aeronautics and Space Administration (NASA) — in the 1960s and 1970s spurred the growth of the U. S. semiconductor industry. "This burgeoning military demand provided a stable market for the small, innovative microelectronics companies that spearheaded the technological development, and it helped launch the industry on its high-growth technology," Norman wrote in his article.

In the 1970s the focus of the industry shifted from military and space technology to goods aimed for the commercial market. In 1981, according to statistics from Semiconductor Industry Association, Charles River Associates and Electronic Industries Association, the semiconductor industry, which was growing at a rate of about 30 percent a year, accounted for approximately $10 billion in sales; at that time, about $1 billion worth of semiconductors—or 10 percent of the market—went to military programs. From 1972 to 1982 employment in the semiconductor industry rose at an annual rate of 5.6 percent. In 1982 employment totaled 168,300.

Jerry Sanders, president of Advanced Micro Devices Inc. of Sunnyvale, Calif., was quoted widely when he testified before the U.S. International Trade Commission that he "liked to think of semiconductor technology and its evolution as being the crude oil of the electronics industry. . . ." Wall Street electronics industry analyst Ben Rosen spoke of the far-reaching economic importance of this "crude oil" when he

The Parent Industry: Electronics

Computers and their components made up but one segment of one of the nation's healthiest industries: electronics. This industry manufactures and markets products that direct and control the conduction of electricity in gas, vacuum, liquid or solid-state materials. According to the Electronic Industries Association, the "distinguishing feature of electronic products as opposed to purely electrical ones is that electronics products also include tubes and semiconductors which can discharge, direct, control, or otherwise influence the flow of that electricity."

The American electronics industry manufactured about 30,000 different products. They varied enormously in function, size and use ranging from microscopic components to giant computing and control systems. The electronics industry employed about 1.5 million workers in 1979, and shipped some $80.6 billion worth of merchandise — from television and radio receivers to hearing aids, computers, calculators and guidance systems for unmanned missiles. The industry's manufacturing plants were located in nearly every state, with the greatest concentration in California, New York, Illinois, New Jersey, Pennsylvania, Massachusetts and Indiana.

Among the electronics industry's most successful companies were those that manufactured integrated circuits. The industry was dominated by a group of small, independent firms located in an area south of San Francisco known as "Silicon Valley." A number of large electronics firms also manufactured semiconductors. The leading companies in the field were: Advanced Micro Devices Inc., Sunnyvale, Calif.; American Microsystems Inc., Santa Clara, Calif.; General Instrument Corp., New York, N.Y.; Intel Corp., Santa Clara, Calif.; International Rectifier Corp., Los Angeles, Calif.; Intersil Inc., Cupertino, Calif.; Motorola Inc., Schaumburg, Ill.; National Semiconductor Corp., Santa Clara, Calif.; and Texas Instruments, Dallas, Texas.

appeared on the television news show "The MacNeil/Lehrer Report" in October 1980. "Unlike the old crude oil that comes from the Middle East," he said, "this is crude oil that we have and they want — 'they' being the rest of the world."

New Japanese Challenge in Microprocessing

But Japan too was banking on high technology to be the key to its long-term exporting future. This plan put the Japanese on a collision course with the United States because the United States had dominated the microelectronics industry since its inception. Indeed, American entrepreneurs invented the semiconductor, and American businesses taught Japanese firms the mechanics of semiconductor manufacturing. *(Foreign Trade and U.S. Unemployment, p. 57)*

Japan made little secret of its future plans. A 1981 study by the U.S. House Ways and Means Committee called "Report on Trade Mission to the Far East" underscored what the challenge meant to the U.S. industry: "... [I]n the high technology products that count — the products which will dominate the world trade and economy for the rest of the century — the Japanese are second to none .... The trend lines indicate that they will surpass the United States and that the gap will widen dramatically, UNLESS the United States responds."

Until recently, American companies — including Texas Instruments, National Semiconductor and Intel — built and sold about 70 percent of the world's semiconductors. Japan was in second place in worldwide semiconductor sales. But by the early 1980s the Japanese producers — especially Nipon Electric, Hitachi and Fujitsu Fanuc Ltd. — with the help of hundreds of millions of dollars in government research money, had cut deeply into the U.S-controlled market. This came at a time when American semiconductor firms were being hurt by rising research and equipment costs, which in combination with intense domestic competition, had forced U.S. companies to sell their products at very low profit margins.

One example of Japan's success in the field involved the 64K RAM, a random access memory chip that could store 64,000 bits of digital computer data. It served as the main memory bank in many of the computers in use in the early 1980s. By the end of 1981 the Japanese controlled about 70 percent of the world market in 64K RAMS.

During the 1974-75 recession, U.S. semiconductor companies cut their budgets and work forces. When the recession ended and demand returned, the domestic industry could not meet it. Only two American companies — Motorola and Texas Instruments — were manufacturing the 64K RAM chips in 1981, but three more firms joined the competition in 1982. According to the Commerce Department, the U.S. share of the market grew to 40 percent during 1982 from 1981's 30

Japan's Success with Video Recorders

The newest and brightest star in the consumer electronics equipment field in the early 1980s was the videocassette recorder (VCR). In 1981 Japan sold nearly $1.8 billion worth of audio and video recorders in the United States — a phenomenal 69.9 percent increase over 1980 sales. Japan was dominating the booming U.S. market because no American electronics firms manufactured VCRs; all those sold by U.S. companies were built by the Japanese.

American inventors developed the original idea and technology for videocassette recorders. But the first two U.S. ventures into the home VCR market, by CBS and Ampex, were costly failures. In the early 1970s, after the Americans had given up on the idea, Sony and Victor Co. of Japan (JVC, a division of Matsushita Electric Industrial) came out with successful home VCRs.

Worldwide, Japan shipped more than 7.4 million VCRs in 1981, more than double 1980's total. For the first time, in 1981, Japanese VCR exports surpassed those of color televisions. Matsushita, Japan's leading electronics firm, had its best year ever in 1981 with nearly $13 billion in sales. Matsushita's sales of VCRs — marketed under the brand names Quasar, Panasonic and National — rose 80 percent over 1980; total overseas sales jumped 36 percent.

percent. But while Americans were playing catch-up in this market, Hitachi forged ahead with work on a 256K RAM chip with mass production set for 1983. Another Japanese firm, Toshiba Corp. of Tokyo, was planning to build an $86 million facility to manufacture the first 1 megabit unit — a chip capable of containing one million bits of data.

Most of the leading U.S. semiconductor manufacturers, at least initially, were relatively small, independent firms. But most Japanese manufacturers were part of larger electronics companies, and this gave them a big advantage. "These [parent] companies are ready to provide the big sums needed for developing new microchips — and not just to earn profits from sales," a March 1982 issue of *The Economist* noted. "They also believe that the future of other products depends heavily on developing good components. Japanese companies can back this hunch by borrowing at low rates unheard of in America for a decade or more."

There were signs that European manufacturers — who long stood as a distant third behind the United States and Japan — were trying to widen their share of the world computer market. "European nations are favoring local semiconductor producers, fostering corporate marriages, and new ventures, assessing huge tariffs on imports, and launching some of the grandest industrial aid programs since World War II," observed Bro Uttal in the July 28, 1980, issue of *Fortune*. The Europeans did not have financial support from their defense and space programs like the Americans. Nor did they initially have the advantage of government largess as was the case in Japan. But the European Community eventually started a project to coordinate its member countries' activities in the field.

Cooperative Research Efforts by U.S. Firms

One way that U.S. data processing companies and integrated circuit manufacturers decided to right this competition was to take a page from Japan's book. Competing U.S. industries began to cooperate in research and development programs for their common good. Edwin L. Harper, Reagan's senior White House staff official in charge of domestic policy alternatives, wanted to enable more U.S. companies to coordinate their research and development ideas without fear of government allegations of violating the antitrust and price-fixing laws. In an April 18, 1983, *Washington Post* article, Harper said: "One of the things we have set as policy is that we ought to be supporting research and development that is not immediately commercially utilizable."

Six American companies, including International Business Machines (the world's largest computer producer), Xerox Corp. and Burroughs Corp., sent financial assistance as well as company scientists to a California Institute of Technology program designed to foster microprocessor research. Similar industry-sponsored research programs got under way at Stanford University, Duke University and North Carolina State University. The University of Minnesota set up a Microelectronics and Information Science Center with the help of Control Data Corp., Honeywell Inc., Sperry Corp. and other companies. The center focused its research in microelectronics physics, integrated circuit design and other related technologies.

These programs were designed not only to advance microelectronic knowledge, but also to produce more trained computer scientists to work in a field chronically short of personnel. In the field of engineering, for example, the United States in 1980 graduated 69,000 engineers, or about 7 percent of the college graduates, compared with 81,000, or 15 percent of graduates, for Japan. The population of the United States was double that of Japan.

The shortage of trained computer personnel was not limited to top-level jobs. According to John W. Hamblem, chairman of the computer sciences department at the University of Missouri at Rolla, the shortage existed at nearly all levels and was expected to be a problem for years. "Right now, at the bachelor's level, we are producing one candidate for every four jobs," Hamblen was quoted as saying in a February 1981 article in *Savvy*. "At the master's level it's one for 10, and at the doctoral level it's been one for four, and the supply is decreasing. People aren't even bothering to go for graduate degrees when they can start at $20,000 with a B.S. I think we'll start to close the gap at the B.S. level around 1986."

Computer industry analysts estimated that the industry would have openings for about 54,000 college graduates a year; 34,000 openings for those with master's degrees; and 1,300 openings for those with doctorates. Salaries in the computer field were for the most part above average, especially at companies with large computer operations. *(Salaries box, p. 41)*

The Robot Revolution

The technology of microelectronics was continually evolving in the 1980s, the threshold for advancement constantly shifting. One related development receiving increasing attention was the potential of robotics; the microprocessor had given robots the added dimension of being reprogrammable, and therefore multifunctional.

Robotics was but one part of a larger industrial scheme, called programmable automation, that derived from the development of the computer. Programmable automation, or computerized manufacturing, was an umbrella term that applied to several types of automated equipment and systems that drew on computers, including: robots; computer-aided design or CAD; computer-aided manufacturing or CAM; computer-aided process planning or CAPP; and automated materials handling, storage and retrieval systems. Of this group, robots had attracted the most attention from the media and the public.

It took the first American robot manufacturer 14 years to show a profit, and other companies' earnings from robots were only beginning to materialize in the early 1980s. But the portion of corporate revenues from robots was growing significantly, and interest in robotics reached an all-time high. By 1974 U.S. robot manufacturers joined together to form a trade association, the Robot Institute of America (RIA), in Dearborn, Mich.

By 1982 membership had grown to include more than 180 companies and corporations that supplied or used industrial robots. Copies of RIA's magazine, *Robotics Today,* were so much in demand that non-subscriber copies sold out soon after printing, and attendance at trade shows more than doubled between 1981 and 1982. The Robots VI conference, held in Detroit in March 1982, was so packed, observers noted, that the exhibition area had to be closed off to visitors for hours at a time.

Many companies' robot divisions were growing at a faster rate than the rest of the organization, and new companies were entering the field just as quickly. According to Laura Conigliaro, a financial analyst with the New York investment firm Bache Halsey Stuart Shields Inc., it was once difficult for small firms just starting out in robots to attract adequate financial backing. But by 1982, she said, the tables had turned and venture capital firms were seeking out robot-makers.

"We're going to end up producing much of our national wealth without human interference," said Joseph Engelberger, founder and president of Unimation Inc., the nation's oldest and largest robot manufacturer, in a December 1981 issue of *Science Digest*. "Over the next 50 years, it will be as profound a change as the Industrial Revolution." Experts predicted that new developments in robotics in the 1980s likely will result in even greater productivity across a widening range of applications. "Advances are being made hourly," said George Brosseau, a project manager with the National Science Foundation in Washington, D.C., in 1982. "Within the next three years, robot technology will take off like a shot."

Use of Industrial Robots in Factories

Robots don't call in sick, go on strike or take long lunch breaks. They can work efficiently for indefinite periods and never complain about salaries, demanding bosses or poor working conditions. Experts saw them as a way to boost the United States' lagging productivity. Productivity is broadly defined as output per man hour. From the end of World War II through the mid-1960s, U.S. productivity increased by an average of 3.4 percent a year, but the rate of increase began declining in

1983 Average Starting Salaries in the Data Processing Field

Job Description	Size of Company*		
	Large	Medium	Small
Management Information Systems Director	$49,000-$70,000	$38,000-$48,000	$27,000-$34,000
Systems & Programming Manager	$31,000-$38,500	$30,000-$36,000	$26,000-$35,000
Project Manager	30,000-38,000	28,000-35,000	23,000-30,000
Project Leader	29,000-36,000	28,000-35,000	23,000-30,000
Systems Analyst	29,500-36,000	27,000-33,000	23,000-28,000
Programmer Analyst	22,000-30,000	21,000-29,000	19,000-26,000
Programmer	18,000-24,000	18,000-21,000	15,000-19,000
Technical Support Manager	$35,000-$45,000	$32,000-$40,000	—
Systems Programmer	26,000-36,000	27,000-35,000	—
Data Base Support Data Base Administrator	$29,000-$36,000	$28,000-$34,000	—
Data Base Specialist	27,000-37,000	25,000-30,000	—
Telecommunications Manager	$30,000-$35,000	$27,000-$35,000	—
Telecommunications Specialist	28,000-32,000	21,000-30,000	—
Operations Manager	$27,000-$36,000	$26,000-$34,000	$22,000-$29,000
Shift Supervisor	21,000-27,000	19,000-23,000	—
Operator	15,000-19,500	14,000-18,000	13,000-17,000
Control Analyst	15,000-19,000	14,000-18,500	12,000-15,000

* There is a difference in salaries between large, medium and small installations. The size of the installation is determined by a combination of hardware (central processing unit only) and the professional staff (management, analysts, programmers). The hardware is judged by the size of the central processing unit, and the professional staff mostly by the number of professionals employed. (Large — more than 50; medium — 15 to 49; small — under 15).

Source: Prevailing Financial and Data Processing Starting Salaries, by Robert Half International Inc., 1983.

the 1970s. In 1981 U.S. productivity rose by only .9 percent. Analysts estimated that robots in use in American factories in the early 1980s had helped boost production by 10-90 percent.

Industrial robots did hazardous, difficult and monotonous jobs that most humans preferred not to do; they did them more reliably and, in some cases, more cheaply. Unlike the stereotypical 1950s vision of the robot, industrial robots in factories by the 1980s looked nothing like humans. They were machines with a guiding brain — a computer — and one or more mechanical arms with grippers for hands. The computer was plugged into an electrical outlet, and cables transmitted instructions from the computer to a control system that operated the gripper. Hydraulic pressure activated robots for heavy work.

As defined by the Robot Institute of America, a robot was "a reprogrammable multi-functional manipulator designed to move material, parts, tools, or specialized devices through variable programmed motions for the performance of a variety of tasks." That robots were reprogrammable and could perform a variety of tasks were the keys to their importance. Factories had been using automated machines, such as bottle cappers, for years in mass production, but these machines did only one task at a time. New tasks required new machines or extensive retooling of old ones, both of which were expensive and time-consuming. But as the technology progressed, it became possible to reprogram robots at any time, often in a few minutes, to either switch or expand their work routines.

What allowed robots to be reprogrammable were microprocessors — tiny silicon wafers about half the size of a fingernail, which contained the resistors, transistors and diodes that served as the brains of computers. The steady and rapid decrease in the cost of microprocessors and related computer technology, along with skyrocketing labor costs, were responsible for the growing popularity of industrial robots.

Most of the 5,000 or so robots in U.S. factories in 1981 were used in the automobile industry, although increasingly they also appeared in electrical firms. Robots did jobs such as die casting, spray painting, forging, spot and arc welding, machine loading and unloading, and various types of assembling. Experts predicted that by 1990 more than a third of factory assembly work would be done by robots, compared with about 5-10 percent in 1982. One system was being designed to assemble a 17-piece automobile alternator in less than three minutes. Unimation already was making an assembly robot called PUMA — an acronym for

Jobs Done by Robots Now and in the Future

Job Description	Through 1981	1990
Spot welding	35-45%	3-5%
Arc welding	5-8	15-20
Materials handling, including machine loading and unloading	25-30	30-35
Paint spraying	8-12	5
Assembly	5-10	35-40
Other	8-10	7-10

Note: Percentage figures are based on total dollars spent on robots, broken down by job category.

Source: Bache Halsey Stuart Shields Inc.

"programmable universal machine for assembly" — that could pick up parts and pass them along, spray paint, weld, load and unload parts from furnaces, stamping presses and conveyors — all without supervision.

One factor making robots more feasible for assembly work was off-line programming, which increased robots' flexibility. The customary way of teaching a robot was to put it in a "learn mode" and then lead it by hand through the task it had to do. When the robot was put in an operating mode it then would do exactly what it was taught. But with off-line programming a technician could sit down at a central computer console and punch in the coordinates of a job without having literally to hold the robot's hand.

One of the obstacles in the development of off-line programming was the difficulty in putting together compatible systems from separate parts, which oftentimes were built by different companies. What was needed was a high-level computer language that was standardized for the industry. Paul Wright, a professor at Carnegie-Mellon University's Robotics Institute, described the situation in the April 11, 1983, *Wall Street Journal* this way: It was "like trying to run a restaurant with a Russian chef, a French baker, a Chinese dishwasher and an Egyptian waiter, each of whom speaks only his native language and is also hard of hearing." To make matters worse, companies sometimes tried to encourage customers to buy only from them by making equipment incapable of communicating with other companies' products.

Gains in Intelligence, Vision and Touch. One of the chief drawbacks of most robots was that they could do their jobs only if things were exactly where they had been programmed to find them. For example, a robot could not tell whether the right car body was in the right place on an assembly line and if not move it. To deal with such limitations, roboticists were trying to develop senses for robots as well as the ability to integrate what they could see and touch with even more sophisticated electronic logic, thus enabling robots to make limited decisions.

Such intelligence — the ability to perceive and appropriately respond to changes in the environment — was expected to allow robots to do complex assembly work without expensive human or automated supervision. "Over the next 10 years, sensors will enlarge by an order of magnitude the number of places where you can put robots in a factory," said Charles Rosen, chief scientist at the Machine Intelligence Corp. in Palo Alto, Calif., in the December 1981 issue of *Science Digest.*

Robot vision essentially was accomplished by training television or other optical receptors (such as lasers) on an object or group of objects and using that information to direct the robot's activities. The television camera scans the object and transmits to a computer the thousands of dots that form the television image. The computer transforms these dots into binary code, consisting of one, representing the black dots, and zero, representing the white dots.

"Now the computer is ready to 'see' the picture and make sense of it," Stephen Solomon wrote in the December 1981 issue of *Science Digest.* "Where the zeroes in the picture give way to ones, the computer detects the silhouette of the object and its orientation. Instantly it calculates many of its features — an area, perimeter, diameter, and so on — and compares them with the measurement of various objects that have been programmed into its memory. When the computer discovers a similar set of parameters, it 'knows' what it is looking at." The computer then directs the robot's fingers to the edges of the object so it can pick it up.

This crude form of vision was not too useful in factories because it required high-contrast lighting between objects and their backgrounds; objects piled in a bin or moving down an assembly line rarely provided the required contrasts. But it was believed that eventually robots would be able to see even better than humans did. An electronic eye was not bound by biological limitations, and scientists could make it sensitive to infrared and ultraviolet light, which the human eye could not perceive.

Some companies already were making and using seeing robots. IBM had test-marketed an advanced system called RS 1, designed for precision automatic assembly work. It combined sophisticated tactile and optical sensing abilities with the ability to move its arm in six directions. GM had developed a system called Consight, which enabled a robot with an electronic camera to look at scattered parts on a conveyer belt, pick them up and move them in a specific sequence to a different work area.

Robots also were getting a rudimentary sense of touch. By the early 1980s they were able to tell when a part in its gripper did not feel right so that they could alert a human supervisor, and they could jiggle a part until it fit into place by using sensors that followed the contour of the object being worked on. Researchers at the Massachusetts Institute of Technology (MIT) had developed an artificial robot skin consisting of rubber laced with touch-sensitive wire. Blake M. Cornish described the skin in an August 1981 article appearing in *The Futurist* magazine: "The top sheet has an electric current running through it, so that as pressure is applied, the top sheet passes the current down to other levels of the rubber sheets. The amount of pressure applied determines which sheets of rubber and wire are electrified. A microprocessor measures the voltage of the different levels of skin and can form an image of the object being touched."

Researchers also were developing robots able to respond to simple voice commands. With microphones for eardrums, a robot was able to convert sound waves into sequences of numbers and then could compare those with number sequences stored in its memory to determine meaning. Another trend in robot technology involved distributed intelligence. Instead of one computer controlling an entire robot system, roboticists were starting to build microprocessors into each working part. "By distributing the intelligence among the robot's components," explained George Brosseau, "you can improve the way you can control it."

Future Applications. The new breed of intelligent robots being hatched in laboratories around the world was expected to enable robots to do more varied work than the strictly industrial tasks they were limited to initially. Two professors at the Tokyo Institute of Technology developed a snakelike robot capable of passing through pipes and other narrow openings to inspect and do repair work in places inaccessible to people. Unimation was designing a robot that could pluck chickens, and Australian roboticists were at work developing a robot to shear sheep.

James Albus, as head of the robot division of the National Bureau of Standards in Gaithersburg, Md., predicted that during the 1990s robots would be doing construction work, such as carrying materials, lifting and positioning panels, cutting boards to size and laying bricks. It also was possible that robots would be working in mining and ocean and space exploration. By the turn of the century, Albus maintained, factories might be completely automated. Sen. Bentsen, at the March 1983 Joint Economic Committee hearing on robotics and unemployment, said: "By 1990, we could easily see from 100,000 to 150,000 robots being utilized here [in the United States], with sales topping $2 billion annually. Ford and GM alone may well be using 30,000 robots between them by 1990."

While industry was likely to remain the largest market for robots, some of the most interesting developments were taking place in the medical field. Professor Hiroyasu Funakubo of Japan's Medical Precision Engineering Institute developed a robot arm almost as flexible as a human one. These arms were mounted in pairs on a bedside table and linked to a cart that shuttled back and forth between a storage cart and a patient's bed. The system was capable of being activated by a keyboard, voice commands or even by whistles and gasps, for patients unable to speak.

Tokyo's Waseda University was developing a 25-fingered breast-cancer detector. Each of the fingers was equipped with a gauge hooked to a computer. As the fingers examined the breast, the computer drew a picture of the location of any lumps. Breast inspection by a robot could reduce from 200 to fewer than 30 the number of X-ray pictures needed to make a diagnosis.

Japan as Industry Leader

The investment firm Bache Halsey Stuart Shields mailed a questionnaire in December 1981 to selected robot vendors and users to assess trends in the robot industry. In the answers the single most-mentioned word, in contexts ranging from pricing to technology, was "Japan." Japan, as the world leader in robot production and sales, produced about 57 percent of the world's robots and used about three times as many ro-

U.S. and Japanese Robot Production

	Units		Value (in millions of dollars)	
	U.S.	Japan	U.S.	Japan
1980	1,269	3,200	$ 100.5	$ 180
1985	5,195	31,900	441.2	2,150
1990	21,575	57,450	1,884.0	4,450

Source: Daiwa Securities America Inc.

bots as the United States in 1982.

Yet it was the United States, not Japan, that pioneered the building of robots in the early 1960s. U.S. technology still was thought to be the most advanced, particularly in the computer software that ran the so-called smart robots. But Japan clearly led the United States in production and applications. Robotics expert Paul Aron predicted that by 1985 Japan would have five times as many robots as the United States and that by then Japan would be producing about 32,000 robots a year.

Like their U.S. counterparts, Japanese robot-makers were working on advanced models with vision or tactile-sending sytems to do assembly work. By 1985 Hitachi reportedly hoped to use robots for 60 percent of its assembly operations. In 1981 Fujitsu Fanuc Ltd., whose president was known in Japan as the Emperor of Robots, opened a plant in which robots actually reproduced themselves — about 100 a month — though humans still were needed for the final assembly. The plant operated around the clock with only 100 workers, one-fifth the number needed for a normal plant of the same size.

Factors Contributing to Japan's Successes. Japan's successful robot industry partly resulted from its labor practices. Employees in large Japanese corporations were guaranteed lifetime employment until age 55 or 60 and received regular bonuses based on the company's profits. Since employees tended to identify with a company rather than a skill and often were moved from one job to another, they did not generally fear losing their jobs because of automation. They also knew their bonuses would grow with the profits robots produced. In addition, companies provided retraining for workers displaced by robots, while few U.S. companies assumed that responsibility.

The Japanese government consistently provided incentives to the robot industry in the form of tax write-offs and subsidized loans. It also pressured 24 manufacturers and 10 insurance companies to form Japan Robot Lease, which leased welding robots to small companies for $90 a month. Not only could a round-the-clock robot provide $1,200 worth of work for $90, but employers could swap for improved versions when they became available without tying up their money in an outright purchase.

The biggest Japanese government move so far was a Ministry of International Trade and Industry (MITI) program designed to push the development of the "fifth generation" of computers: machines that can "think" for themselves. By 1991 the government wanted to have a working robot that could automatically translate languages, convert speech into the printed word, as well as make decisions. The project's estimated costs ranged from $500 million to $1 billion.

Perhaps the most crucial element contributing to Japan's exploding robot industry was rooted in the Japanese psyche. While many Americans were unenthusiastic about the prospect of robots in their lives, the Japanese were fascinated by them and reacted to them in an intensely personal way. "We give them names," said Seiichiro Akiyama, a Tokyo psychologist, in a *New York Times Magazine* article that appeared on Jan. 10, 1982. "We want to stroke them. We respond to them not as machines but as close-to-human beings."

A common view among psychologists was that Buddhism played an important role in the Japanese attitude. Osamu Tezuka, a cartoonist who used robots as a theme in his work, explained in the same article: "Unlike Christian Occidentals, Japanese don't make a distinction between man, the superior creature, and the world about him. Everything is fused together, and we accept robots easily along with the wide world about us. . . . We have none of the doubting attitude toward robots, as pseudohumans, that you find in the West."

But there were signs that Japan's love affair with robots was faltering. During the spring of 1982, under heavy pressure from Japan's biggest labor unions, the Labor Ministry began a two-year study of robots' impact on Japanese workers. Several unions, fearing loss of jobs to robots within the next five to 10 years, had begun studies of their own. One cause for alarm was that companies that once transferred displaced workers within factories were starting to transfer them to other factories and even other cities.

Although robots did not directly affect Japan's January 1983 unemployment rate of 2.72 percent, some industry leaders privately admitted they were slowly running out of jobs for an increasing number of workers. As reported in the April 13, 1983, *Wall Street Journal*, a survey by Japan's Labor Ministry found that about 29 percent of Japanese manufacturing companies thought they had excess workers, and 16 percent of them were considering cutbacks. About 30 percent of the Japanese workers were protected by the "lifetime" employment system, but many of the smaller and medium-sized companies traditionally laid people off during economic slumps. Constrained by the lifetime employment system, Hitachi used primarily attrition and incentives for early retirement to trim its employee rolls from 1972 to 1982 by almost 15 percent, to 76,000 workers, while simultaneously nearly tripling its sales.

Big-Name Companies Entering the Market. In the 1980s Japan's robot industry was likely to be faced with increased competition from the United States. Commenting in a January 1982 *U. S. News & World Report* article, Naohide Kumagai, an executive with Tokyo's Kawasaki Heavy Industries, said the Japanese realized that if Americans overcame their reluctance to use more robots and decided "to go ahead with robotization in earnest, they would easily overtake Japanese competition."

Japanese robot exports more than doubled between 1977 and 1982, to $9.2 million. But exploding U.S. demand, superior Western technology in areas such as software, and the difficulty of servicing robots overseas could limit future growth. While U.S. industry was not happy with being a far second to Japan, it credited the Japanese with focusing world attention on robots and for broadening their applications. Industry leaders also saw competition with the Japanese as positive because it spurred U.S. vendors to increase their technological research. Although the U.S. robot industry caught on slower than Japan's, it was healthy and growing steadily. Sales more than doubled during 1981 and 1982 and were expected to reach $540 million in 1985, increasing at an average rate of 25-35 percent annually for the rest of the decade.

The number of U.S. companies selling robots tripled to more than 50 during the early 1980s, but the most significant trend for the industry was the entry of giants such as IBM, GM, Westinghouse Electric Corp. and Bendix Corp. Their participation was expected to increase robot use in the United States and help make U.S. companies more effective competitors internationally. But to the dismay of some of the smaller U.S. robot manufacturers, many of the big-name corporations were buying robot technology from the Japanese and Europeans.

IBM made its debut into the market in 1982 with a low-cost robot manufactured by Sankyo Seiki of Japan. General Electric announced in March of the same year a licensing agreement allowing it to produce and improve on robots by Volkswagen, Europe's largest robot manufacturer, and it had concluded similar deals with Japan's Hitachi and Italy's Digital Electronic Automation. Westinghouse planned to market welding robots built by two Japanese companies, but it also purchased the largest American robot firm, Unimation, in the early 1980s. GM agreed to a joint venture with Japan's Fujitsu Fanuc Ltd. to design, build and market robots in the United States. The new company, GMFanuc Robotics Corp., was to be equally owned, and its headquarters were in Troy, Mich. It initially planned to sell robots built in existing Japanese facilities. GM had been a major customer of the already-existing American robotics plants, but planned to buy most of the robots for its own plants from the new joint venture company.

Buying foreign robot technology allowed companies to make a fast entry into the market, since "developing a complete robot is not done overnight," explained Jules A. Mirabal, general manager of GE's automation systems division. In the long run, however, American companies planned to develop and market their own technology. Texas Instruments and Bendix had developed their own technology by 1982, and some analysts thought that IBM only adopted a Japanese-built robot after realizing it would not be able to produce its own until 1983. Industry analysts also predicted that in the future U.S. vendors would be setting up robotics operations abroad and that more licensing agreements would flow from this country to foreign companies instead of the other way around.

Increased Competition. Plenty of speculation existed about what the effects of the increased competition in the robot industry would be. According to Peter L. Blake, executive director of Robotics International, "There's enough business for the next two or three years, but then there will be a shakeout." Unimation and Cincinnati Milacron, the U.S. leaders with about one-third each of the domestic business, already were

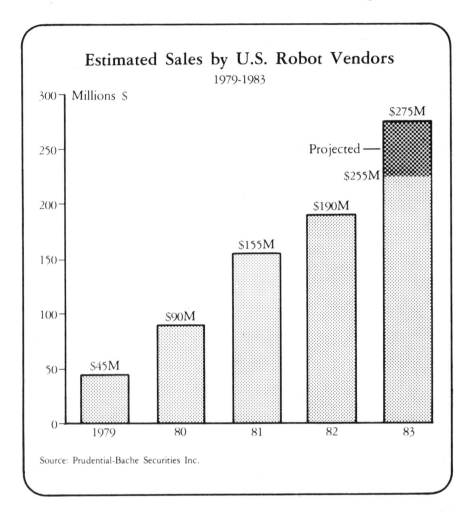

Estimated Sales by U.S. Robot Vendors
1979-1983

Millions $

$275M

Projected —

$255M

$190M

$155M

$90M

$45M

300
250
200
150
100
50
0

1979   80   81   82   83

Source: Prudential-Bache Securities Inc.

fearing the pinch. GM maintained that it would continue to buy robots from companies other than its own GMFanuc; but one Milacron representative admitted that the idea of a major customer becoming a competitor was "kind of spooky," according to a *Wall Street Journal* article of April 7, 1983.

Survival was expected to favor companies financially strong enough to develop and market intelligent robots and the smaller companies that had a specialization — in region, price or application. Electronics firms were likely to become the primary producers of robots because robot brains — their microprocessors, which electronics firms produced —

were expected to develop much more rapidly than robot brawn — their mechanical aspects, such as manual dexterity.

While no one predicted a major interruption in the industry's growth, analysts agreed that the nation's faltering economy had limited demand for robots. Most said that some investments had been delayed and predicted that many small robot companies would suffer from cashflow problems. New business from the auto industry and related spot welding had slowed, despite overall increased sales. Even GM, which was committed to installing 20,000 robots by 1990, was putting only a few new robots into production at a time.

The recession's second effect on the robot industry was partly a result of the first. Vendors were forced to market their products to a wider variety of industries and generally to step up their marketing activities. Broader marketing did not replace the temporary order reductions from the auto industry, but it helped to educate potential users and increase product visibility. "It is our belief that this wider and more aggressive marketing approach, despite its having been forced on portions of the industry through economic circumstances, will be extremely positive for the health and sustainability of the robotics industry in the long term," wrote Laura Conigliaro, in the Jan. 25, 1982, edition of the *Robotics Newsletter*. The entry of companies such as IBM and Westinghouse into the business also was expected to help to open up new markets.

But confronted with increased choices, many potential customers were holding off buying a robot, waiting for the best product or most reliable manufacturers to emerge. The April 7, 1983, *Wall Street Journal* quoted an engineering manager from Boeing Co., who put it this way: "Every year there's a whole new slate of products on the market. . . . We want to avoid buying one and then finding out two years later that there's a better machine that costs less."

Eventual Consequences for American Workers

Despite increased interest in robotics, most U.S. companies still approached the new technology with caution. Although robots were cheaper than people in the long run, few companies had enough capital to invest in many at one time. Management resistance was a big factor. "If you are going to automate, you are not going to get your payback for a while," said Brosseau of the National Science Foundation. "Managers, particularly middle-managers, are very reluctant to make that decision."

Another reason for sluggish U.S. acceptance of robots was the nation's plentiful labor supply. "Because of America's large labor resources, we were able to postpone the robotic revolution — until approximately 1980," said Ken Susnjara, president of Thermwood Corp., a robot maker in Dale, Ind. By then industry began to realize that the number of young entrants into the work force would be shrinking through the 1990s.

Lack of understanding and technical knowledge about what robots could do and how they could solve problems also was an inhibiting factor. Prospective users began to spend millions of dollars to bring their engineers and production managers up to date. Companies such as General Electric and Westinghouse were investing heavily in their own robot research and management training programs, and in some cases industry supplied academia with funds for their robotics programs. In the mid-1970s only a few robotics training programs at colleges and universities existed; by 1982 there were more than 30, including those at MIT and Carnegie-Mellon University in Pittsburgh. Even the lesser-known technical colleges were turning out graduates able to command starting salaries of more than $30,000.

Certainly one source of resistance to robots was lodged in people's fear of being displaced by them. J. Timothy Heile, marketing communications manager at Cincinnati Milacron's Lebanon, Ohio, facility, told those attending the Robots VI conference in March 1982 that "The high degree of publicity about robot technology over the past several years has spawned interest, suspicion, fear, and ultimately defensive attitudes throughout society."

The Robot Institute of America and others had criticized industry for not addressing these concerns and the social costs and implications of the robot revolution. As evidence of this shortsightedness they pointed to industry's slowness in providing retraining for workers who might be displaced by robots. "We are seeing a massive introduction of highly productive technology with little regard for the impact on individuals or the community," Harley Shaiken, a consultant to the United Auto Workers and a research associate at MIT, told a meeting of the American Management Association.

The Office of Technology Assessment, which was set up in 1972 to help Congress plan for the consequences of uses of technology, undertook a long-term study of manufacturing automation expected to be completed in the fall of 1983. The first product of the study, entitled "Automation and the Workplace: Selected Labor, Education, and

Training Issues," was released at the Joint Economic Committee hearings in March 1983. In his opening statement, Sen. Bentsen outlined the committee's two objectives. The first was to evaluate the training and re-training needs caused by the increased use of automated manufacturing. The committee also intended to address the tricky question of whether the rush to automation and robotics would, in the end, increase or decrease the number of jobs for American workers.

On this second question, Bentsen reported: "Evidence ... is mixed.... An analysis by the Arthur D. Little consulting firm predicts that up to 4 million jobs, or one-quarter of our factory work force, could be lost by 1990 to robots.... And experts at the National Bureau of Standards project that every new robot will create from two to four man-years of work somewhere in our economy — that robots will create more jobs than they displace."

Albus of the National Bureau of Standards said in an interview: "Robots create profits, profits create expansion in industry and expanding industries hire more people." Others were more cautious. According to Brosseau, "In the past, whenever a new technology has been introduced, it has always generated more jobs than it displaced. But we don't know whether that's true of robot technology. There's no question but that new jobs will be created, but will there be enough to offset the loss?"

Albus said it was premature to worry about running out of jobs. The problem as he saw it was "in finding mechanisms by which the wealth created by robot technology can be distributed to the people who need it." A solution he proposed was to make everyone stockholders in national, automated robot factories that would pay people substantial dividends. If they wanted more money, people could take jobs or start their own businesses, but no one would have to.

Just about everyone agreed that the long-term impact of robots in factories and in society would be profound, although in what ways no one was able to predict with certainty. As of 1983, the approximately 5,000 robots in American factories had taken jobs that most workers did not want. Robots, therefore, were not now considered a serious threat to American workers, and most labor unions admitted that competition compelled their presence on the assembly line. But the UAW estimated that assembly line labor could be cut by as much as 50 percent in nine years, 1982-1990, because of robots and other automation projects. To deal with this, the UAW hoped to make job retraining part of its national contracts.

"[T]he robot revolution," Albus wrote in *Brains, Behavior, & Robotics* (1981), "could free the human race from the regimentation and mechanization imposed by the requirement for human decision-making in factories and offices. It has the capacity to provide us all with material wealth, clean energy, and the personal freedom to enjoy what could become a golden age of mankind." The vision of robots gliding about in empty factories while people basked in robot-subsidized fulfillment seemed a far-fetched one. But whether robots were welcomed as saviors or feared as human replacements, increasing numbers of them would be around.

Molten pig iron being poured into a modern basic oxygen furnace, where it will be refined into steel. The U.S. steel industry needed to invest in new, up-to-date equipment to compete with foreign producers.

Chapter 3

FOREIGN TRADE AND U.S. UNEMPLOYMENT

President Ronald Reagan, in his State of the Union message on Jan. 25, 1983, pointed to the close connection between U.S. trade policy and jobs. "Every American has a role and stake in international trade," Reagan told Congress. "One out of every five jobs in our country depends on trade. We export over 20 percent of our industrial production, and 40 percent of our farm land produces for export."

The theme was woven throughout the speech. "In at least half the pages of his text he made references to programs that impact on trade," noted U.S. Trade Representative William E. Brock III. The reason, said Brock, was that 1982's decline in trade contributed greatly to unemployment in the United States. "The very essence of trade is to deal with that problem," said Brock.

Reagan was not alone in emphasizing the importance of trade to the staggering unemployment problems in the United States. Earlier, on the same day as Reagan's speech, the Senate Finance Committee met to discuss the trade issue. "I really believe trade is going to be the most important issue we face this year," said Sen. Lloyd Bentsen, D-Texas.

In their response to Reagan's speech, Democrats also staked out international trade as important ground. "It's time the United States began to deal with the reality of the international economy that we live in today," said Senate Minority Leader Robert C. Byrd, D-W.Va. "America must get just as tough on trade as our world competitors. . . . That could be the difference in thousands and thousands of jobs a year."

In the early 1970s trade issues did not receive such attention. In 1973 trade accounted for only 6 percent of the U.S. gross national product; by 1983 it represented more than 12 percent. U.S. exports doubled during the 1970s, and in 1983 they played a crucial role in the nation's economic health. Eighty percent of the jobs created in the United States between

1977 and 1980 were due to increased exports, according to government statistics. And more than a million of the jobs lost during the recession that began in 1981 could be traced to the deterioration of trade.

The world recession, which caused global trade to drop sharply in 1982, drove home the full implications of the United States' increased dependence on trade. The effects of recession were exacerbated by a new spirit of mercantilism in the world, with governments adopting extreme measures to increase exports and decrease imports. Because one nation's imports were another's exports, the conflicts inherent in this strategy were clear and difficult to escape.

In 1983 some members of Congress were coming to espouse what a number of U.S. trading partners had for years: Create jobs cheaply by subsidizing exports. "The United States has been a patsy for what our trading partners have been doing for too long," said Sen. Mack Mattingly, R-Ga. — and his sentiments typified those of many members.

Yet the United States continued to preach the virtues of free trade. "As the leader of the West and as a country that has become great and rich because of economic freedom, America must be an unrelenting advocate of free trade," Reagan said in his State of the Union speech.

But like its trading partners such as the European Community (EC), which acted as the economic representative for certain Western European countries, the United States already had taken several large steps down the path of economic nationalism. Textile, steel and automobile imports all were restricted as of January 1983. The administration that same month approved a heavily subsidized sale of wheat to Egypt. And Reagan had alluded to plans for a war chest at the Export-Import Bank to subsidize U.S. goods that faced subsidized competition abroad. Reagan also indicated his intent to request new negotiating authority to reduce tariffs and eliminate barriers affecting services, investment and high technology trade.

Congress was threatening to enact even more severe trade measures. The automobile local content bill, a measure requiring automakers to use a percentage of U.S. parts and labor in cars sold in this country, which passed the House in 1982, was one of many trade-restriction measures likely to surface again in 1983. A "contract sanctity" provision, which prohibited the president from imposing sanctions that would break contracts on agricultural goods already signed by exporters, was added to the Export Administrtion Act in January 1983. Business leaders in 1983 advocated including manufactured goods as well.

None of the proposals was made in the name of "protectionism," a doctrine that, in principle, almost everyone opposed. But the definition of the term was becoming increasingly fluid. "Protecting American jobs against unfair foreign competition is not, in my view, protectionism," Sen. George J. Mitchell, D-Maine, said at a January 1983 Finance Committee hearing.

Regardless of what they were called, measures restricting trade carried the danger of triggering countermeasures abroad. For example, China already had imposed sanctions on U.S. agricultural imports in response to U.S insistence on low textile quotas. The result was even less trade, and more problems.

A growing number of members of Congress favored a strategy that approximated defense policy. The U.S. should restrict imports and subsidize exports, they argued, so that it would have bargaining strength when negotiating with other nations for freer trade. How far they carried that strategy remained to be seen. But given the predictions of a record trade deficit in 1983, those issues were certain to remain near the top of the agenda.

Auto, Steel Industries Face Decline

Although the U.S. economy was less dependent upon foreign trade for its health than those of most industrialized nations, a number of domestic industries relied heavily on export of their products for survival. Others were particularly vulnerable to imported products with which they had to compete on the domestic market.

In particular, two industries — automobile and steel — had been forced to compete against imported products, some of which were heavily subsidized by foreign governments to undercut American prices. The number of workers laid off by those two industries alone had reached alarming proportions.

The auto industry, despite a slightly optimistic showing in 1982, continued to lose its share of the domestic car market. In 1981 Japan sold $9.5 billion worth of automobiles to the United States and more than $2 billion worth of trucks. Even with the "voluntary" auto-import restrictions, whereby Japan agreed to limit the number of cars it exported to the United States, 1.9 million Japanese cars and 443,500 Japanese trucks were sold in this country in 1981, compared with 6.9 million American cars and 1.8 million American trucks, according to the U.S. Motor Vehicle Manufacturers Association.

In 1982 the value of auto imports rose to $20.6 billion from $18.4 billion the year before. Imports accounted for 27.9 percent of all cars sold in the United States. If this trend continued, said Gene Kasraiss, legislative representative of the United Auto Workers (UAW), imports could account for 35-40 percent of the U.S. automobile market by the end of the 1980s. This, he said, would have a disastrous effect on jobs. About 300,000 UAW members already were out of work as of March 1983.

In 1982 U.S. car producers sounded an optimistic note by listing a combined profit of $321 million, the first profit shown since 1979. But the gain appeared less sanguine when compared with combined losses of $1.8 billion in 1981 and $4.2 billion in 1980.

The automobile industry may have suffered its most difficult peacetime year ever in 1980. In January of that year it seemed that only Chrysler, the smallest of the Big Three automakers, was in really serious trouble. But in the months that followed Ford and General Motors also found themselves awash in red ink.

The full extent of the industry's financial bind became clear at the end of October 1980. General Motors reported a third-quarter loss of $567 million, the company's second consecutive quarterly deficit. The following day Ford announced a third-quarter loss of $595 million, the largest quarterly net loss in the U.S. auto industry and one of the biggest quarterly deficits for any U.S. corporation.

Later that month Chrysler reported a third-quarter loss of $489.7 million, the company's second-largest quarterly deficit. Chrysler announced Dec. 8 that it needed $350 million in additional federal loan guarantees within the next 30 days if it was to remain in business; the $1.5 billion federal bail out came in January of 1981.

More bad news came on Nov. 10, 1980, when the U.S. International Trade Commission rejected a request by Ford and the United Auto Workers union for temporary protection against Japanese auto imports while the domestic industry implemented its $80 billion conversion to small, fuel-efficient cars. The commission ruled that imports were not the major cause of injury to American automakers.

The flood of Japanese auto imports, in combination with the sagging U.S. auto industry, gave rise to more calls for the government to cut back on Japanese imports. In 1981 restrictions were voluntarily agreed to by the Japanese on the number of automobiles they would export to the United States. House Speaker Thomas P. O'Neill Jr., D-Mass., told an autoworkers' group in March 1982 that if he were president he would put an embargo on Japanese autos. Charles Peters, editor of *The Washington Monthly,* also called for an embargo on Japanese cars in the March 1982 issue of the magazine. "I know all my liberal friends will scream and say, 'Don't you believe in free trade?' " Peters wrote. "My answer is: not when it's killing us."

The swelling ranks of unemployed Americans were at the root of the concern over Japanese imports. As one bumper sticker put it: "When you bought your Japanese car, 10 Americans lost their jobs." That concern was heightened when unemployment figures swelled to 10.2 percent in February of 1983.

U.S. Trade Representative Brock in February 1983 extended for an additional year the 1.6 million limit on Japanese auto imports in the United States. The limitation was an extension of the two-year "voluntary" agreement first reached in 1981. Labor leaders and several senators had urged that the limitation be lowered to 1.28 million cars a year and extended through 1985, but the Japanese would agree only to the 1.6 million limitation through March 31, 1984.

U.S. Manufacturers Fight Back

Many believed the Japanese agreed to an extension of the limitation because they feared that proposed protectionist measures, such as the domestic content bill before Congress in 1983, would become a reality.

The measure, passed by the House in December 1982, would have required that automakers use a high percentage of U.S. labor and parts in cars they sold in this country. It would have set domestic content ratios for automakers based on the number of cars they sold in the United States. Given 1982's level of sales, Toyota and Nissan (Datsun) would have been required to have 70 to 75 percent domestic content to their cars by 1985, while smaller makers such as Toyo Kogyo (Mazda) and Honda would have had to achieve ratios of between 20 and 40 percent.

The major U.S. makers also would have faced a domestic content requirement of 90 percent, limiting their ability to buy parts from abroad. Stiff quotas would have been applied to companies that failed to meet the bill's required ratios. The bill failed to pass the Senate in the remaining days of the 1982 lame-duck session, but support for it still was strong in the 98th Congress.

Others believed Japanese cars had sold well in this country because American automakers were not giving consumers what they wanted —

reliability and economy. When asked if the Japanese were to blame for Detroit's troubles, Trade Representative Brock said, "I don't think you've ever heard anybody in this administration blame the Japanese for our domestic automobile problems. This is just not a valid point of criticism."

One sign that Detroit was learning from Japan's success was an agreement signed in February 1983 between GM and the Toyota Motor Corporation of Japan. The agreement marked the first time an American car manufacturer had sought outside help in manufacturing cars within the United States. The joint venture allowed GM to build the small front-wheel-drive Corolla II in its Fremont, Calif., plant — under Japanese management with the chief executive to be chosen by Toyota. Other executives would be chosen from both companies.

One reason GM was receptive to joint production was that its J-car — a $5 billion investment — had been a big disappointment. "GM has not been so successful yet with its small lines like the J-car," said Yukio Kobayashi, an analyst for Nomura Securities Co., in the March 9, 1982, *New York Times*. "If GM had full confidence in its ability to develop small cars by itself, it would not talk to Toyota."

In addition, GM said that the agreement would create 3,000 jobs in its Fremont plant and another 9,000 jobs elsewhere to make components for the new model. The plant was expected to hire back half of the people laid off when GM closed the facility, but re-employment was not guaranteed by the Toyota executives. Workers would have to adapt not only to Japanese management techniques but also to the use of robots, which were expected to do one-third of the work.

From Toyota's perspective, the use of a GM plant provided a chance to start American production without making a heavy investment in equipment. Moreover, it was anticipated that cooperation with a U.S. automaker could cool some of the growing anti-Japanese sentiment in the United States. The GM deal marked the second time Toyota had tested the waters in the United States. In 1981 preliminary joint production talks had been held with the Ford Motor Co., but the talks fell through.

Steel Industry Suffers From Imports

Another basic industry troubled by the recession and foreign competition was the steel industry. While iron and steel imports fell by $1.3 billion between 1981 and 1982 to $9.9 billion — partly as a result of a

1982 agreement with European producers to limit exports to the United States — domestic steel mills operated at only 40 percent capacity and reported a staggering 50 percent unemployment rate for 1982.

The steel industry as a whole was faced with an urgent need to replace outmoded equipment — and quickly — if they were going to have any chance of competing successfully against highly efficient manufacturers in Japan, subsidized producers in Europe and cheap-labor mills in the Third World. But industry representatives said that companies could not afford to make costly investments in modern equipment unless they were protected in the meantime against imports, which foreign producers allegedly were "dumping" on the U.S. market at below-cost prices. While steel spokesmen conceded that new tax laws and revised environmental regulations had provided significant incentives for investment, they said that protection from unfair foreign competition also was a prerequisite for modernization.

Demand for U.S. Steel Declines. After the end of World War II, demand for steel continued to grow despite substitution of new metal alloys, plastics and other materials. Steel remained vital to the construction of buildings, bridges, roads, automotive equipment, rails, rail vehicles, ships, industrial and mining machinery, farm equipment, household appliances, weapons and a variety of other products. Even so, U.S. demand for steel grew much more slowly than demand for manufactured goods in general, and during the two decades after 1960, foreign suppliers tended to capture what little growth there was in the American market.

A number of factors made it hard for U.S. producers to compete with foreign suppliers. During the 1940s and 1950s, U.S. prices for iron ore climbed sharply, while new sources were discovered in countries such as Venezuela, Australia and Canada. By the 1960s world iron ore prices were dropping relative to U.S. prices since shipping costs also were declining during this period.

During the years immediately after World War II, U.S. steel producers also suffered the disadvantage of being located in the country with the world's highest standard of living and highest wage rates. The gap between the United States and other nations narrowed after 1960, and workers in a number of industrial countries began to earn more than U.S. workers. But U.S. steel workers continued to be paid more than their counterparts in many competitor nations.

Steel workers were a well-paid blue-collar elite almost everywhere.

They worked under hazardous and unpleasant conditions, were highly skilled and very highly unionized. Steel workers were by far the most highly paid blue-collar workers in the United States, and the difference between their wages and the wages paid other working-class groups was much larger than it was in Germany and Japan. According to a study by Merrill Lynch, Pierce, Fenner & Smith Inc., which was released in June 1979, average hourly earnings in the U.S. steel industry were 59 percent above the average in all manufacturing industries.

In countries such as Japan, wage rates in steel increased quickly after World War II, but because of extensive modernization of plant and equipment, productivity climbed even faster. According to Robert Crandall, an authority on the industry with the Brookings Institution in Washington, D.C., Japanese wages went up nearly 250 percent in the decade after the 1958 recession, but unit labor costs — the amount of wages needed to produce a given amount of steel — declined 30 percent.

During the same period in the United States, wages increased just 39 percent, but unit labor costs remained unchanged. In 1978, according to Crandall, a U.S. worker had to put in about 8 hours to produce a ton of finished steel, while a Japanese worker put in between 7.0 and 7.5 hours. According to an article published in *Time* magazine in March 1980, a Japanese worker produced about 4.8 tons of steel in a 40-hour week, a U.S. worker 4.6 tons and a West German worker 3.8 tons.

Labor-Management Reach Agreement. In early March 1983 the battered steel industry signed a historic 41-month agreement with the United Steelworkers Union (USW) that cut the wages of close to 260,000 steel workers. The new agreement reduced wages by 9 percent and was expected to save the seven companies that make up Big Steel an estimated $2 billion. Before the contract was signed the companies were operating under labor costs averaging $26.12 an hour. The agreement represented the first time the USW had given in to management's demands to cut wages.

The companies won an immediate $1.25 an hour in wages and gains in cost-of-living payments and vacation pay. The union, in return, received guaranteed improvements in unemployment benefits for laid-off workers. Also, management agreed to use all its savings to rebuild the steel industry — a move demanded by labor after U.S. Steel purchased Marathon Oil Co. in 1982.

The contract followed on the heels of threats by major American consumers, such as General Motors, that they would buy their steel overseas if union and management did not reach an agreement by March 1, 1983, and eliminate the threat of a mid-summer strike. Experts believed the contract would relieve some of the industry's cost burdens, but would only be a small advance toward facing the larger problem of the industry's decreasing production capability.

After the "oil shock" of 1973-74, which threw the world economy into a protracted slump, total U.S. steel-making capacity remained essentially unchanged at about 156-158 million net tons a year. Total employment in steel, however, fell from 544,000 in 1969 to 361,000 in December 1981; the number of workers paid hourly wages in December was 258,000. During 1981 alone, over 80,000 workers were laid off or put on abbreviated work schedules.

Plant capacity utilization also continued to drop; the lower capacity utilization fell, the higher the unit costs rose, creating a vicious circle in which manufacturers became more and more vulnerable to foreign competition. During 1981 as a whole, imports accounted for close to 20 percent of the steel sold in the United States. By January 1982 imports accounted for 26.3 percent of the U.S. steel market. The statistics probably understated the amount of steel imports because they referred only to raw steel, excluding steel imported in the form of Japanese automobiles, German appliances and the like.

Many steel companies reported improved results for 1981, but that was largely because 1980 was such a bad year for the industry. Steel production fell 18 percent in 1980, and while it increased by 6.7 percent in 1981, it remained 20 percent lower than it was in 1973. Steel companies tended to do relatively well in the first half of 1981, but as the year wore on the situation deteriorated. U.S. Steel, Bethlehem, Republic Steel and Inland Steel all announced steep drops in their earnings for the final quarter of 1981.

Conditions did not improve in 1982; steel companies lost $3.3 billion collectively, mills were operating at 40 percent capacity and 140,000 USW members were laid off.

Steel Production Worldwide

By 1977, a critical year for the industry worldwide, it was apparent that steel was overbuilt on a global scale. In the United States, the industry had been limping along ever since a national steel strike in 1958-59. Dollar devaluations in 1971 and 1973 gave the American industry a boost (a devaluation decreases the price of exports and increases the price of imports) and from 1969 to 1974 European countries and Japan entered into "voluntary restraint agreements" limiting their exports to the United States. Still, between 1974 and 1979, the EC's steel industry lost 16 percent of its workers, roughly 125,000 people. Employment in Japan's industry dropped 9.5 percent between 1974 and 1978. In 1977 falling world demand led to increasingly fierce competition, and, as world prices dropped, exports to the United States began to climb.

The industry asserted, with considerable basis in fact, that steel companies in Europe and in other foreign countries were benefiting from massive government subsidies. In principle, the EC countries agreed to end subsidies by 1985 and not to introduce new steel-aid programs after July 1, 1983. But it remained to be seen whether they would hold to their commitment.

U.S. steel makers accused their European counterparts of seeking to solve their own problems of unemployment by dumping steel on the U.S. market, where it accounted for close to 20 percent of all domestic sales in 1981. This was made possible by government subsidies of the industry, which enabled European manufacturers to sell their products abroad at below cost of production, thus making U.S. steel uncompetitive at home. As a number of U.S. companies announced plant closings, a "steel caucus" formed in Congress to generate pressure to help the industry.

President Jimmy Carter said that the administration was planning a broad program of relief for the U.S. industry, which would include tax incentives for modernization and some relief from environmental requirements. His administration also introduced the "trigger-price" mechanism, which established a minimum price for which steel imports could be sold on the U.S. market. Sale of imports below the trigger price allowed U.S. steel makers to initiate anti-dumping suits against the allegedly offending producer countries. Industry spokesmen contended that officials in the U.S. Treasury and State Departments had been reluctant to enforce trade laws vigorously for fear of jeopardizing wider foreign policy objectives. A partial resolution of the dispute was achieved, however, when the Reagan administration agreed in August 1982 to drop anti-dumping suits in exchange for EC quotas on steel exports to the United States.

Nonetheless, American complaints aroused alarm in Europe. EC Commissioner Etienne Davignon was quoted in a Feb. 14, 1982, article in *The New York Times* as declaring that "protectionism is no longer a risk; it is a probability." In the United States as well there was some concern about the industry's methods and ultimate objectives. Richard I. Kirkland Jr., who wrote regularly about steel for *Fortune* magazine, argued in the Feb. 8, 1982, issue that the industry really hoped to maneuver the government into imposing quotas on steel imports. While the American Iron and Steel Institute denied that this was the industry's intention, there had been support for quotas from some corporate executives, notably Thomas C. Graham, chief executive officer of Jones & Laughlin Steel Corp.

In December 1982 the U.S. steel industry announced that it was asking the government to put restrictions on imports of Japanese steel. The request, based on a complaint of unfair trade practices, was filed with the Office of the U.S. Trade Representative and asked for a one-third reduction in imports from Japan. Japanese steel imports had been averaging about 6 million tons annually since 1978. Steel industry spokesmen brought the case at a time when "protectionist" sentiment was rising in Congress. Japanese steel exporters counterattacked the complaint, urging the government to reject the U.S. steel industry's request. Reagan was still considering what to do about this request as of April 1983.

Agriculture Suffers From Competition

The United States was born an agrarian nation. In 1790 more than 90 percent of all Americans were involved in agriculture, and it was not until the 1880s that agricultural employment dropped below half of the work force. But mechanization, scientific farming methods, periodic economic calamities, the lure of the cities, the creation of huge farm co-operatives and "agribusiness" corporations, and recent inflation and high interest rates all contributed to the dramatic decline in the agricultural work force.

In the 1970s, farm employment dropped to 3.1 million workers. Only 3 percent of American workers were involved in agriculture in 1983, and their ranks were expected to thin by 200,000 to 500,000, or 7 to 16 percent, by 1990.

Despite their decreasing numbers, farmers continued to play a critical role in the U.S. economy. U.S. farm exports in 1982 represented 17.7 percent of all U.S. exports. During the 1970s Americans were able to pay their foreign oil bills largely thanks to a significant rise in agricultural exports, which quadrupled between 1973 and 1979 to over $40 billion. In 1982, however, agricultural exports, while maintaining a comfortable surplus over imports, fell to $36.6 billion from $43.3 billion in 1981. Every billion dollars in farm export sales created at least 26,000 jobs, according to Sen. Thad Cochran, R-Miss.

Surplus, Recession Diminish Exports

The reasons for the decline in agricultural exports, according to Jim Donald, chairman of the Department of Agriculture's World Food and Agricultural Outlook and Situation Board, were "very weak world economic conditions, along with the strength of the dollar." Due to the increased value of the dollar over nearly all major currencies in 1982, U.S. agricultural commodities tended to be priced higher in overseas markets than competitive products from other countries. *(Dollar value box, p. 77)*

At the same time favorable weather conditions among grain exporting nations and weakening demand due to the worldwide recession caused sizable surpluses of grain stocks, further depressing prices for those commodities.

If America's farmers stopped planting wheat and corn in 1983, Americans, in theory, would have been able to keep right on eating. The mountains of surplus grain built up in the nation's storage bins by the end of 1982 equaled nearly a year's worth of domestic consumption. Officials at the Agriculture Department (USDA) estimated that "ending stocks" — grain for which there was no commercial demand at the end of 1982 — would amount to nearly 150 million metric tons. In 1981 America used 177 million metric tons for food, feed and fuel, and exported nearly 10 million metric tons. Federal outlays for price supports for grain and dairy products — also in surplus — cost an unprecedented $12 billion in fiscal 1982, about four times their average annual level.

For nearly a decade, the government had relied on export commodity sales to siphon off excess production while boosting farm income. During that period, exports had grown 12 to 14 percent annually. But in 1982 commodity exports were 10 percent to 11 percent lower in value than in 1981.

When farm exports were balanced against imported goods, they made a positive contribution of $26 billion to the U.S. balance of trade, according to the Commerce Department. But even as American farmers were becoming dependent on foreign markets, those markets were eroding. The protective, highly subsidized farm policy of the EC, adopted to stabilize markets and assure domestic food supplies, matured during the 1970s. Europe reduced its need for other nations' food and became

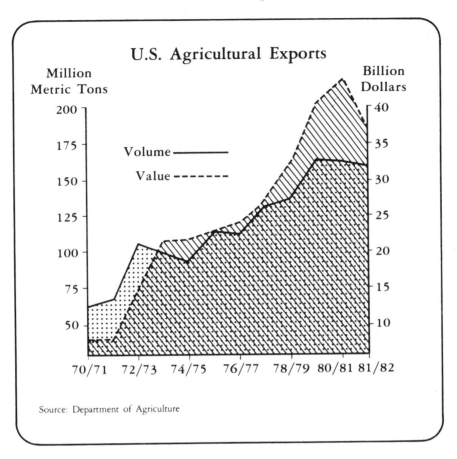

U.S. Agricultural Exports

Million Metric Tons

Billion Dollars

Volume ———
Value - - - - - -

70/71 72/73 74/75 76/77 78/79 80/81 81/82

Source: Department of Agriculture

an aggressive exporter of its own agricultural products.

Also, developing nations borrowed heavily during this period to finance development, energy or food imports. The resulting debts meant that many countries were unable to finance new U.S. food purchases. Finally, there were U.S. trade restrictions, of which President Reagan's effort to withhold natural gas pipeline components from the Soviet Union was only the latest example. The pipeline sanctions, originally imposed in December 1981 in retaliation for the military crackdown in Poland, finally were removed in November 1982. *(Pipeline, box, p. 71)*

Reputation Damaged by Restraints on Trade

The farm community, Congress and the administration generally agreed that U.S. agricultural trade had suffered from a decade of using trade restraint as a political tool, which caused foreign purchasers to view the United States as an unreliable supplier. They pointed to the U.S. embargo on grain sales to the Soviet Union, which President Carter imposed in 1980 in response to the Soviet invasion of Afghanistan. This embargo served as a crucial factor in diverting foreign buyers to other, more reliable grain suppliers, in particular Argentina and Canada.

The 1980 grain embargo cost the U.S. economy $11.4 billion, but trade experts maintained that a 1973 soybean embargo sent earlier exceptionally damaging signals abroad: that even America's friends, such as Japan, could not count on contracted food deliveries.

The soybean embargo was imposed in the belief that domestic supplies were too low to permit exports. Contracts were suspended briefly, then partially restored, with permission to ship only half the contracted quantity of soybeans. Before the embargo, Japan bought 98 percent of its soybeans from U.S. suppliers; afterwards, it bought large quantities from Brazil and invested in major expansions of soybean production in Brazil.

Smaller U.S. crops and rising food prices prompted informal federal export controls beginning in 1974 and a voluntary but effective embargo on grain sales to Russia in 1975. Some observers viewed the cutoff as an unsuccessful effort to extract lower oil prices from the Soviet Union.

The cutoff ended in October 1975 when the United States and Russia agreed to a five-year pact calling for minimum U.S.S.R. grain purchases of 6 million to 8 million tons a year. The agreement was meant to make Soviet grain buying more predictable so as to prevent market distortions of the type that occurred after the 1972 purchase.

Carter's 1980 grain embargo changed perceptions of the grain pact. Because he allowed delivery to the U.S.S.R. of the minimum quantity of grain during the embargo, the agreement came to be viewed as an essential guarantee for export contracts.

Carter also used less publicized trade restrictions against certain nations, such as withholding spare parts for American machinery. Those actions were meant to convey American disapproval of terrorism or human rights violations, according to Jules Katz, who served in the Carter State Department as assistant secretary for economic and business affairs.

President Reagan ended the grain embargo April 24, 1981, and extended the expiring terms of the pact twice, each time for a year. Farm prices did not recover when Reagan lifted the embargo, and members of

Controversy Over Siberian Gas Pipeline

The Export Administration Act, first enacted in 1940, gave U.S. presidents the authority to limit exports for defense or foreign policy reasons. While the act repeatedly was modified to reduce the number of export items that the president may ban at any time, presidential application of the law provoked controversy in recent years. President Jimmy Carter twice banned exports to the Soviet Union for political reasons, once in 1978 after the imprisonment of Soviet dissident Anatoly Scharansky and again, in retaliation for the Soviet invasion of Afghanistan in December 1979, when he imposed an embargo on U.S. grain sales to the Soviet Union.

By far the most controversial application of the Export Administration Act was President Ronald Reagan's ban on U.S. exports for use in the construction of the Siberian gas pipeline linking the vast natural gas reserves east of the Ural Mountains with markets in energy-poor Western Europe. The sanctions originally were imposed in December 1981 in retaliation for the military crackdown in Poland. They prohibited U.S. companies from exporting oil and gas drilling equipment to the Soviets and were expanded in June 1982 to include foreign subsidiaries of U.S. firms as well as independent companies producing equipment under license from U.S. firms.

The sanctions were roundly condemned by America's European allies, who accused the administration of violating international law in forcing foreign firms to break previous contracts with the Soviet Union, as well as by U.S. firms that had provided licenses to the affected European companies. Reagan finally removed the sanctions on Nov. 13, 1982, and came to an agreement with the North Atlantic Treaty Organization (NATO) allies on a blueprint to study the entire question of East-West trade and its implications for Western security. The study was being conducted by the Organization for Economic Cooperation and Development (OECD) and Cocom, the NATO organization responsible for determining the potential strategic value of exports to the Soviet Union.

Congress blamed what they called a de facto embargo on grain sales. Sellers and buyers were reluctant to trade, they said, because of fears that a new embargo would result from the unsettled political situation in Poland. They insisted that only a new multi-year grain agreement could quell market jitters. Reagan, however, broke off negotiations for a new long-term U.S.-U.S.S.R. grain pact in December 1981 to protest the imposition of martial law in Poland.

The cumulative effect of these actions was to isolate America with the reputation of a tarnished trader. When European Community nations agreed to go along with Great Britain's trade sanctions against Argentina during the 1982 Falklands crisis, the decision affected only new contracts, not existing agreements. Even Britain permitted delivery to Argentina on existing British contracts.

That behavior was standard for every nation except the United States, according to Joseph Halow, executive director of the North American Export Grain Association.

Congressional and Administrative Actions

Many members of Congress and farmers wanted to attack the problem of America's tattered trading reputation. They wanted Congress to guarantee that export contracts would be honored despite any embargos or other foreign policy actions, a tactic opposed by the administration.

Sen. Dave Durenberger, R-Minn., proposed a bill in the fall of 1982 that was meant to improve the U.S. trade image abroad by guaranteeing that trade contracts would be honored. The proposal required that except in time of war or national emergency delivery be made on agricultural exports under contract at the time an embargo was imposed, if delivery had been scheduled within 270 days.

The bill's sweeping guarantee of delivery of agricultural exports was objectionable to the State Department because it restricted the president's freedom to act. But because the trade guarantee had wide support within the financially troubled farm community, administration officials avoided public objections to it. Despite the State Department's objections, the bill was passed in December 1982 and in January 1983 the president signed it into law.

Reagan, in the meantime, had sought to repair the Soviet market with oral assurances of reliability. His actions included a March 22, 1982, statement to farm editors ruling out embargoes except in "extreme situations," only if other nations cooperated and only for all goods, not just agricultural commodities. On Oct. 15, 1982, Reagan said that U.S.

negotiators would assure Soviet buyers of delivery of up to 23 million metric tons of grain, if they met certain conditions.

Administration officials also sought to enlarge non-Soviet markets, repeatedly threatening to fight what they said were unfair European and Japanese trade barriers. They filed trade complaints with the General Agreement on Tariffs and Trade (GATT), the international treaty organization that administers guidelines on tariffs, subsidies and other aspects of trade. *(GATT box, p. 83)*

On Oct. 20, 1982, Agriculture Secretary John R. Block announced a new, three-year $1.5 billion "blended credit" program. Foreign purchasers could buy U.S. commodities at favorable interest rates, using a combination of interest-free loans and market-rate, federally guaranteed commercial loans. The 1982 omnibus reconciliation act required the administration to devote $175 million to $190 million in Commodity Credit Corporation (CCC) funds to promote exports by subsidized financing. Some $100 million of the administration's blended credit program for the first year came from those funds.

Moreover, the sheer size of the surplus had begun to prompt questions about federal farm programs that relied on exports as a safety valve. Farm lobbyists were beginning to talk of options such as multibillion-dollar trade subsidies or strict limits on how much farmers could grow.

Block suggested giving some of the surplus grain back to farms to "pay" them for reducing the amount they grew in 1983. The plan called for expanding an existing paid land diversion program that Congress included in the August 1982 budget reconciliation bill. Under that program, wheat producers were required to idle 15 percent of the acreage they customarily planted, and corn producers 10 percent, to qualify for federal farm programs such as price support loans. Farmers retiring an additional 5 percent in wheat acreage or 10 percent in corn acreage would be paid in cash for doing so.

Block proposed that farmers be paid in surplus grain for retiring even more cropland — up to 100 percent in the specified crops. The farmers could sell the grain and not have to plant a crop the next year.

The Reagan administration failed to win congressional endorsement of the proposal in the final moments of the 1982 session. But on Jan. 11, 1983, President Reagan announced that he would go along with the plan anyway. Block said that no congressional action was needed on the surplus giveaway plan. Department lawyers, according to Block, had resolved legal problems that had prompted him to unsuccessfully seek hurry-up approval of the plan by Congress.

The "payment in kind" (PIK), dubbed a "crop swap" by Reagan, was in addition to previously announced cash payments for production cuts. With federal support, a farmer could retire up to half his normal acreage in 1984 or in some cases, whole farms. In March 1983 Congress passed legislation exempting farmers in the PIK program from federal tax laws that would have required them to pay income taxes on PIK commodities in the same year they received them from the federal government.

The same week he announced the PIK program, in a speech to the annual American Farm Bureau Federation convention in Dallas, Reagan also announced a $250 million increase in a program to finance farm exports with a combination of interest-free federal loans and federally guaranteed commercial loans. Department officials also were considering increased food donations abroad. But they stressed that no combination of government actions could make the surplus vanish quickly.

Reagan's attempts to induce major cutbacks in farm production were a marked change in his farm policy, which had stressed all-out production and little government interference. Block had estimated that PIK would take 23 million acres out of production, but the actual amount, announced March 22, 1983, far exceeded expectations. Farmers pledged to put 69.1 million acres under PIK and 13.1 million acres under the acreage diversion program. Together the 82.2 million acres to be left unplanted represented 36 percent of the farm land eligible for the two programs.

Adminstration Plans Farm Export Subsidies

In October 1982 the Agriculture Department (USDA) began offering export loans at about 2 percentage points below commercial rates for purchases of American commodities. In January 1983 the USDA arranged a one million metric ton flour sale to Egypt by giving some surplus wheat to millers who would provide the flour below world prices.

The Reagan export subsidies were relatively modest in scope, compared with those in Europe, which totaled about $6 billion in 1982. Between October 1982 and February 1983, some $350 million in interest-free U.S. loans had been committed for foreign customers, which, when combined with federally guaranteed private loans, provided "blended credit" export loan packages below commercial interest rates. The cost

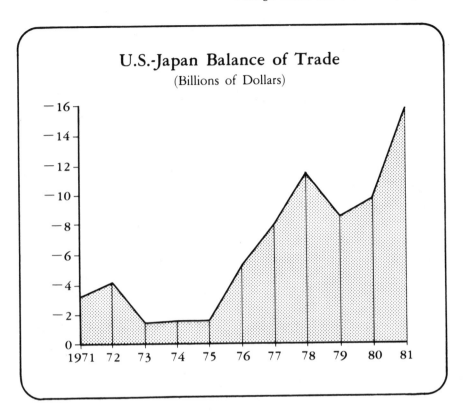

U.S.-Japan Balance of Trade
(Billions of Dollars)

of the subsidy in the Egyptian flour sale was not determined, because it involved bonuses of wheat to U.S. millers to supply the flour cheaply to Egypt.

The last time the United States directly subsidized farm exports, it did so for more than 20 years. Between 1949 and 1972 the government paid commodity exporters the difference between high, federally supported domestic prices and lower world prices. The payments were suspended in September 1972 when the U.S.-U.S.S.R. grain sales pushed world prices well above domestic prices; the payments never were reinstituted.

Until 1982, other nations guaranteed high prices for their own farmers, subsidized cheap overseas sales, and believed that the United States would not fight back. The Egyptian flour sale elicited a swift complaint to the GATT by the EC, which was shut out of the Egyptian market for the year by the sale. The U.S. deal was similar to subsidized EC flour sales that were the subject of a U.S. complaint to GATT.

The $6 billion a year that it would take to match EC subsidies, or "rebates" as European officials termed them, seemed cheap, compared with budget estimates of $18 billion in outlays for fiscal 1983 for domestic price support loans and payments to farmers who could not sell their crops. But it was double what the price supports had averaged during the 1970s.

Leading Competitors in World Trade

With the contraction of economic growth and exports brought on by the global recession, numerous conflicts erupted among the principle trading blocs, which were locked in increasingly fierce competition to maintain their overseas markets while protecting their domestic ones. Japan, the strongest of these, incurred a surplus of nearly $30 billion in 1982 in its trading with the United States and the EC — $19 billion with the United States alone. It was an embarrassment of riches for Japan, which was accused of building its surplus by unfairly excluding many of their goods from the Japanese market. *(Chart, p. 75)*

Regardless of the economic consequences of this trade imbalance, its political significance was indisputable. Trade had become increasingly important to the United States during the 1970s. There were numerous reasons, other than import barriers, for the trade imbalance, but the strength of the dollar was perhaps the most important. Japan's need to import virtually all of its oil and other natural resources, and to export manufactured goods to pay for those resources, was another.

Japanese Problems

While previous conflicts between the United States and Japan centered on Japanese textiles, color television sets and steel, problem areas in early 1983 were Japanese auto exports and U.S access to Japanese markets, especially for sales of citrus fruits and beef. Although Japan agreed in 1981 to export no more than 1.6 million autos a year to the United States, Japanese cars still accounted for one-fourth of the new car sales in America, and Detroit had asked for further restrictions. On the other hand, the American suggestion that Japan open its markets to a greater share of U.S. beef and citrus products had provoked mass demonstrations in the streets of Tokyo by Japanese farmers who protested that the Japanese market already absorbed about half of all U.S. exports of these items.

Business and government officials and members of Congress had

Overvalued Dollar vs. Undervalued Yen

While falling demand for U.S. exports was attributable largely to the dampening effects of the worldwide recession, much of the blame for the declining trade balance was placed on the overvaluation of the dollar on foreign exchange markets.

According to Treasury Department statistics, the dollar appreciated 20.4 percent from the beginning of 1981 through January 1983 against the currencies of the 23 other countries belonging to the Organization for Economic Cooperation and Development (OECD). With each successive appreciation of the dollar's value, U.S. exports became more costly and less competitive with similar goods produced abroad. Dollar appreciation also made domestically produced goods less attractive than imports to American consumers.

During the last quarter of 1978, the Japanese yen traded at a rate of 190 to the dollar. As of April 18, 1983, that rate stood at 225 yen to the dollar. The implications of that huge swing were clear; Japanese products were far cheaper for the American buyer than they were four years earlier, and U.S. products in Japan were far more expensive. That alone, according to many economists, accounted for the lion's share of the $20 billion trade deficit between the two countries.

The reasons for the misalignment of exchange rates were not clearly understood, but at least part of it was due to trade policies.

The Reagan administration followed a loose fiscal policy, cutting taxes and permitting huge deficits, and left the inflation fight to a tight monetary policy. That resulted in extraordinarily high real interest rates (after adjustment for inflation). High interest rates encourage foreigners to invest in the U.S. money markets, increasing the demand for dollars and pushing up exchange rates.

In Japan, the opposite policy was followed. Faced with huge budget deficits, the government launched a tight fiscal policy to eliminate red ink. A loose monetary policy, accompanied by low interest rates, was relied on to stimulate the nation's sagging economy. And low interest rates reduced the demand for yen.

C. Fred Bergsten, director of the Institute for International Economics, noted that the dollar also had been boosted by world troubles.

complained loudly about the barriers foreign businesses faced in Japan. These included Japan's vigorous inspection of foreign-made goods and agricultural products and a distribution system that was bewildering to many foreigners. U.S. trade officials pointed to the Japanese cigarette industry as a particularly egregious example of that nation's non-tariff barriers. American-made cigarettes accounted for less than 2 percent of the Japanese market in 1981, compared with about 20 percent of sales in some European countries. One reason American cigarette manufacturers had found it difficult to sell to Japan was the Japan Tobacco and Salt Public Corp. (JTS), a government monopoly that tightly controlled the cigarette market.

JTS was required to buy all the tobacco produced by Japan's 113,000 small tobacco growers, a commitment that supported the domestic industry at the expense of importers. JTS also limited the number of licensed retail outlets that could sell imported cigarettes, allowed only new brands of imported cigarettes to be advertised on television, and imposed a 57 percent excise tax and a 20 percent distribution and handling fee on imported brands.

The U.S. clamor for market access did not go unnoticed in Japan. The Japanese agreed to put into effect in April 1982 tariff cuts on semi-conductor parts that had been scheduled to go into effect in fiscal years 1983 and 1984. On Jan. 22, 1982, Japan announced it would eliminate 67 non-tariff barriers and set up an ombudsman's office to handle individual complaints on trade matters from abroad. Among other things, the Japanese agreed to simplify testing procedures for certain types of automobiles, accept animal test data from abroad on medicines and cosmetics, and relax certain safety standards for electrical appliances.

The Japanese Ministry of International Trade and Industry (MITI) attributed the trade imbalance to factors other than tariffs or non-tariff barriers, such as import quotas and stiff quality-control standards, according to a study published in 1981 by the Japan Economic Institute of America Inc. The report pointed out that the Japanese economy also was troubled by rising unemployment and a slowdown of its basic industries, including steel and autos. Japan's exports in fact fell by more than 13 percent in the second half of 1982, their biggest postwar decline. Japanese officials, fearing isolation by Japan's trading partners, pointed to tariff cuts on more than 300 imported items, but U.S. and EC officials responded that Japan had not gone far enough toward removing its trade barriers.

The Japanese took the position that American business executives had not worked hard enough to tailor their products to the Japanese market. "Forty years ago the American Army and Navy penetrated the Japanese islands physically," said Naohiro Amaya, a trade adviser to the Japanese government, during a March 3, 1982, MacNeil/Lehrer Report. "We . . . shuddered at the vitality and guts of the American soldier. . . . Now, they are complaining about the difficulty of getting into the Japanese market. I think we wish them to revitalize their vitality and guts. . . . What is important is to study the Japanese market and study what the consumers are wishing to have. . . . If they appeal to the consumers, there is no doubt that they can get penetration into the Japanese market."

European Trade Difficulties

Western European countries also were pressing for greater access to Japanese markets. France, in particular, retaliated by erecting non-tariff barriers of its own to Japanese products. The French government in 1982 required that all Japanese video-tape recorders be processed through a small, provincial customhouse and that all documents and instruction manuals accompanying imports be translated into French.

While the 10 member countries of the EC focused their complaints of unfair trade practices on Japan, they were in turn the object of similar complaints from the United States. While the United States still enjoyed a $5.3 billion trade surplus with the combined economies of the EC in 1982, its margin of advantage shrank from its 1981 surplus of $9 billion. While 1982 saw a partial resolution of the steel dispute between the United States and the EC, the battle still raged over the EC's subsidization of agricultural exports, which U.S. farmers blamed for their own falling exports on world markets.

To this complaint the Europeans replied that their trade deficit with the United States in agricultural products had continued to rise, after reaching $6.8 billion in 1980. They attributed the American decline in world agricultural trade not to European subsidies but rather to the increased value of the dollar, high interest rates, reduced U.S. grain sales to the Soviet Union and record harvests at a time of contracting overseas markets. This deepening trade conflict was further underscored by European condemnation of the Reagan administration's imposition of sanctions against European subsidiaries of U.S. companies selling equipment for use in construction of the Siberian gas pipeline.

Sluggish growth in the industrialized nations also depressed demand for the commodities produced by the less developed countries (LDCs) of the Third World, whose lack of industrial development made them dependent upon export of raw materials such as iron ore, copper and bauxite. With the exception of the oil-exporting countries, those less developed nations were faced with a staggering combined external debt of about $500 billion, which they were unable to repay for lack of export-generated income. Unable to export commodities, the LDCs reduced imports, 40 percent of which came from the industrialized nations. For the U.S. economy, which directed one-third of its exports to Third World nations, the effect of the debt crisis in these countries precipitated a further deepening of its own trade deficit.

Reciprocity Bills Introduced

A number of bills were introduced in Congress asking for retaliatory action against nations that did not provide equal access to their markets. According to former U.S. Deputy Trade Representative David R. Macdonald, these so-called "reciprocity" bills would ensure that the United States had access to other countries' markets to sell those products it exported most efficiently, in return for allowing other countries to export to the U.S. market those products they produced most efficiently.

The bill that gained the most attention originally was sponsored by Sen. John C. Danforth, R-Mo., and was approved by the Senate Finance Committee in June 1982. That bill was designed to strengthen the procedures for enforcing violations of existing trade law and to require the government to seek international agreements on services, high-technology and investment trade.

The legislation at first received mixed reviews from the administration. Testifying before a congressional subcommittee in March 1982, Brock said the Reagan administration was committed to the concept of free trade and was firmly against protectionist legislation. Although the president was pushing Japan to give American companies more access to its domestic market, Brock said, the administration would not support any law that would force U.S. trade policy to require "bilateral, sectoral or product-by-product reciprocity."

But when the bill was reintroduced into the Senate in March 1983, U.S. Trade Representative Brock said that it had the president's strong support. The administration's attitude toward the bill had changed by

1983 because, unlike other trade proposals, the bill did not propose trade sanctions. Rather, it left the authority and the initiative for imposing sanctions in the president's hands. It asked for an expansion of the president's authority to retaliate against unfair trading practices by other countries and would require the administration to seek new international agreements on trade in services and high technology.

Throughout 1982 and early 1983, negotiators from Brock's office had stepped up their demands on the Japanese. In spite of their general opposition to legislation that restricted trade, administration negotiators found Congress' protectionist sentiment a very useful tool. The Japanese, already faced with automobile export restraints, were increasingly frightened of the possibility of more restrictions. As a result, they were anxious to please the United States.

As for the concept of reciprocity, there was evidence that American business leaders were not overly enthusiastic about it. An "informal sampling of business leaders" taken in April 1982 by *Fortune* magazine found "no one openly in favor of reciprocity legislation; most business-men seemed fearful of retaliation." A House Ways and Means sub-committee report released in December 1981 concluded: "While we concede that Japan's trade barriers threaten the free world trading system, we believe that our prime focus should be on ways to make the U.S. economy more competitive."

The report called for improvements in American management techniques, labor, management relations, productivity and quality control. According to Harvard Professor Ezra Vogel, "American companies must work harder to achieve global competitiveness. They must, for example, train more people capable of doing business in the Japanese language and developing close relationships with Japanese businessmen and officials. And, of course, Washington must actively support these efforts."

Events Leading to the GATT Ministerial

Responding to the fall in the volume of world trade and the rise in protectionist sentiment among U.S. trading partners, the Reagan admin-istration — notably Trade Representative Brock and Commerce Secretary Malcolm Baldrige — began to call for the strengthening of U.S. and in-ternational trade rules. By March 1982 more than 250 reciprocity bills had been introduced in Congress to establish rules limiting or barring imports from countries whose trade barriers to U.S. exports were stricter than

U.S. rules on imports from those countries.

Brock, citing the growing importance of the services sector of the economy (65 percent of the gross national product), also began to call for inclusion of this sector in the agreements governing international trade overseen by the GATT, whose rules cover only merchandise and commodity trade. *(GATT rules, box, next page)*

To discuss these developments and others, the 88 members of GATT, for the first time in nine years, agreed to hold a ministerial-level meeting in Geneva on Nov. 24-29, 1982. Convened largely at the insistence of the United States, the meeting had an ambitious agenda: to further liberalize international trading rules, to impose the same regulations already applied to manufactured goods to the services sector, to stem the wave of protectionist measures imposed by member governments, and to liberalize trade restrictions in agricultural products.

But the GATT ministerial meeting served principally to underscore the growing rift among the main trading blocs, especially between the United States and the EC over agricultural policy. In their final declaration, the participants agreed only to "resist protectionist pressures" and to "refrain from taking or maintaining any measures inconsistent with GATT." Issues such as expanding GATT rules to include trade in services and liberalizing trade in agricultural goods were relegated to further study. While Brock, who led the U.S. delegation to the Geneva meeting, gave the ministerial a "grade of C" at its conclusion, he later said that "given the economic atmosphere in which the ministerial took place, perhaps our most important achievement was in keeping the GATT system together and moving in a positive direction."

Although GATT represented a multilateral attempt to mediate differences among the contracting nations over changing trade patterns, many observers believed more attention should be paid to the structural changes that had brought them about, so that a more coherent and effective trade strategy could be elaborated for the future. For example, the postwar reindustrialization of Western Europe and Japan, the emergence of newly industrialized nations and the lack of industrial development in the LDCs all had an enormous impact on trade.

Before the oil shocks of the mid-1970s, postwar international trade had grown about 7 percent a year, thanks in part to the removal of barriers under various GATT negotiations. The undisputed winner in this situation was the United States, which claimed in the economic boom years of the 1950s and 1960s about one-fourth of the world market in

GATT's Role in World Trade

The General Agreement on Tariffs and Trade (GATT), initially signed by 23 countries on Oct. 30, 1947, had, as of March 1983, 88 members that together accounted for 80 percent of world trade. In addition to these "contracting parties," many other countries complied informally with GATT regulations. The Agreement contains rules on both tariff and non-tariff barriers to trade across individual nations. These have been modified in seven successive rounds of negotiations aimed at reducing barriers on a reciprocal basis. The best known of these were the Kennedy Round (1964-67) and the Tokyo Round (1973-79), which resulted in an overall 39 percent reduction in tariffs on manufactured goods.

The main provisions of GATT rules can be summarized as follows:

Member nations must confer "most-favored-nation" status to all other members, allowing equal access to all on their domestic markets.

Once tariffs have been removed or reduced by negotiation, they must not be reimposed in the form of compensatory domestic taxes.

Where imports are shown to threaten domestic industries producing similar items, member nations may impose anti-dumping or countervailing duties to offset this damage. Similarly, an "escape clause" permits the suspension or modification of tariff concessions when a surge in imports threatens domestic industries. GATT rules do not, however, prohibit competing nations from retaliating against those invoking the "escape clause" if consultations do not produce compensatory action on the part of the nation invoking the clause.

Import quotas are permitted only for agricultural or fishery products when necessary to protect domestic production-control programs and to avoid balance-of-payments crises.

GATT lacks power to enforce its rules because Congress refused to allow the U.S. government to participate in its proposed adminstrative bodies, which consequently never came into being. The 300-member GATT secretariat, based in Geneva, provides a forum for the airing of disputes among contracting nations, allowing GATT to perform a mediating role in world trade.

manufactured goods, and 95 percent of all domestic sales of autos, steel and consumer electronics in 1960. By 1979, in contrast, the U.S. world market share had fallen to approximately 17 percent, and domestic manufacturers could claim only a 70 percent share of auto sales, 86 percent of steel products, and less than half of consumer electronics goods sold domestically.

At the same time, the growing role of the Third World nations in the world economy had increased its interdependent nature. In 1982 alone, the less developed countries bought more than one-third of American exports and more than one-quarter of the total exports from the Organization for Economic Cooperation and Development (OECD), a group of 24 nations including Japan, the United States, Western European countries, and Australia.

Domestic Pressure to Create Jobs

While the predictability of economic trends had been shown to be spotty at best, economic forecasters were almost unanimous early in 1983 in their assessment that the lengthy recession had just about "bottomed out" in the United States. Although domestic business activity was expected to pick up in 1983, the problems in export-dependent industries were likely to continue for some time, as countries that imported U.S. products continued to be plagued by high unemployment and slow growth. Since unemployment in the United States was expected to remain high in 1983, perhaps peaking in the first half of the year, industries already hurt by imports were likely to continue to experience difficulties throughout the year.

The concern that the decline in the international competitiveness of key U.S. industries added significantly to the unemployment problem brought about this dilemma: Should the United States pursue free market evangelism and attack its trading partners for interfering with industry, or should it attempt to emulate the successes of others, and adopt its own industrial policy? While the Reagan administration railed against industrial policies overseas, a growing number of members of Congress advocated adopting some of those same policies in the United States.

Most supporters were congressional Democrats, who believed — along with presidential hopefuls Walter F. Mondale and Sen. Gary Hart, D-Colo. — that proposals for boosting U.S. industry would be key issues in the 1984 elections. They shied away from the term "industrial policy," for fear that it would carry implications of "creeping socialism." But what they advocated was clearly a more active role for government in promoting industry.

Congressional efforts to create an industrial policy were aided by a petition filed with the Trade Representative's Office in May 1982 by Houdaille Industries, a Florida-based machine tool manufacturer. The petition requested President Reagan to deny investment tax credits to U.S. companies that purchased certain Japanese computerized tools. The petition documented, with more than one thousand pages of supporting evidence, the entire range of Japanese government industrial policies that had been used over the previous three decades to promote development of the computerized machine tool industry. The report claimed that Japan's industrial policy itself amounted to an unfair trading practice.

Attorney Richard D. Copaken of the law firm of Covington and Burling spent months gathering evidence for the document. Frustrated by the refusal of the Japanese government to provide the information he needed, Copaken walked unannounced into some Tokyo offices armed with a video camera and a long list of questions. The result was a de-tailed — if at times overstated — account of Japanese policies to promote the machine tool industry.

In the 1950s Japan's Ministry of International Trade and Industry (MITI) began efforts to encourage its machine tool manufacturers to develop computerized (known as numerically controlled, or NC) machine tools. Those tools promised the highest return per worker, and MITI wanted to propel their development. Manufacturers with small shares of the fragmented market were forced to drop out, and those remaining were encouraged to cooperate in product research and development.

To help accomplish its goals, the government provided tax benefits, concessionary loans and research and development grants. It shielded the industry from international competition in its early stages of develop-ment. It also used off-budget funds, gained from bicycle and motorcycle race betting, to promote the use of computerized machine tools by other industries. The Houdaille petition documented, for instance, how a government-subsidized institute in Tokyo developed software for a watch company to use in making watches, thereby convincing the watch maker to buy an NC machine tool.

As a result of such efforts, Japanese industry made the transition from traditional to computerized machine tools far more quickly than the industry of any other nation. By 1980, according to a study by a

French consulting firm, Japan was consuming as many NC tools as the United States, even though its economy was less than half the size of the U.S. economy. And Japanese production was more than twice U.S production.

A symbol of the Japanese industry's rapid advancement was the Fanuc company's futuristic manufacturing plant at the foot of Mount Fuji. The plant used computerized machine tools and robots to manufacture more computerized machine tools and robots. It operated 24 hours each day, and at night it was manned by only two employees who could control the entire operation from the computer room.

U.S. manufacturers, once considered the best in the world, were lagging. A Department of Commerce analysis reported, "U.S. manufacturers find themselves in a disadvantaged position relative to their government-supported competitors. . . . Few of them have the resources to pursue an aggressive catch-up program in the current economic environment."

Faced with this situation, the U.S. manufacturers were crying foul play, and the government moved to support their cry.

Toward a U.S. Industrial Policy?

Robert B. Reich, Harvard professor and sometime adviser to Democratic members of Congress, said denying the investment tax credit to U.S. companies that buy certain Japanese machine tools would be "another in a long line of steps we are taking down the road of protectionism." In Reich's view, it represented the wrong way to respond to international competition: U.S. machine tool makers would be protected at the expense of U.S. machine tool buyers, and nothing would be done to ensure that the industry became more efficient.

Reich was one voice in a growing chorus of economists, business school professors and former government officials calling for an industrial policy to improve the United States' international competitiveness. The ideas of these advisers varied greatly — some emphasized rebuilding traditional "smokestack" industries, while others talked more of promoting high-tech industries. But they all agreed on one thing: the United States already had a vast array of policies that promoted and subsidized specific industries. All it lacked was a mechanism for coordinating those policies to improve international competitiveness.

The law books were full of research subsidies, loans with concessionary rates as low as 5 percent, loan guarantee programs, tax breaks and outright grants that benefited narrow sectors of the economy. Research and development financing by the U.S. government was more than twice as large as that in Japan, according to a joint study by two trade consulting firms, Malmgren Inc. and Developing World Industry and Technology Inc. Most of that research was carried out by the Department of Defense, a fact that prompted Reich to comment that defense was the U.S. equivalent of industrial policy.

The primary difference between the United States and its trading partners was that the U.S. policies were not coordinated for the sake of economic development. They were created on an ad hoc basis, in response to specific problems at specific times. They were directed at a variety of differing goals, and no one even knew what they all were, much less what their effect was on the economy.

In the view of Reich and others, the real question facing the United States was not whether to have an industrial policy. Rather, it was whether to face up to the fact that an industrial policy already existed and by that admission make possible a more rational coordination of policy.

Labor leaders, too, were joining the debate for more stringent coordination and control of industrial policy. Spokemen for the ailing labor unions were beginning to insist on "fair trade" in addition to "free trade." The AFL-CIO's 1983 platform contained an entire section on the trade issue, in which the "simplistic dialogue of 'free trade' vs. 'protectionism' " was condemned. Because other governments routinely intervened in the flow of trade, it stated, so too "the United States needs clear limits on certain imports until the nation's future is assured."

The document went on to describe the confederation's chief trade priorities for the year: temporary restrictions on "harmful imports"; enactment of a "domestic content" law; assurances that a greater portion of U.S. raw materials be processed domestically before exportation. "Reciprocity should have some teeth in it. . . ," stated AFL-CIO President Lane Kirkland in an interview in *AFL-CIO News* in January 1983. "We ought to play by the same ground rules as our competitors and negotiate from that basis."

Fighting Fire with Fire

To combat job erosion, Congress was toying with various proposals that would, in effect, fight fire with fire. Among them were proposals to authorize subsidies for agricultural exports and to expand low-interest export loans — designed to improve the ability of U.S. companies to out-bid their competitors overseas. One of the new measures, passed by Congress in October 1982, encouraged creation of export trading companies, previously barred by antitrust laws, to facilitate small business exporting.

Business executives contended that European, Canadian and Japanese firms had snatched multimillion-dollar export contracts from U.S. companies simply by offering government-sponsored, low-interest loans to foreign buyers. If the United States could provide similar government credit, they argued, its exporters could bring in more business and create thousands of jobs at a cost to the government far lower than any of the highly touted "jobs programs" that were under consideration by Congress and the administration in early 1983. *(Jobs bill chapter, p. 95)*

Many members of Congress supported the strengthening of the U.S. Export-Import ("Ex-Im") Bank. Compared with government credit agencies in other nations, the U.S. bank's efforts were small. In 1980, for instance, government export credit in the United States covered only 12.8 percent of all manufactured exports. Meanwhile, the French government financed 25.2 percent of its exports; the British, 50.8 percent, and the Japanese, 42.4 percent, according to a study by Gary Clyde Hufbauer, a senior fellow with the Institute for International Economics, and Joanna Shelton Erb, an economist at the Treasury Department.

The bank, a federally chartered independent corporation, does not get appropriated funds from Congress. Rather, it borrows money from the Federal Financing Bank (FFB), which in turn borrows from the Treasury; the Treasury raises its funds by the sale of government securities. Because the interest the Treasury must pay on the securities it sells generally is lower than commercial loan rates, Ex-Im makes loans somewhat below market rates. Congress sets ceilings for the bank, and for fiscal 1983 Congress limited the bank's direct lending to $4.4 billion and guarantees on commercial loans to $9 billion.

Ex-Im provides direct loans and loan guarantees for five years or more to finance the export of major capital equipment, such as airplanes and power plants. In October 1982 the bank also instituted a new program for "medium-term" exports — exports that required only one to five years of financing.

Historically, the bank followed conservative policies, attempting to keep its interest rates high enough to cover the cost of borrowing from the FFB. In the last few years, however, increased foreign export credit

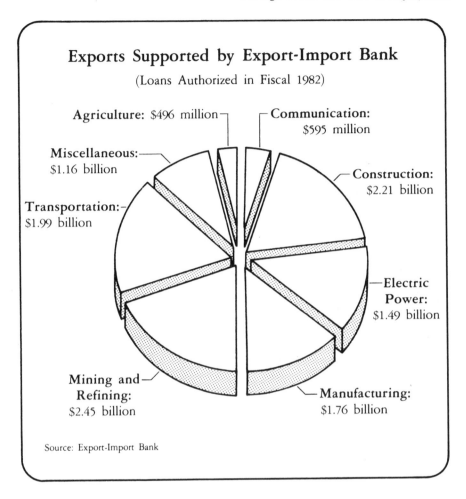

Exports Supported by Export-Import Bank

(Loans Authorized in Fiscal 1982)

Agriculture: $496 million

Communication: $595 million

Miscellaneous: $1.16 billion

Construction: $2.21 billion

Transportation: $1.99 billion

Electric Power: $1.49 billion

Mining and Refining: $2.45 billion

Manufacturing: $1.76 billion

Source: Export-Import Bank

subsidies abroad pressured Ex-Im to keep its rates low to be competitive — while high interest rates in the United States pressured it to keep its rates high to cover costs.

A variety of plans for strengthening the institution also surfaced. The bank's charter was up for reauthorization by Congress in 1983, and two members who chaired subcommittees that had to approve Ex-Im legislation — Sen. John Heinz, R-Pa., and Rep. Stephen L. Neal, D-N.C. — both had proposals that would force Ex-Im to compete more aggressively against subsidized competition. The U.S. Chamber of Commerce also was urging Congress to allow the bank to mix its loans with official U.S. development aid, bringing down export financing costs.

Trade Prospects for the Future

Continued differences between the United States and its allies were expected to dominate the Western economic summit to be held in May 1983 in Williamsburg, Va. The major industrialized nations — the United States, Canada, Japan, West Germany, Great Britain, France and Italy — were to gather there to discuss problems in coordinating each country's economic policy. Such summits have been held annually since 1975. Especially troublesome would be the conflict between the United States and the European countries over agricultural exports, intensified by the Reagan administration decision to subsidize the export of wheat flour to Egypt, a market previously dominated by subsidized EC flour sales. *(Egyptian wheat sale, p. 74)*

The subsidy was a clear indication that the administration had somewhat softened its free-trade philosophy. But officials were clearly reluctant to declare an all-out trade war. Agriculture Secretary Block told the House Foreign Affairs Committee on Feb. 15, 1982, "I don't think we should go around picking off markets in the world indiscriminately. However, if you find that a market that was ours has been taken away . . . we have no other choice but to compete." Secretary of State George P. Shultz told the Senate Foreign Relations Committee the same day that if subsidies were used commonly to market agricultural products, "the net result will not be good, and we will be in effect giving products away."

Another factor impeding U.S. export activity was the strong dollar, although some forecasters predicted that interest rates would continue their downward trend, weakening the dollar against major currencies before the end of 1983. Lawrence B. Krause of the Brookings Institution, for example, predicted that the dollar's depreciation would mean improvement for the U.S. trade picture by 1984. Others took a more pessimistic view. The U.S. ambassador to West Germany, Arthur F. Burns, said in a speech in December 1982 that "political tensions on account of economic difficulties may well continue to trouble the alliance."

According to Agriculture Department estimates, agricultural exports were expected to sustain a $20.6 billion surplus in fiscal 1983, following the previous year's fall to $23.7 billion from fiscal 1981's $26.6 billion surplus. While he sees some hope in falling interest rates, Jim Donald, chairman of the USDA's World Food and Agricultural Outlook and Situation Board, maintained that "it will take a while to cut back on stocks" and that agricultural sales abroad will depend on the pace of recovery in the rest of the world.

The United States also found itself involved in a dispute over agricultural exports with the People's Republic of China, which on Jan. 19, 1982, suspended all imports of U.S. cotton, soybeans and chemical fibers in 1983. This move was in retaliation for the administration's refusal to allow imports of Chinese textiles to exceed the 1.5 percent growth rate permitted China's competitors for the U.S. market — Taiwan, South Korea and Hong Kong. With bilateral trade totaling $5.2 billion last year, the breach in negotiations could lead to a further erosion of the U.S. trade picture. The administration gave in to pressure from the domestic textile industry, which had idled some 200,000 workers since the recession began in 1981.

Another source of attrition in the bilateral trade relationship involved U.S. policy on high-technology exports to Peking, which the Reagan administration had thus far failed to define and which was not clarified during Secretary of State Shultz' first official trip to Peking in early February 1983.

Greater success was claimed by the administration from the outcome of the January 1983 visit to Washington by Japanese Prime Minister Yasuhiro Nakasone. Although he did not reduce import restrictions on U.S. beef and citrus products, he introduced shortly before his departure from Tokyo reform measures reducing tariffs and liberalizing customs procedures, product standards and testing criteria affecting some 60 percent of U.S. products exported to Japan.

President Reagan was unable to produce much in the way of tangible evidence of noticeable change in the Japanese attitudes on import quotas. But the visit did relieve some of the political tensions between the two countries. Citing domestic unrest over growing economic troubles, Nakasone appeared to have persuaded Washington that any substantive liberalizing measures in trade policy must await parliamentary elections in the summer of 1983 in order for Nakasone, himself elected in November 1982, to consolidate his political position.

One of the few areas of agreement between the United States and its industrialized trading partners was over the threat posed to international trade by the growing external debt of the less developed countries. In a striking policy reversal, the administration agreed in mid-January 1983 to support an increase in the special emergency fund that the International Monetary Fund made available to borrowing nations to help repay their debts. Considerable opposition to increased funding was expected from members of Congress who were concerned about ballooning budget deficits; the administration's support came as a surprise, however, since it previously had espoused the notion that Third World development could best be handled by the "magic of the marketplace." The move was an indication of the heightened concern.

Reagan's Position; Outlook in Congress. World events after 1980 undoubtedly affected the administration's trade policy. But while the president bent somewhat to protectionist pressures from voters and members of Congress, he remained basically committed to a free-trade policy. This was made clear in the economic report Reagan sent to Congress Feb. 2, 1983, in which he said he was "committed to a policy of preventing the enactment of protectionist measures in the United States."

> While the United States may be forced to respond to the trade distorting practices of foreign governments through the use of strategic measures, such practices do not warrant indiscriminate protectionist actions, such as domestic content rules for automobiles sold in the United States. Widespread protectionist policies would hurt American consumers by raising prices of the products they buy, and by removing some of the pressures for cost control and quality improvement that result from competition. Moreover, protectionism at home could hurt the workers, farmers and firms in the United States that produce goods and services for export, since it would almost inevitably lead to increased protectionism by governments abroad.

Reagan's position was not likely to quell critics' calls for more specific measures aimed at protecting domestic industries and workers in urgent need of help.

Aside from the immediate implications of trade-related legislation likely to be discussed in 1983, the entire debate on international trade was certain to influence the campaign for the 1984 presidential election. Even when President Reagan had yet to declare publicly whether or not he intended to run for a second term, his Democratic critics and potential opponents were gearing up for battle over trade policy.

Former Vice President Mondale, considered the leading Democratic contender in the early phase of the 1984 presidential campaign, had already come down on the side of strict reciprocity laws. In a November 1982 article in *The New York Times* he wrote that he also favored using a well-funded Ex-Im Bank "to match the export subsidies of our trade competitors, product for product, dollar for dollar." President Reagan also was being challenged on trade policy by conservatives within his own party. Speaking for this group, conservative commentator Kevin Phillips took the administration to task for failing to formulate a coherent trade policy in an article published in *The Washington Post* in January 1983.

The issue of "protectionism" vs. "free trade" continued to unfold in congressional debate. Its outcome depended to a large extent on the pace of economic recovery and the prospects for employment of American workers. In the absence of an overall policy with established priorities for the direction of the U.S. economy and its role in international trade, domestic industries hurt by a falling share of the domestic market, as well as those whose exports failed to compete effectively on world markets, seemed likely to continue pressing for special concessions from Washington.

People unable to find jobs queue up for unemployment benefits.

Chapter 4

FEDERAL JOBS PROGRAMS CONTROVERSY

Persistent high unemployment figures in 1982 and early 1983 renewed a long-standing debate over the value of federal jobs-creation programs during economic downturns. While most economists had come to agree that a certain level of unemployment was, in fact, necessary to maintain a labor pool to replace workers who retired, died, were fired or otherwise left their jobs, the high "cyclical" unemployment brought on by the recessions of the 1970s and early 1980s, combined with the steadily increasing "structural" unemployment induced by industrial shifts, created a mood of urgency in Congress.

The contemporary debate over job-creating legislation had a familiar ring to it; arguments made for and against the proposals were remarkably similar to those that surrounded the New Deal programs half a century earlier. Critics in the 1980s once again questioned the effect of public works spending on industrial recovery, the merits of creating jobs directly or stimulating the private sector for indirect relief, and finally the effectiveness of government intervention on unemployment.

Throughout history, federal job-creating programs had dual goals of making permanent improvements to roads, subways and other components of the country's physical infrastructure and immediately helping people who needed jobs. Carefully planned, long-range capital improvements provided a boon to future generations but proved slow in helping hungry people in need. Quick-starting repair and service projects were successful in ameliorating suffering but were criticized for having accomplished little lasting good and for being open to fraud and waste. Finally, they often became branded as "make-work, leaf-raking" jobs.

Initially resisting the pressure to use federal jobs programs as a solution to rising unemployment, President Ronald Reagan advocated relying on overall economic recovery for employment relief. To accomplish this, cuts in the federal budget were accompanied by decreases in personal and corporate income taxes intended to stimulate industrial investment and to create jobs indirectly. As late as December 1982, with unemployment figures still hovering at a post-Depression record of around 10 percent, Reagan said in an interview with *The Washington Post*: "All our past experience shows that make-work jobs programs in the past, whatever they did in creating eventually some employment, usually it was so late that recovery had already taken place or was still underway.... Also, the taking of these funds from the economy to be used by government in that way resulted in uncounted unemployment in other sectors of the economy.... You simply shifted the jobs from one group to another."

Finally, in reaction to congressional pressures as well as to the high jobless rate, Reagan proposed in February 1983 a recession relief bill, abandoning his earlier opposition to jobs bills. The measure grew into the Emergency Jobs and Recession Relief Act, passed March 24, 1983. He further proposed the Employment Act of 1983 in March, designed to relieve the structural unemployment problem.

By 1983 there was one thing on which virtually all interested individuals agreed: the unemployment problem could not begin to be solved until the country experienced a strong economic recovery. Structural unemployment, however, promised to be a more enduring problem.

As Congress and President Reagan approached the 1984 elections, it appeared certain that consideration of short-term relief measures would continue. Yet the economic and political controversy over the federal role in economic management and employment that first surfaced in the 1930s had not been resolved by the 1980s. President Franklin D. Roosevelt's advice to his New Dealers still held appeal to a new generation of legislators: "Take a method and try it. If it fails, admit it frankly and try another. But above all, try something."

Contemporary Jobs Proposals

Congress generally went along with the president's resistance to make-work programs for the first 22 months of the Reagan administration. Prior to the 1982 midterm elections, demands and support for jobs measures came primarily from Democrats in the 97th Congress. But rising unemployment and Republican losses in the 1982 elections, which many political analysts attributed at least in part to opposition to

MY UNEMPLOYMENT INSURANCE HAS RUN OUT... I CAN'T PAY THE BILLS...

WE WERE FORCED TO SELL THE HOUSE, AND OUR KID HAD TO QUIT COLLEGE

HEY- THINGS COULD BE WORSE-

YOU COULD HAVE A MAKE-WORK, DEAD-END JOB

Wasserman © 1982, Los Angeles Times Syndicate, Reprinted with permission.

Reagan's economic policies, seemed to make jobs programs somewhat more attractive to their traditional opponents.

Transportation Assistance Act of 1982

President Reagan ultimately backed, and the lame-duck Congress approved before its December 1982 adjournment, a 5-cent-a-gallon increase in the federal gasoline tax to finance repair of the nation's deteriorating roads and transit systems. The bill was expected to provide 300,000 jobs for some of the 12 million unemployed Americans. Yet Reagan insisted that the Transportation Act of 1982, a bipartisan measure, was not a jobs bill; he maintained he supported the legislation as a start in repairing the transportation system.

Nevertheless, to many congressional liberals the bill was reminiscent of the many New Deal era public works initiatives. Members of Congress had toiled unsuccessfully for months to move legislation to create jobs and increase transportation and public works funding. But the escalating unemployment problem, along with the Democratic election victories in the House and the near wins in the Senate, pushed jobs and the issue of of structural decay further up on the congressional agenda.

The law finally enacted involved a substantial portion of the infrastructure, authorizing more than $71 billion to finish the interstate highway system and to improve the roads, bridges and mass transit systems. The measure increased the gas tax a nickel a gallon to a total of 9 cents, thereby raising an additional $5.5 billion a year to help pay for the programs.

The economic necessity of maintaining the transportation system was an accepted fact. For example, it was estimated that 90 percent of what Americans consume, wear or use was transported on the nation's highways. The infrastructure needs were many and Transportation

Secretary Drew Lewis, the Associated General Contractors of America and others cited examples:

● One out of five bridges in the nation needed immediate major repairs. The life of a bridge was about 50 years, and 40 percent already were more than 40 years old.

● More than 4,000 miles, or 10 percent, of the interstate highway system needed replacement or major repairs. More than 26,000 miles would require major repairs through 1995.

● If highway conditions continued to decline at their current rate, the average motorist's costs could increase by up to 25 percent by 1995 because of the wear and tear on automobiles and increased gasoline use.

● Twenty percent of all subway cars were more than 25 years old, while the design life generally was about 20 years. Sixty-seven percent of all tracks needed upgrading.

● Capital needs for transit replacement and repairs would total $50 billion over the next 10 years.

● A study for the House Wednesday Group, which was made up of Republican members, said more than one-half of the nation's communities had wastewater treatment systems at full capacity and could not support further economic development.

While the urgency of attending to the crumbling infrastructure and addressing the unemployment problem lent support to the bill, economists questioned whether there would be a net gain of jobs through the gasoline tax increase. Martin S. Feldstein, chairman of the president's Council of Economic Advisers, said that the increased cost of gasoline would reduce consumer spending on other goods and services, possibly increasing unemployment during the first years of the gasoline tax increase.

Others pointed out that much of the gasoline tax money raised by the tax would go into continuing projects, such as the completion of the interstate highway system. While this might forestall an increase in unemployment, critics said that it would not result in a net increase in jobs. They also pointed out that road building is not particularly labor intensive, because a large proportion of expenditures goes for materials rather than wages.

Senate Democrats unsuccessfully tried to attach an additional jobs plan to the Transportation Act legislation, a $5.3 billion job-creation/supplemental jobless benefit amendment. The amendment would have eliminated the 5-cent-a-gallon increase in fuel taxes and financed the highway repair program by trimming the scheduled July 1983 tax cut for upper-income taxpayers. The Democrats' core proposal was a $2 billion light public works program funding small-scale projects such as bridge painting and public housing repair. In a party-line vote, the Senate rejected the amendment.

The gas-tax bill capped a year of halting Democratic efforts to develop politically acceptable anti-recession legislation. Democratic leaders, with an eye to the 1982 midterm elections, had won House passage of a $1 billion jobs package in September 1982 that Republicans derided as "economic moonshine." The bill was the centerpiece of a Democatic package aimed at creating jobs and stimulating the economy by providing an estimated 200,000 temporary public-works jobs. The Republican opposition was overwhelmed by Democrats, who openly challenged the GOP to oppose such a program shortly before the congressional elections while the nation's unemployment rate approached double digits.

"I find it amazing that there are actually members of this Congress in September 1982 who are going to go and campaign on the basis that they voted against this bill," Rep. John Conyers Jr., D-Mich., exclaimed with relish. "Fantastic!"

Speaker of the House Thomas P. "Tip" O'Neill Jr., D-Mass., chided Republican Minority Leader Robert H. Michel personally. O'Neill said there were four bridges needing repair in Peoria, Illinois, part of Michel's district, and 16 percent unemployment. "You have an opportunity to repair some needed work in your own area," O'Neill declared. Michel responded, "In my home community of Peoria, I can assure you that Reaganomics is going to play much better than Tip O'Nomics."

Shortly thereafter, the Republican-controlled Senate blocked an attempt by Edward M. Kennedy, D-Mass., to attach the measure to the first fiscal 1983 continuing resolution, which was required to maintain funding for agencies whose regular appropriations bills had not been enacted. No further action was taken on the House bill.

During the 1982 post-election session, Democrats once again pressed for enactment of jobs legislation as part of the second fiscal 1983 continuing appropriations resolution. Although each chamber approved its own version, the jobs funding was dropped from the measure in a House-Senate conference to avert a threatened presidential veto. But in debate on the conference report, proponents vowed to fight for jobs legislation in the 98th Congress, which convened in January 1983.

Job Training Partnership Act of 1982

The 97th Congress was successful in passing the Job Training Partnership Act of 1982 to replace the job-training provisions of the expired Comprehensive Employment and Training Act (CETA). Modern programs of this type began in earnest with the passage of the Manpower Development and Training Act in 1962, which was later replaced by CETA in 1973. Since that time, job-training and retraining proposals had become important ways for Congress to affect the growing ranks of the structurally unemployed and unskilled people. The Job Training Partnership Act provided job skill training for the low-income unemployed. Unlike CETA, it did not pay for public service employment. The act also differed from CETA in that it gave more power to run the programs to state, rather than city and county, governments.*(History of CETA, p. 125)*

The 1982 bill's final provisions addressed the problems of economically disadvantaged youths and adults, and the growing number of dislocated workers. It authorized a state and local grants program, and services such as training, job counseling, remedial education or on-the-job training. The bill also established a training assistance program for those who had lost their jobs and were unlikely to get them back because, for example, of a factory's permanent closing.

National programs also were created by the act, including job-training funding for native Americans, migrant workers and veterans. National Job Corps centers were to be set up for the training and education of disadvantaged young people.

Business involvement was required, because the act called for the establishment of Private Industry Councils (PICs), composed of business, labor, educational and community representatives to be responsible, along with the local governments, for guiding the training programs.

While the Job Training Partnership Act had the endorsement of Reagan and Congress throughout its legislative history, action was delayed repeatedly. But the approaching midterm elections gave prominence to employment issues, prompting final action. President Reagan signed the bill into law Oct. 13, 1982.

Youth Projects Proposals

Many lawmakers compared contemporary conditions among jobless youths in 1983 with those of the 1930s, when at least one-quarter of the roughly 13 million unemployed were young men. While total unemployment stood at 10.3 percent in March 1983, overall youth

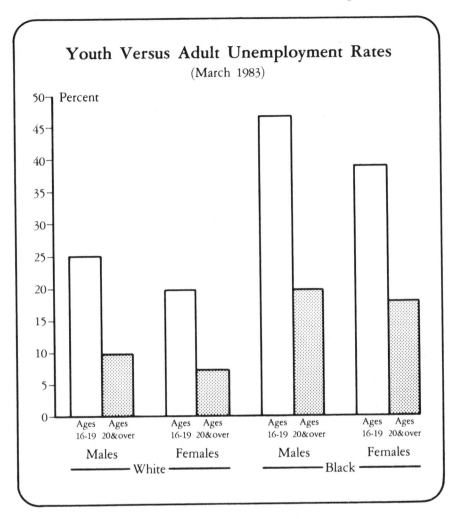

Youth Versus Adult Unemployment Rates
(March 1983)

unemployment was 23.5 percent. Black youth unemployment had hit a staggering 43.5 percent. While the Job Training Partnership Act dealt with youth unemployment, many legislators also supported youth conservation and public project programs, reminiscent of those implemented during the Depression.

Pending before Congress during the spring of 1983 was a bill to create an American Conservation Corps (ACC). As passed by the House the legislation authorized $50 million for fiscal 1983 and $250 million for each of fiscal years 1984-89. A smaller version of President Franklin D. Roosevelt's Civilian Conservation Corps (CCC), the bill provided 100,000 jobs refurbishing the nation's parks and forests to unemployed and disadvantaged youths. The ACC legislation "addresses simultaneously two distressing problems now confronting this nation: youth unemployment of epidemic proportions and the accelerating deterioration of public lands," said Rep. Carl D. Perkins, D-Ky., chairman of the House Education and Labor Committee.

The bill directed the Interior Department, in cooperation with the Agriculture and Labor departments, to set up and run a program of year-round and summer jobs. It additionally directed the Interior Department to set up conservation centers in both urban and rural locations to attract disadvantaged youth and those from high unemployment areas. The proposed ACC projects included maintaining and improving forests, range lands, recreational areas, roads, trails and urban centers.

A more ambitious Senate bill was introduced by Robert T. Stafford, R-Vt., to create some 300,000 jobs a year for young people repairing and improving neighborhood parks, public buildings and other facilities, as well as doing the traditional conservation work in national parks and forests.

The Stafford bill would create a Youth Community Conservation and Improvements Program of community-based work for unemployed 16- to 19-year-olds. Proposed projects included public facilities rehabilitation, weatherization and rodent control of low-income housing, and conservation work. Another program included in the bill was the Young Adult Conservation Corps, which called for the Interior and Agriculture departments to administer a youth work conservation program geared to those residing in rural and urban areas with substantial unemployment. It provided for work developing recreation areas, revitalizing urban parks and related conservation activities.

Besides the CCC, the proposals were modeled after two youth jobs programs of the 1970s — the Youth Conservation Corps (YCC), which was created to employ young people aged 15 to 18 to perform conservation work during the summer, and the Young Adult Conservation Corps (YACC), which put youths aged 16 to 23 to work on year-round conservation projects. In 1981 the Reagan administration asked Congress to end both programs, citing inefficiency and cost. Congress agreed to kill the YACC, and the YCC was in the process of being terminated in 1983 with only $10 million appropriated in fiscal 1983 and no funds requested for 1984.

Yet youth conservation programs clearly had congressional support

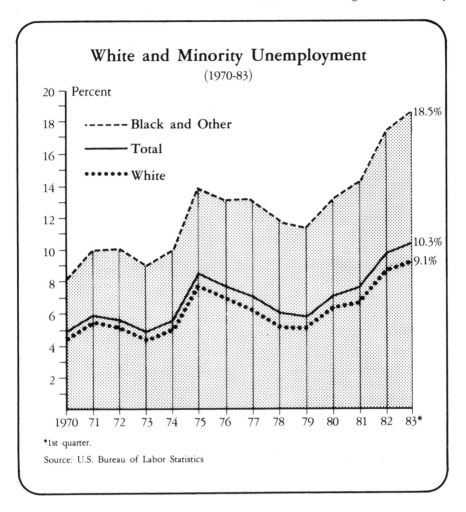

White and Minority Unemployment
(1970-83)

Percent

- ------ Black and Other
- —— Total
- •••••• White

18.5%

10.3%
9.1%

1970 71 72 73 74 75 76 77 78 79 80 81 82 83*

*1st quarter.

Source: U.S. Bureau of Labor Statistics

in early 1983 when both the House and Senate bills were pending. The Reagan administration, however, remained strongly opposed to youth jobs programs at that time, criticizing them as too expensive and ultimately inadequate.

Reagan Administration Joins the Fight

A more heavily Democratic 98th Congress convened in January 1983 amid a growing national sense of economic crisis and concern about unemployment figures that had reached post-Depression highs. Faced with these political realities, Reagan appeared to moderate his formerly rigid, ideological stance against government-supported jobs programs and adopt a pragmatic approach more reminiscent of earlier Republican administrations.

Phase I. Reagan sent a $4.3 billion recession relief program to Congress in February. The program grew into the Emergency Jobs and Recession Relief Act passed by Congress and signed into law March 24, 1983. The $4.6 billion jobs and humanitarian relief package was viewed by both Democrats and Republicans as merely "Phase I" of a comprehensive effort to address high unemployment levels. "This bill will meet neglected urgent needs, result not in make-work but productive jobs, and provide for the indigent and homeless," said Jamie L. Whitten, D-Miss., chairman of the House Appropriations Committee. *(Humanitarian relief aspects of bill, p. 134)*

The package's largest single item — $1 billion for Community Development Block Grants — was spread evenly between "bricks and mortar" projects and public service programs, such as home health and day care. Women's groups had pushed for these public service provisions, pointing out that few of the bill's construction and public works jobs would benefit women. Said Rep. Edward P. Boland, D-Mass.: "This will guarantee a better break for women." Boland also defended the heavy appropriations for public service programs, which the administration had opposed as make-work jobs, saying it was one area where people could begin working quickly.

The Emergency Jobs and Recession Relief Act additionally appropriated funds for employment and job-training assistance. Addressing the problems of the structurally unemployed, it included provisions for retraining and relocating displaced workers and waived the state matching funds, which had been called for in the Job Training Partnership Act.

Although this bill was the 98th Congress' first major effort to deal with the severe economic and unemployment situation, it appeared to be only the beginning of legislative employment initiatives.

Phase II. The proposed Community Renewal Employment Act, introduced by Rep. Augustus F. Hawkins, D-Calif., and under committee consideration in spring 1983, was part of a Democratic follow-up to the Emergency Jobs and Recession Relief Act.

Hawkins predicted that one million jobs would be created under the proposal, designed to reduce long-term, structural unemployment. The bill provided for grants to states and local governments with populations of 50,000 or more as well as high unemployment rates, and the money would be used for labor-intensive "community renewal" projects such as road and sewer projects, public building repairs, health and social service activities, emergency food and shelter, and land and water reclamation.

Funding for the proposal would begin with a fiscal 1983 authorization of $5 billion. Subsequent spending, linked to the level of long-term unemployment, would provide jobs for 20 percent of those unemployed for at least 15 weeks. Hawkins estimated fiscal 1984 expenditures would total $9 billion.

The bill became ensnarled in debate over a controversial amendment that would prohibit local governments from using jobs money to replace permanent staff with federally subsidized workers. Referring to the shortcomings of CETA where governments frequently cut expenses by replacing existing staff with federally funded CETA employees, Rep. William Clay, D-Mo., proposed to penalize governments that abused programs funded under the Hawkins bill.

"We don't consider this a quick fix," said Hawkins. "At a time when 11.4 million people are officially out of work, it is absolutely essential that Congress be responsive to people who are willing and desperate to work."

Not everyone agreed that the Hawkins bill would provide many solutions. John N. Erlenborn, R-Ill., called it "a boondoggle" and said it "gives money to cities to hire people they would have hired anyway." While the Democrats considered the Hawkins proposal the cornerstone of their Phase II package, other related bills included:

● A bill to authorize $4 billion in fiscal 1984 for labor-intensive projects to repair and renovate public facilities in states with high unemployment.

● A $2.7 billion fiscal plan to provide health insurance for unemployed workers in 1983, and an additional $2.7 billion in fiscal 1984.

● A $760 million bill designed to provide mortgage relief for homeowners facing foreclosure. *(Box, p. 150-151)*

● A bill that would relax federal banking laws to allow farmers to defer mortgage payments for one year.

House Republicans announced their own $5.4 billion package of Phase II bills on March 15, 1983. Their package aimed to create more than three million jobs and retraining opportunities for unemployed workers in 1983 and 1984. "Over the past two decades the world has been changing from an industrial to a highly technological base," said Rep. Erlenborn, chairman of the Republican task force on employment opportunities. "Economic recovery won't help people who are no longer marketable. We're going to have to train and retrain millions of people."

Erlenborn added that the Republican plan emphasized tax credits and private sector initiatives. This contrasted with the public spending and government-run programs proposed by the Democrats. The Republican package included bills:

● To allow pension fund investment in labor-intensive housing projects and home mortgages.

● That would grant special tax and regulatory benefits to companies establishing business in designated "urban enterprise zones," a proposal similar to the Reagan administration program.

● To establish a $50 billion revolving fund, financed through user fees and matching state-federal grants, that would rebuild roads, bridges and other deteriorating public facilities.

Employment Act of 1983. President Reagan presented to Congress in March 1983 his own proposal, the Employment Act of 1983, to relieve unemployment. The proposal carefully distinguished between cyclical and structural unemployment. According to his March 11 message announcing his proposal, cyclical unemployment was an inevitable consequence of the ups and downs in the business cycle. Hence, any attempted government intervention to relieve it risked creating inflationary pressures, a view consistent with orthodox economic theory. He still advocated alleviating the problems of victims of cyclical unemployment by ending the recession through the stimulation of private enterprise.

Structural unemployment, in contrast, resulted "from the continuous change in a dynamic economy where some industries are declining while others are expanding; from a mismatch of skills needed for available jobs versus the skills in the available work force; from barriers to labor market entry; and from increases in the proportion of the population looking for work."

In Reagan's view, the structural unemployment problem had its roots in events that antedated his administration, but he still hoped to help its victims. In his speech, Reagan identified three groups of structurally unemployed workers that the administration was prepared to assist: the long-term unemployed, workers displaced by the decline of certain industries and trades, and young people unable to find jobs due to their lack of skills. The message proposed a three-pronged attack on the problem of the long-term unemployed: additional unemployment compensation, a job voucher system and the creation of enterprise zones.

Projecting an average jobless rate of 10.7 percent in 1983 and 9.9 percent in 1984, Reagan proposed a six-month extension until the end of fiscal 1983 of the emergency supplemental unemployment benfits. This proposal, signed into law on April 21, 1983, as part of the Social Security system rescue bill, was intended to continue helping those unemployed workers who had exhausted their regular unemployment insurance benefits.

To stimulate the creation of jobs, Reagan proposed a voucher plan. Under this plan, individuals could elect to receive vouchers in place of their supplemental weekly benefits. The vouchers would equal one half the value of the weekly benefits, but would be received for twice as many weeks. For example, if an individual was eligible for 16 weeks of supplemental benefits, he or she could receive vouchers for 32 weeks. The vouchers could then be turned over to a full-time employer, who would receive a tax credit equal to the amount of the voucher. The idea was to provide an incentive for employers to hire the long-term unemployed.

The enterprise zone concept, which Reagan first suggested in March 1982, proposed that significant federal, state and local tax and regulatory relief be provided to businesses that invested in distressed inner cities and rural towns. Provisions included benefits and incentives to employers to hire and train the unemployed. Administration officials described the plan as "an experimental, free-market initiative" to create jobs and stimulate new economic activity. Under the proposal, up to 25 zones a year would be selected by the secretary of housing and urban development in the first three years. Cities and states would nominate areas hard-hit by poverty and unemployment. *(Map, p. 109)*

Two methods were proposed to assist displaced workers. The first, already embodied in the Job Training Partnership Act, offered federal matching funds for retraining and placement assistance at the state and local levels and provided that those programs involve the private sector's significant participation. The second proposal called for states to use up to 2 percent of state unemployment tax revenues for training, job search and relocation assistance to displaced workers.

In the youth unemployment area, Reagan stressed that parts of the solution already were provided by the enterprise zone and Job Training and Partnership programs, but he did request an additional $724 million appropriation to target the latter program on disadvantaged youth. He also noted that the previously extended Targeted Jobs Tax Credit had been modified to provide tax incentives to businesses that provide training to young people.

Finally, the president proposed enactment of what he called a "youth employment opportunity wage," which would allow employers to pay a minimum wage of $2.50 per hour to workers under 22 years of age for summer employment. This wage, which would be 25 percent less than the existing regular minimum wage of $3.25 per hour, was perhaps the most controversial of Reagan's March 11 proposals. He defended it, however, by citing historical evidence that application of the regular minimum wage to young, unskilled workers was a serious impediment to their employment. By accepting work at a lesser wage, such young people, according to Reagan, could gain otherwise inaccessible on-the-job experience and could enhance their future chances of finding better paying jobs.

In summing up his proposals, the president defined the Employment Act of 1983 as a "balanced and realistic approach to addressing our economy's structural unemployment problem."

Debate on Legislative Initiatives

The contemporary jobs bill debate kept returning to the problem of "time lag" — the tendency of public works programs to take months or years to get geared up, providing little immediate relief for the unemployed nor stimulus for the economy. Oftentimes, the recession that occasioned the legislation was ended by the time the projects were begun. Even some supporters of work relief agreed that public works employment was not a perfect avenue for job creation. James K. Galbraith, executive director of the congressional Joint Economic Committee, said, "You don't build a Hoover Dam in order to offset a six-month recession . . . There's a danger that if you get too much into the highway programs as an antidote to unemployment, you will get out of sync with the business cycle."

Others contended that the time-lag issue was irrelevant. Amitai Etzioni, director of the Center for Policy Research and a professor at George Washington University, maintained that the criterion for any job-creation project should be whether it aided in the reindustrialization of America. "If you have something that would cost extra and takes even

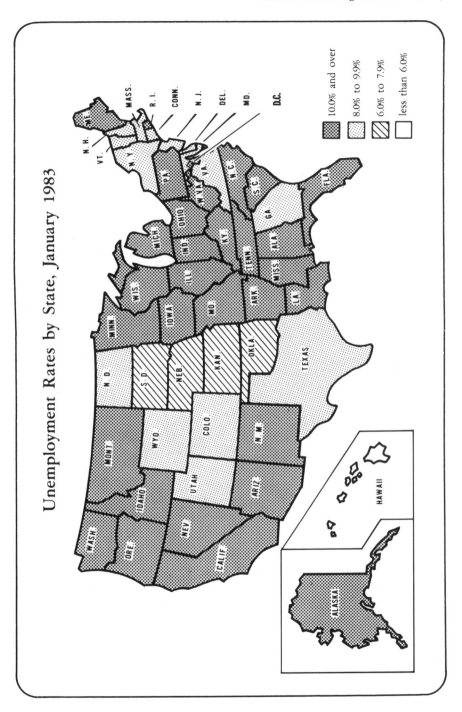

Unemployment Rates by State, January 1983

10.0% and over
8.0% to 9.9%
6.0% to 7.9%
less than 6.0%

longer, but both reduces unemployment and [creates] something of real value, I would prefer that. . . ."

Critics also charged that public works programs did not really create many jobs, and actually could result in a short-term loss of jobs because local and state governments tended to defer their own projects while waiting for federal government action. Roger Vaughan, who worked for two years as a public works adviser to New York Gov. Hugh L. Carey, said that when the federal Local Public Works program was passed in 1976 state and local governments cut back on their capital spending. They deferred their spending, according to Vaughan, to wait and see if the federal government would support all their project costs. Federal agencies attempted, over time, to create some kind of "maintenance of effort" requirements for state and local governments. Measurement of what a state might have spent was almost impossible, making the federal laws difficult to enforce.

Even during the days of the New Deal's Public Works Administration, critics said that public works programs were not labor-intensive enough to be good job-creating mechanisms. Contemporary skeptics noted that construction work was even more mechanized than ever before. In the 1930s rehabilitating an aging bridge required considerable unskilled and semiskilled workers to load and unload materials, mix concrete and paint, for example. Those same processes became, over time, highly automated. The recent repairs made on the Woodrow Wilson Bridge near Washington, D.C., provided a good example.

To keep the bridge open to commuter traffic, it was repaired at night, using a new, tractor-driven, buzz-saw-like machine to cut out large rectangles of bridge surface, which were then removed by crane and replaced by blocks of quick-drying concrete. Although this process most likely saved time and money, it also replaced a number of semiskilled laborers using jackhammers or picks with one skilled machine operator behind the wheel of the saw.

Public Service Employment. The most widely used alternative to public works for creating jobs was public service employment. Instead of waiting around for construction projects to get started, people were quickly hired for "service" jobs, such as working in day-care centers, providing homemaker services for the elderly or doing clerical work in government offices.

Despite the advantages of easy implementation and low cost as compared with public works projects, public service employment often was stigmatized as dead-end and make-work. Critics said that public service jobs rarely provided opportunities for permanent employment or advancement and did not teach workers marketable skills. But advocates of public service employment characterized the make-work charge as unfair. Sar Levitan, director of the National Council on Employment Policy in Washington, D.C., contended there were many services that states and localities should offer their citizens but often did not for lack of funds. Federal grants could be used to provide essential services and, at the same time, relieve unemployment.

Public service employment supporters also pointed out that programs that immediately created jobs lifted morale, which could have important consequences for economic recovery. James Galbraith suggested that if public service employment were available, fewer people would be afraid to commit themselves to long-term purchases such as houses or automobiles for fear of losing their jobs. Hence, consumer spending would rise, thus aiding economic recovery.

Job-Creation Alternatives. While Congress concentrated on traditional work-relief programs, other legislative proposals also were pushed as "job-creation" or "job-preservation" measures. Considering public sentiment about the unemployment issue in 1983, Sen. Dan Quayle, R-Ind., noted that any bill introduced into Congress that touched on employment by any stretch of the imagination would have the word "jobs" attached to it.

Unions in industries hard hit by imports, such as automobiles and steel, backed a bill in the 97th Congress introduced by Rep. Richard L. Ottinger, D-N.Y., that called for imported goods to use a certain percentage of "domestic content," meaning American parts and labor. The proposal used a sliding scale. For example, the more cars that a Japanese automaker sought to sell in the United States, the higher the amount of "domestic content" that would have to go into it. The United Auto Workers of America (UAW) asserted the domestic-content rule would result in 800,000 auto jobs created or saved. But opponents said that such protectionist measures would result in retaliation by our trading partners, resulting in thousands of lost jobs in other industries. The House passed a watered-down bill Dec. 15, 1982, containing an amendment that the legislation could not violate any existing treaty or trade agreement. The Senate did not vote on the bill, however, killing it for the 97th Congress. *(Foreign Trade and U.S. Unemployment, p. 57)*

Another jobs-related proposal was an immigration bill sponsored by Sen. Alan K. Simpson, R-Wyo., and Rep. Romano L. Mazzoli, D-Ky. The bill would have granted amnesty to many illegal aliens in the United States at that time, but would have put stricter limits on future immigration. Although many of the jobs taken by illegal aliens, such as harsh farm labor, had been rejected by most Americans, the legislation's supporters projected that it would preserve as many as 100,000 jobs in the service and manufacturing industries. While this bill stalled in the 97th Congress, a similar Senate proposal was introduced in the 98th. The bill received committee approval in April 1983 with an attached amendment by Kennedy. The amendment authorized an annual review of employer sanctions for five years, with congressional hearings required on the findings.

History of Jobs Programs

The dispute over the federal government's role in public works went back to early constitutional debate. Some of the founding fathers — even those who distrusted too much centralized authority — favored a strong federal role in undertaking public works or, in the parlance of the 18th century, "internal improvements." Most such proposals for a strong federal role were, however, defeated or at best received indifferently.

Constitutional Debate

At the Constitutional Convention of 1787, Benjamin Franklin moved that the Constitution explicitly grant the government the power "for cutting canals where deemed necessary." James Madison extended this motion by proposing that the power over all improvements "to secure an easy communication between States" be included. Both motions were defeated because of the smaller states' fears that such centralized power over communications would work to their disadvantage.

Thomas Jefferson returned to these themes in 1806 when, as president, he suggested a constitutional amendment to grant power to the federal government to encourage "public education, roads, rivers, canals, and such other objects of public improvement as it may be thought proper to add to the constitutional enumeration of Federal powers." His suggestion, however, died when Congress became concerned over the possible U.S. involvement in the Napoleonic wars.

The farthest-reaching proposal for federal power over public works in the early 19th century came from President John Quincy Adams. In his first annual message to Congress in 1825, he called for an ambitious program of road and canal construction to be coordinated by a new Cabinet-level Department of Internal Improvements. Adam's program, however, was considered too visionary by his contemporaries.

Federal support of public works did exist, but usually as a reaction to private industrial initiatives. Many of the public works systems constructed were attempts to stimulate private economic growth. Federal use of public works as a job-creating mechanism also had a long history. Longshoremen and sailors who had lost their jobs because of the Embargo Act 1808, which banned trade with Europe, were used by the federal government to build fortifications in New York City. The use of large-scale public employment programs was considered during the depressions of the 1850s and 1870s, but never was adopted on a federal level.

Post-World War I Policies

The post-World War I depression of 1920-21 spurred discussion of a counter-cyclical mechanism that would increase public works expenditures during economic downturns. President Warren Harding's Conference on Unemployment advised in 1921 that "Federal authorities, including the Federal Reserve Bank, should expedite the construction of public buildings and public works covered by existing appropriations." But the boom of the "Roaring '20s" took the urgency out of those deliberations.

In 1929 national unemployment stood at 3 percent. But in October of that year the stock market crashed, precipitating the massive economic collapse that came to be known as the Great Depression. Even as unemployment was climbing, President Herbert Hoover stuck to the classic laissez-faire economic philosophy that the federal government should leave recovery to the private sector. "Under our political system, government is not, nor should it be, a general employer of labor," Hoover said in 1930.

Hoover preferred to leave the provision of relief to the states, communities and private charities. But when joblessness soared in 1932 to 25 percent, bringing with it widespread suffering that was beyond the capacity of the traditional structures to deal with, Hoover was moved to act. He created the Reconstruction Finance Corporation (RFC), which appropriated $300 million for public construction loans. Hoover's actions were too late, however, to save him from defeat in the presidential

113

Keynesian Economics

Many New Deal initiatives to end the Depression were bitterly opposed in the 1930s, but by the 1950s there seemed to be widespread acceptance of Roosevelt's pragmatic application of Keynesian theory, which had become a permanent facet of federal economic policy.

Roosevelt based his "pump-priming" policies on the theories of John Maynard Keynes, an influential British economic philosopher. Beginning in 1929 as the jobless rate in Britain rose, Keynes increasingly advocated government spending on public works to ease widespread unemployment. Classical laissez-faire economic doctrine, based on the late 18th century writings of Adam Smith, insisted that economic "boom-and-bust" cycles were an inevitable consequence of a free market economy. Smith held that any attempt by government to intervene in the natural law of the market place would be at best ineffective, and more likely deleterious to the economy.

Keynes, in contrast, argued that because both national and international economies had become vastly more complex and interconnected than in the 18th century, many of Smith's basic premises no longer were applicable. He then went on to develop a case for government intervention to affect economic cycles. He contended that besides creating jobs in the short term, appropriate government intervention in a slumping economy could increase national purchasing power and also promote employment in private industry. Government could thereby play a role in long-term economic growth as well as relieve short-term unemployment.

election of 1932 to Franklin Roosevelt. But his ideas did provide the framework for the "alphabet soup" of make-work agencies during the New Deal period that followed.

By 1933 the incoming Roosevelt administration agreed that a policy involving both government/industry cooperation and immediate relief programs was essential. Throughout the 1930s until the onset of World War II, Roosevelt's administration initiated a vast array of programs that augmented the federal government's commitment to the country's economic stability. Called the New Deal, many of these programs were intended either to create jobs directly through work relief or indirectly through economic stimulation.

The National Recovery Administration (NRA) was created to stimulate industry and restore employment. The public works and relief programs included the Public Works Administration (PWA), the Federal Emergency Relief Agency (FERA), the Works Progress Administration (WPA) and the Civil Works Administration (CWA). Finally the Civilian Conservation Corps (CCC) and the National Youth Administration (NYA) were created to help mobilize and relieve the nation's unemployed youth.

New Deal Sets Precedents

One of Roosevelt's earliest actions was to create FERA, which administered the first system of federal relief. It provided $500 million mainly for cash relief, but also for a small number of menial jobs, such a leaf-raking and park cleaning. Roosevelt moved quickly to complement FERA with more substantial job-creation programs, and in January 1935 he abolished the FERA completely. Despite the impression of Roosevelt as the father of the "welfare state," he actually disapproved of the idea of cash relief. "The quicker they are taken off the dole the better it is for them during the rest of their lives," Roosevelt said shortly after taking office. "Most Americans want to give something for what they get. That something, which in this case is honest work, is the saving barrier between them and moral disintegration." Roosevelt also hoped to speed economic recovery and end the Depression by encouraging industrial recovery, stimulating consumer spending and creating an atmosphere of action rather than resignation.

Civilian Conservation Corps. The first New Deal program devoted solely to job creation was the CCC established by an Act of Congress on March 31, 1933, less than a month after Roosevelt's inauguration. The plan to send thousands of unemployed slum youths into the country to plant trees was a product of Roosevelt's devotion to conservation and to his nostalgic notion that he could reverse the pattern of migration from rural to urban areas.

The CCC was one of Roosevelt's most significant personal accomplishments. He was committed from an early stage to the idea of youth conservation jobs programs. As governor of New York, he asked the state Legislature in 1929 for conservation jobs "to be used primarily to employ people out of work." By 1932, 10,000 out-of-work men were planting trees throughout the state.

In accepting the Democratic nomination for president in June of that year, Roosevelt spoke of his vision of engaging a million young men in such work through the country, and his interest in such programs was sustained when he reached the White House. In his March 21, 1933, message sending the CCC bill to Congress, he said the corps would concentrate on "forestry, the prevention of soil erosion, flood control and similar projects." The president lavished attention on the CCC. He personally drew diagrams showing how the new agency should be organized and spurred the CCC to quickly construct camps and enroll young men.

The CCC was not embraced universally at first. Some of Roosevelt's Cabinet members felt it might be dangerous to collect large groups of jobless and possibly resentful young men in the woods. The plan to pay corps members only $1 a day enraged labor leaders. Conservative Republicans and Southern Democrats warned that deficit spending would prevent the recovery of the private sector, and that the stimulus provided by the program would be minuscule compared with an overall business recovery. The plan passed anyway and within three months 250,000 men were employed in 1,468 forest and park camps under Army supervision. They were paid $30 a month ($1 per day), $25 of which had to be sent home to their families.

In the nine-year existence of the CCC, more than 1.5 million youths were employed in creating 65,511 new acres of wildlife refuge, 199,214 acres of national parkland and 7,436,321 acres of national forest. The 200 million trees they planted helped prevent the kind of soil erosion that had turned the Great Plains into a "dust bowl" during the Depression. They fought forest fires, strung 12,000 miles of telephone line and built the Skyline Drive through the Shenandoah National Forest in Virginia.

The CCC made a lasting impression on many of its members, including Rep. Edward R. Roybal, D-Calif. He spent about nine months in a California camp between 1934 and 1935, and credited the CCC with developing his character. *(Roybal box, p. 118)*

Another program that aided unemployed youths was the National Youth Administration (1935-43). This program encouraged financially distressed youths to remain in high school or college by providing them with part-time jobs in school libraries and laboratories or on grounds maintenance. The average NYA monthly stipend was $15.

Civil Works Administration. The CCC provided jobs for young men, but did not solve the dilemma of adults who were displaced by the economic collapse. Roosevelt wanted a job program that, unlike FERA, served some tangible purpose, and on Nov. 8, 1933, he created the CWA by taking $400 million out of a $5 billion general-purpose emergency jobs appropriation that Congress had placed at his discretion.

Roosevelt put Harry Hopkins, his relief administrator when he was governor of New York, in charge of CWA. Within two months about 4 million people were employed on such projects as building or repairing streets, schools and airports; digging sewers; and developing parks and playgrounds. Kansas Gov. Alf Landon, who would unsuccessfully challenge Roosevelt for the presidency in 1936, wrote in early 1934 that the CWA was one of the most important policy decisions of the Roosevelt administration, and he urged the program's continuance. But critics pointed out alleged circumstances of waste and fraud in the implementation of the program and decried the cost when Roosevelt went back to the emergency fund for another $533 million. In 1934 Roosevelt ordered CWA shut down.

National Recovery Administration. The NRA and the Public Works Administration (PWA) both were established under the terms of the National Industrial Recovery Act of June 16, 1933. In signing the bill into law, Roosevelt emphasized that its primary purpose, from his perspective, was to put people back to work. The NRA aimed to create jobs by stimulating industrial recovery, the PWA through a massive public works program.

The NRA was basically an experiment in voluntary industrial coordination and planning through industry-wide trade associations under government supervision. Roosevelt characterized the experiment as "a challenge to industry." Gen. Hugh Johnson, a guiding spirit of the NRA concept and first administrator of the agency, had helped mobilize industry during World War I. After the onset of the Great Depression, he advocated a similar mobilization for industrial recovery. Johnson shared the opinion of many economists, business executives and labor leaders that unbridled competition among companies within an industry had been largely responsible for the Depression.

Labor had been the first casualty in the Great Depression, as in previous crises, since companies that cut wages and increased working hours to reduce their employment rolls could undercut the prices of their competitors. However, the Sherman Anti-Trust Act appeared to forbid any agreement among firms that could discourage free competition. The NRA was empowered to suspend, in part, these strict antitrust policies by

Roybal Recalls His New Deal Days

For at least one member of Congress, talk of new youth conservation jobs programs sparked memories that went back nearly 50 years.

The Civilian Conservation Corps (CCC) not only gave Rep. Edward R. Roybal, D-Calif., a job — helping to revitalize a national park — but in his view it saved him from an almost certain life of crime."Many of my friends ended up on the wrong side of the law," said Roybal, who had lived most of his life in a largely Hispanic section of east Los Angeles.

Roybal joined the Depression-era youth conservation jobs program in 1934, when he was 18 years old. It was either that "or starve," he said.

The program, which employed more than 1.5 million youths, was limited to unmarried men between the ages of 15 and 18 whose families were on relief. Roybal was sent to Sequoia National Park in central California, where for about nine months he cleared fire trails and constructed park roads. He was paid $30 a month, of which $25 was sent back to his family in Los Angeles.

The CCC furnished additional benefits to many of its members. The corps' educational programs taught approximately 40,000 illiterate young men to read and write, and the far-flung work projects provided travel experience that otherwise would have been unaffordable.

But for Roybal the CCC "not only provided employment, but developed character." That, in fact, was the program's greatest quality, he said. Roybal described competitions among CCC camps in the area to try to win a special "good character" flag. The flag would fly from the top of the winning bunkhouse, denoting the group's stellar work habits. There was "a great deal of pride" taken in winning those contests, Roybal said.

CCC corpsmen wore uniforms and adhered to strict rules and regulations. They got up at 5:30 a.m. and started work at 8. The training and physical conditioning doubtlessly helped the men adjust to the armed forces during World War II. "We were self-disciplined," Roybal said, adding that "if we had that discipline in Congress, we would have real party discipline."

endorsing industry-wide codes to raise wages (and thus increase the purchasing power of labor), to shorten working hours (thus create jobs) and to recognize the rights of labor to collective bargaining. In exchange for these concessions, firms within an industry were permitted more latitude than under strict antitrust policies to set minimum prices and production quotas.

Johnson realized from the outset that the codes the NRA exacted from industry were probably legally unenforceable and, therefore, compliance would have to rely strongly on public opinion. With encouragement from Roosevelt, he set about his task. His initial successes were phenomenal. Within days of enactment of the National Industrial Recovery Act, for example, Johnson announced that the cotton textile industry — long regarded as a prime example of unfair labor practices — had agreed to industry-wide codes. These codes not only set a reasonable minimum wage, maximum hours, and collective bargaining promises, but they also forbade child labor.

Unfortunately, Johnson promised too much and sought to extend the reach of the NRA too far. He brought the ridicule and wrath of opponents of industrial planning down upon the NRA by attempting to extend NRA provisions to small businesses such as family dry cleaning establishments. In May 1935 the Supreme Court declared the NRA unconstitutional on the grounds that it gave excessive legislative powers to Congress and unduly regulated commerce. This decision effectively blocked out the New Deal's attempt at national industrial planning. During its brief existence, however, the NRA had accomplished a great deal for the morale of the country. In *The Coming of the New Deal*, Arthur Schlesinger wrote that the NRA's enduring achievements were more in social than economic fields. "It established the principle of maximum hours and minimum wages on a national basis. It abolished child labor. It dealt a fatal blow to sweatshops. It made collective bargaining a national policy and thereby transformed the position of organized labor. It stamped out a noxious collection of unfair trade practices. It set new standards of economic decency in American life — standards which could not be called back, whatever happened to the NRA."

Public Works Administration. The experience with public works programs mandated by the National Industrial Recovery Act provided a different set of lessons. The PWA was established with an initial funding of $3.3 billion to coordinate the construction of large public facilities such as hospitals, schools, dams, bridges and tunnels. The PWA quickly funded a number of socially useful projects, such as the Boulder Dam (now the Hoover Dam) on the Colorado River and the rebuilding of schools in Los Angeles following an earthquake.

The agency, run meticulously by Secretary of the Interior Harold Ickes, was unmarked by scandal. Even though its accomplishments later were eclipsed by the Works Progress Administration (renamed Works Project Adminstration in 1939), the PWA hardly went out of business. Between 1933 and 1939, it was responsible for 70 percent of new school construction, 65 percent of all courthouses, city halls and sewage treatment plants and 62 percent of all hospitals. The Grand Coulee, Bonneville and Fort Peck dams were built by the PWA, as were the Triborough Bridge and the Lincoln and Queens Midtown tunnels in New York City.

But PWA provided first evidence of the limited usefulness of large public works programs as counter-recessionary mechanisms. For one thing, the programs required months or sometimes years of planning. Ickes' tight-fisted control was seen by critics as bureaucratic red tape that further hindered projects. The projects were expensive and, perhaps most damaging of all, highly capital-intensive, with about 70 percent of expenditures going for materials and less than 30 percent for wages. Many of the projects also required skilled construction workers and did little for either the unskilled or for unemployed white-collar workers. While the PWA undoubtedly contributed to improving the infrastructure of the country, its value as an unemployment relief mechanism was felt to be limited.

Works Progress Administration. In January 1935 Roosevelt sent a message to Congress that contained his intention to replace FERA once and for all with a more substantial work-relief program. "I am not willing that the vitality of our people be further sapped by the giving of cash, of market baskets, of a few hours of weekly work cutting grass, raking leaves or picking up papers in the public parks," Roosevelt said. He outlined the requirements for a large job-creation program. Jobs must be of some value to the public, with wages larger than the dole, but not so large as to discourage return to the private sector during recovery. Projects should be labor-intensive, targeted at high unemployment areas, self-liquidating (pay for themselves with user fees), as well as short-term and flexible enough that they could be quickly terminated during a recovery.

To carry out this program, Roosevelt created the WPA in May

1935. The WPA so permanently eclipsed the PWA, in both money and publicity, that many people attribute the former's accomplishments to the latter. The WPA created thousands of programs, most of which were quick to implement, labor-intensive and inexpensive. WPA's construction funding was concentrated on levee building, street and bridge repair, tree planting, swamp drainage, flood cleanup and similar projects. WPA workers also were employed on larger-scale projects, including construction of New York's North Beach (now LaGuardia) Airport.

Many teachers, researchers, professors and librarians also were hired by the WPA. Murals and sculptures by WPA artists adorned public buildings across the nation. Unemployed actors, including Orson Welles and John Houseman, were put to work in The Federal Theater, which produced a number of innovative plays until protests over its alleged leftist leanings forced Roosevelt to abolish it in 1938. The hiring of actors and intellectuals was one of the most controversial aspects of WPA, and projects such as a grant to study the safety pin's history resulted in the popular epithet "boondoggle" being identified with the entire agency.

The "lazy" WPA worker was as pervasive a stereotype as the "welfare Cadillac" of more recent times. A popular song of the 1930s went: "WPA, WPA, Lean on your shovel to pass the time away." A joke of the times told of the WPA worker who fell and broke his hip, because he had been leaning on his shovel so long that termites had eaten through it. Administration officials were angered by the inference. WPA administrator Aubrey Williams countered in 1937 that the WPA workers had been unjustly misrepresented and maligned as boondogglers when great public services and project accomplishments had been achieved.

The WPA had more substantial problems than image. On a practical level, it proved impossible to match every unemployed worker's skills to an available job, resulting in boredom and frustration. Means-testing to determine a worker's eligibility and a regulation that required all WPA workers to be hired from relief rolls rather than the general labor market resulted in an over-proportion of unskilled, aged and infirm workers. Productivity suffered, and many critics accused the WPA of creating make-work jobs just to get people off the dole.

Between 1935 and 1943, an estimated eight million workers received help from the WPA program. The average monthly employment was 2.1 million. The program, which began with a $5 billion appropriation, spent $11 billion before it went out of business in 1943. It created structures and facilities that underpinned the great industrial growth of World War II and the post-war period. Many WPA projects were not only in use 50 years later but comprised a fair share of the nation's infrastructure.

Some observers credited programs such as the WPA with profound social effects. Even if the relief workers did little other than dig holes and refill them, the theory went, the application of this program forestalled unrest, possibly major class riots, during the Depression years. Calling on Congress to extend WPA in 1938, John L. Lewis, president of the United Mine Workers and the Committee for Industrial Organization (CIO), warned of "the greatest threat to democracy, the idleness and misery of our people." And Republican Rep. Usher L. Burdick of North Dakota (1935-58) warned of the threat of communism if job-relief programs were cut back, potentially bringing suffering to thousands of people.

The New Deal programs were credited with reducing the magnitude of suffering and the possibility of social unrest, but it was World War II that ultimately ended chronic unemployment and the Depression. As late as 1940, 9 million people remained unemployed, in addition to the 3 million working for the WPA. An illustration of the ineffectiveness of work relief in solving the fundamental problems of the depressed economy occurred in 1938. Roosevelt, who was under pressure to balance the federal budget, cut funds for WPA and other jobs programs. Work relief employment dropped from 3.6 million in fiscal 1937 to just over 3 million in 1938 — and the economy spun into recession, sending unemployment soaring. By fiscal 1939 the work relief rolls had rebounded to 4.1 million, an all-time high.

Employment Policies After the Depression

World War II ended the need for work relief, as the manpower needs of the military and the munitions industry sent unemployment plummeting to 1.6 percent. The federal government's concern with unemployment, however, had become a permanent issue. Between the post-war era and the 1980s, many public works and public service programs were initiated.

After the war Congress considered a full-employment bill. The Employment Act of 1946, like the Humphrey Hawkins bill passed in 1978, was a symbolic measure that promised "useful employment opportunities" for all persons "able, willing and seeking work." The bill had as its central goal the reduction of the unemployment rate to 4 percent. But attempts to use the Employment Act of 1946 to establish a permanent public works program that could be triggered during an economic downturn were thwarted.

Accelerated Public Works Act. The boom of the 1950s, aided by federal programs such as interstate highway construction and mortgage assistance, reduced concern about public works programs, but a recession that began in late 1960 revived interest in them. President John F. Kennedy proposed legislation in early 1962 that called for a $2 billion permanent fund that could be used to create public works jobs at the first signs of recession.

Like many of Roosevelt's programs, Kennedy's plan placed full control of fund distribution in the hands of the president. Congress objected to both the proposal's cost and to the presidential monopoly on the prized public works pork barrel. When the Accelerated Public Works Act finally passed in September 1962, it contained only $900 million for a one-time, immediate public works acceleration program, with Congress controlling the distribution of funds. By the time jobs were created under this law, the recession they were supposed to treat already had ended — a constant complaint about federal public works programs.

Economic Development Administration. In 1965, during the heyday of the "Great Society," President Lyndon B. Johnson pushed through two programs that came as close to permanent counter-recessionary mechanisms as there ever had been. The Public Works and Economic Development Act of 1965 created the Economic Development Administration (EDA), which was authorized to provide funds under a formula to states, counties, cities and communities suffering from substantial, persistent or potential unemployment and underemployment. The EDA provided funds for industrial parks, sewer construction, building reconstruction, and other facilities that could assist economic growth in poor communities. The sister bill, the Appalachian Regional Development Act of 1965, played a similar role for the high-poverty rural areas of Appalachia.

Public Service Employment and Local Public Works. The 1969-70 recession resulted in a different strategy by jobs program advocates. Congress passed a bill in December 1970 that would have provided $2 billion through 1974 for a "public service" jobs program to create non-construction jobs, similar to the WPA's. But President Richard Nixon vetoed the measure, stating, "WPA-type jobs are not the answer for the men and women who have them, for government which is less efficient

123

as a result, or for the taxpayers who must foot the bill." In July 1971, Nixon also vetoed an "emergency" employment bill that would have appropriated $2 billion for public works jobs.

Nixon at the time was pushing his revenue-sharing proposal, designed to provide cash directly to cities. Nixon considered this a more effective way of combatting recessions, because local officials would know better where the money was needed most. In July 1971 he relented under congressional pressure, signing the Public Service Employment Act. The act provided $2.25 billion for public service jobs, with expenditures to be triggered when unemployment reached 4.5 percent for three consecutive months. Then in August 1971 Nixon signed a bill that included emergency public works employment provisions similar to those he had earlier vetoed. Critics again complained that the public works process was so slow that the "emergency" jobs were not created until the recession's end.

The jobs-creation issue resurfaced in 1974-75 when a recession sent unemployment to 9 percent, a post-Depression record at the time. In February 1976 the Senate sustained President Gerald R. Ford's veto of a $6.1 billion public works bill. Later that year, a $2 billion public works jobs measure was passed over Ford's veto. Funding a total of 10,616 projects, the Local Public Works (LPW) program vastly expanded the role of the EDA, which administered the program. President Jimmy Carter added another $4 billion in 1977. Most of the projects involved work on sewers, streets and bridges, and local government buildings.

There was disagreement over the number of jobs created by the Local Public Works program. An EDA study maintained that LPW had created the equivalent of 96,000 year-long jobs on-site, 66,000 jobs with project suppliers and 200,000 jobs from the program's economic stimulus, for a total of 350,000 jobs. A 1979 Office of Management and Budget (OMB) study determined that only 30,000 jobs actually had been created. The main problem in determining the number of new jobs created was the issue of "job substitution." Critics said that state and local governments used federal money to pay workers who otherwise would have been on their payrolls. Job substitution saved state and municipal funds, but reduced the net impact of job-creation programs. While the EDA assumed little substitution in its study, OMB suggested substitution rates as high as 65 percent.

Two other issues that traditionally caused problems for public works projects resurfaced during the LPW program. Once again, the projects proved to be capital-intensive. According to the OMB study, only 22 percent of expenditures went for wages, and most of that went to skilled workers who had not been previously unemployed. In addition, spending on the program peaked in 1978, after the economy had begun to recover.

Comprehensive Employment and Training Act

The best-known jobs legislation to emerge from this period was CETA, enacted in 1973. CETA developed out of a vast array of job and training programs spawned by the Great Society legislation in the 1960s. It featured both program centralization, concentrating overall supervision in the Labor Department, and decentralization, giving control of implementation to local governments.

Studies of Kennedy and Johnson administration manpower programs, which included the 1962 Manpower Development and Training Act, the Jobs Corps and Job Opportunities in the Business Sector (JOBS), showed that the programs had a substantial effect on participants' subsequent economic performance, although they had only a limited impact on overall unemployment. But these early job programs were difficult to administer, scattered as they were through various government offices. Agencies were forced to make separate contracts with thousands of training centers, making oversight difficult.

CETA's original provisions included a limited program of public service jobs. It addressed structural unemployment problems by providing jobs for those with long-term employment difficulties. Only persons unemployed for more than a month were allowed to participate.

As the recession deepened in the mid-1970s, congressional leaders saw in CETA a vehicle for fighting increasing unemployment. In 1974 Congress added a new title to CETA further authorizing public service jobs, which it continued to extend and expand. In contrast with CETA's original interest in structural unemployment, the 1974 addition was a counter-cyclical measure to attack unemployment caused by recession. In 1977 a provision to aid disadvantaged youth, a Young Adult Conservation Corps, was initiated.

Although the public service provisions were quickly implemented, the program was beset by problems. Pressed by the Ford and Carter administrations to fulfill hiring quotas, local officials created numerous paper-shuffling and leaf-raking jobs that critics characterized as makework. Lack of tight federal supervision and regulations led to newspaper exposés of local instances of nepotism, favoritism and other kinds of fraud. Many jobs went to middle-class people instead of the hard-core, low-income unemployed for whom they were intended. Job substitution was rampant; in the early stages of the program buildup, more than two-thirds of CETA employees were moved from local or state to federal payrolls. The high unemployment rate that triggered public service employment often peaked during economic recovery and fueled inflation.

Changes in CETA's authorization in 1978 tightened standards, aiming job creation more directly at low-income unemployed and cracking down on waste, fraud and substitution. But the program never outlived the stigma it had acquired. Carter reduced CETA public service employment to 325,000 by the time he left office. In 1981 Reagan proposed elimination of public service employment as part of his federal austerity program, and Congress went along. By September 1981 there were no more federal public service jobs.

Increasing numbers of homeless people resorted to makeshift housing. This scene is in Houston, Texas.

Chapter 5

PROBLEMS FOR THE UNEMPLOYED

From stories about families sleeping under bridges in Tulsa to descriptions of overflow crowds at Detroit soup kitchens, problems among the unemployed surfaced in every part of the country.

A 1982 survey by the U.S. Conference of Mayors found that the most basic human necessities — shelter and food — led the list of emergency services most needed in cities. City officials also reported that they needed money to help families pay fuel bills and for medical care, clothing, transportation and day care. The mayors' report said the economic slump, high unemployment and federal program cuts had helped create a group it called the "new poor." These were "people who are losing their jobs, exhausting their financial resources, exhausting their unemployment benefits and losing their hopes," the mayors' report said.

The recession the report referred to began in July 1981, although that date was a meaningless milestone for the millions of Americans who had lost their jobs well before then. As of January 1983, unemployment stood at a 41-year high of 10.8 percent and reached throughout both goods-producing and service industries. Of the 12 million unemployed, 2.6 million had been out of work for 27 weeks or longer.

Analysts said that the recession differed from those of the past because many laid-off workers in troubled industries such as steel or farm equipment or automobile manufacturing would most likely not get their jobs back after the recession ended.

Long-term unemployment had led to psychological trauma among many of the nation's families. Family violence in 1983 was on the increase. According to the April 2, 1983, *New York Times*, community health leaders interviewed at a national meeting in Detroit had reported an increase in the level of severe quarrels, wife-beating, child abuse, excessive alcohol use, insomnia, depression and suicide.

Blue-collar workers were much more affected by this recession than were white-collar professional, managerial, sales and clerical workers. The most severe unemployment was in states dependent on heavy industry. And adult men working full time, who usually were better insulated from the ups and downs of the economic cycle, were more affected than women and teen-agers, whose relative increase in unemployment rates during 1982 was slightly less than was experienced by men. This trend reflected the recession's severe impact on the nation's industrial base and its effects on the mainstream of America's work force.

A *New York Times*/CBS News Poll, published Feb. 2, 1983, showed that of the 1,597 people who responded to the poll, 574 of them lived in households where one adult was unemployed. Of those households, 63 percent had bought lower quality food, 50 percent had cut medical or dental care and 53 percent had taken money out of savings during the last year. Thirty-three percent had borrowed money and 32 percent had missed payments on homes, cars, apartments or loans. Eighteen percent had taken food stamps or welfare and 47 percent reported more family quarrels.

"While the problem has not reached Great Depression proportions, the similarities are obvious," said Mary Ellen Hombs, of the Community for Creative Non-violence, a Washington, D.C., organization. She spoke at a Dec. 15, 1982, House subcommittee hearing on homelessness. "The 'Okies' of another time are now called 'Black tag people,' a reference to the color of Michigan's license plates," Hombs said. "Bread lines — and the 1980s equivalent, cheese lines — stretch for blocks."

While comparisons to the 1930s were commonplace, many experts viewed the psychological impact of the 1980s recession as more severe. They pointed to the technological changes and restructuring of industry that would permanently eliminate many previously well-paid jobs. That permanence added to the depression felt by many of the unemployed, especially those who were either middle-aged or older.

According to the Oct. 8, 1982, *Washington Post*, between January and October 1982 the unemployment rate for workers 55 and older had increased 24 percent, more than twice the 11 percent increase for those 16-24 and 50 percent more than for the national work force, which had a 16 percent rate of growth. As of August 1982, out of 10.8 million unemployed, 117,000 were 65 or older and 771,000 were 55 and older.

And while the problem was nationwide, it seemed most acute in cities. Legions of unemployed workers flocked to urban centers in search of jobs. The problem was becoming as much an issue in the Sun Belt as in the Frost Belt.

"I was surprised to find mayors from relatively healthy cities talking about people living under bridges, living in cars, looking for jobs," Seattle Mayor Charles Royer, president of the National League of Cities, said at a January 1983 meeting of the Conference of Mayors.

In particular, problems were created by unemployed people who wandered to cities in the West and Southwest in search of jobs. Mayors in those cities said there was not enough work for newcomers and they were placing a strain on city social services. Tulsa authorities, for instance, reported a heavy demand for prenatal and pediatric care among families arriving from Northern cities. They also told the Conference of Mayors there had been a significant increase in domestic violence and murders involving transients.

Federal Cutbacks Add to Problems of Unemployed

Many social service agencies in 1983 reported that, as a result of the recession and federal budget cuts, they were being overwhelmed by demands for their services. In addition to requests for cash assistance to help pay rent or electricity bills, which social agencies typically received during rough times, they also saw a big increase in the number of people requesting the basic necessities: food, clothing and shelter.

In 1981, when President Ronald Reagan first began pressing for budget cuts, he promised to provide a "safety net" for the "truly needy." But social welfare advocates were not convinced. "I don't think that there ever was a safety net," said Father Gary Christ of the National Conference of Catholic Charities. "Someone without food or without shelter and without clothing and without the possibility of getting a job is someone who is truly needy."

An Urban Institute study published in 1982 said that non-profit, private organizations such as hospitals, universities and social service agencies stood to lose about $33 billion in federal funds in the following three years. During the same period the government was expected to cut back an additional $115 billion in funds for federally run social service programs. "Most hard hit by these changes will be non-profit social service agencies and community organizations, which will lose one-fourth to one-third of their total revenues," the report said.

Those who lost federal benefits often turned to state and local governments for help, but those jurisdictions also were reducing their budgets for social service programs in 1983. "One source after another of service or financial support for the disadvantaged has been withdrawn," said Jennifer R. Wolch, assistant professor and associate dean of the University of Southern California's health and mental health services system. "They [the disadvantaged] drift and are generally less well off. Some find temporary refuge in transient-renter areas or the remaining group homes. But more and more are ending up on the streets."

Leaders of black and Hispanic organizations said that minorities were generally the most needful people in the country and had been hit the hardest by the recession. "When you get right down into the streets where we operate, it's incredible, the needless suffering in this country," said Milton Bondurant of the National Urban League. But they also pointed out that the problem was not exclusively a minority one. The ranks of the "truly needy" were swelled by the "newly needy" — lower middle- and middle-class Americans whose lives underwent drastic change during the recession.

Much of the demand on social agencies from the middle class in 1983 was for counseling services. Many people were having a hard time dealing with the psychological consequences of unemployment. Christ reported that in Buffalo, N.Y., requests for the marriage counseling services of Catholic Charities affiliates were up 20 percent over 1982.

But growing numbers of middle-class people were turning to charities for the basics. Christ said that a visit to a soup kitchen would shatter the stereotype of aid recipients as all welfare cases. "We're seeing people who, a couple of years ago, would have never dreamed that they'd be coming anywhere for help," Christ said.

Non-profit Organizations Hurt by Budget Cuts

Although the budget cuts pinched organizations across the voluntary spectrum, the most affected were those dependent on government funds, those least able to compete for block grants and other government funding, those least experienced at fund raising and those that were least popular. According to James Castelli of Independent Sector, an association of private sector organizations that contribute to charities and philanthropic organizations, "Social welfare organizations, civic and political organizations will feel the greatest impact."

By 1983 the National Urban League had for years been involved in federally funded job training projects for minorities. In the fiscal year that ended in July 1982, the Urban League funded 39 programs with a total of

Non-Profit Groups Rely on Government Funding

Proportion of total revenue provided by government grants, contracts and other programs:

Civil and Social Action	44 percent
Health Services	43 percent
Human Services	43 percent
Culture	10 percent
Education and Research	9 percent

Source: "The Fiscal Capacity of the Voluntary Sector," a study prepared by Bruce L. R. Smith of the Brookings Institution and Nelson M. Rosenbaum of the Center for Responsive Governance for a Brookings Institution conference, Dec. 9, 1981.

$34 million; in fiscal year 1983, $9 million was spent on 22 projects. Other charitable organizations reported similar troubles in late 1982. Responding to a survey by Independent Sector, the National Council of La Raza, a Hispanic social welfare organization, said it had suffered a 40 percent reduction in staff with a 45 percent reduction in services. Opportunities Industrialization Centers, a Philadelphia-based job training organization, lost $65 million, or 50 percent of its 1981 budget.

Another problem for voluntary agencies was caused by the elimination of the Comprehensive Employment and Training Administration (CETA) public service jobs program. Critics of the CETA program complained that many of the jobs created were of the "make-work" variety. But non-profit organizers said that CETA workers were vital to many of their functions. "Many organizations were taking advantage of the CETA program in a very useful way," said Robert O. Bothwell, executive director of the National Committee for Responsive Philanthropy.

Reagan signed new job training legislation on Oct. 13, 1982, to replace CETA. The new program authorized by the bill provided training in job skills to the low-income unemployed. Unlike CETA, it did not pay for public service employment for the jobless. The purpose was to aid youth and unskilled adults in entering the job market, and to provide job training to low-income individuals who faced serious problems in finding work. *(Federal Jobs Programs Controversy, p. 95)*

The Homeless

There was no official census of the homeless in America. But experts estimated the number in 1983 ran between 500,000 and two million. These people were found everywhere from a tent city outside of Houston to Salvation Army clothing deposit boxes in the Cleveland area.

"We used to think of the homeless as the Bowery-type derelict who is down on his luck," said the Rev. Donald Sakano, director of the New York Archdiocese neighborhood preservation office. But the new victims often were whole families, he said, noting that he had recently seen a woman who was eight months pregnant living in the New York City subway tunnels.

Kim Hopper, a research associate for the Community Service Society of New York, told a housing subcommittee of the House Banking, Finance and Urban Affairs Committee that unemployment and the loss of income was only one of several factors that contributed to homelessness.

A key influence, she said, was deinstitutionalization, or the release of patients from mental hospitals. This policy contributed to an upsurge in the number of so-called street people in 1983.

A 1982 report by the Community Service Society of New York estimated that every year about 2.5 million Americans were involuntarily displaced from their residences because of renovation, redevelopment or rent increases — victims of housing restoration projects in inner cities. "At the same time," the report said, "a half-million units of low-rent dwellings are lost each year through the combined forces of conversion, abandonment, inflation, arson and demolition. . . . When it was added that the major victims of mass development are the poor, those with the fewest resources to absorb new hardships or to recover in its wake, it is no mystery that the ranks of the homeless continue to swell."

The problem of housing the very poor had been compounded by the nationwide shortage of public housing. In Washington, D.C., where the apartment vacancy rate was low in October 1982, some 8,500 families were on a waiting list for public housing. Many were forced to live in motel rooms at public expense while they waited for available housing.

Estimated Homeless Population

Atlanta	1,500 - 2,000	Philadelphia	8,000
Baltimore	9,000 - 12,000	Phoenix	3,300 - 6,200
Boston	4,000 - 8,000	San Francisco	4,000
Chicago	12,000	Seattle	5,000
Denver	5,000	Washington, D.C.	10,000
Detroit	8,000		
Los Angeles	22,000	National Total	240,000 -
New York City	36,000		1,000,000

Analysts said there also was a growing shortage of cheap rooming houses and hotels, "flophouses," in the nation's big cities. Some had been abandoned, others were being converted into luxury apartments. Rising unemployment had compounded the situation. "The single male who used to pick up enough casual labor to pay for a low-cost room cannot even do that anymore," said City Commissioner Margaret Strachan of Portland, Ore. "Those jobs have dried up, too."

In 1983 cities were responding in a variety of ways. Armories were converted to shelters in New York City and firehouses were used in the winter of 1982 in Philadelphia, according to Mitch Snyder, a leader of the Community for Creative Non-violence. Private charitable and religious groups, such as the Salvation Army and the Travelers Aid Society, took a large share of the responsibility for providing shelters. But officials from these agencies said they had been unable to meet the growing demand for beds. And, they noted, the shelters provided only a temporary haven for the homeless.

As of spring 1983, Congress had begun to respond to the problem, introducing the following related bills:

● Rep. Henry B. Gonzalez, D-Texas, chairman of the housing subcommittee, introduced a bill to provide $100 million to cities for shelters for the homeless and $760 million in emergency mortgage foreclosure relief. *(Anti-foreclosure legislation, box, p. 150)*

● Sen. Paul E. Tsongas, D-Mass., offered the Homeless Relief Act of

135

More Help Urged to Pay Heating Costs...

In March 1983 Peter Smolen lived in a small house in east Buffalo, N.Y., with his wife and two young children. He had worked for a small steel factory, but was then unemployed, and his unemployment benefits had expired. The family survived on the income of his wife, who worked four hours a day cleaning offices.

Several years earlier, Smolen used a portion of his savings to insulate his home against the fierce Buffalo winters. Since losing his job, he had taken more drastic measures, shutting off most of the house and trying to keep his family warm in a single room. In spite of this, Smolen's heating bills continued to rise. During the winter of 1982-83, his gas bill exceeded $100 a month.

"He is up against the wall," said the Rev. Robert K. Golombek, to whom Smolen had taken his problem. "What is he going to do? He is draining his life's savings."

"The problems are widespread all over the city" Golombek said. "Many of our old people ... put new windows in, put in new doors. Then what they find is they are using less gas and paying more and more for it."

The story was similar throughout much of the nation in 1983. For eight preceding years, energy costs had gone from taking $1 of every $6 of a poor family's income to taking $1 of every $3, according to the Citizen/Labor Energy Coalition. A study by the National Council of Senior Citizens found that a quarter of the nation's elderly households devoted more than 40 percent of their income to heating costs.

Federal Aid Programs

Between 1977 and March 1983, the federal government had given grants to states to provide low-income households with help in meeting the burden of rapidly rising energy costs. Those funds, however, had remained at about the same level since 1980, while both heating bills and the number of people needing assistance had risen rapidly. According to witnesses testifying before four House subcommittees Feb. 24, 1983, funding was woefully inadequate.

The low-income energy assistance program operated by the Department of Health and Human Services (HHS) was funded by Congress at $1.975 billion in fiscal 1983. A separate program run by the Department of Energy included $146 million to help "weatherize" the homes of low-

... As Bills Continue to Climb

income families. Government figures indicated the funds assisted 7 million out of some 20 million eligible households, paying about 20 percent of their heating bills.

The administration wanted to cut energy assistance to $1.3 billion in fiscal 1984 and eliminate the weatherization program. "The energy assistance program was never intended to pay the entire energy bill for all low-income households," said Linda S. McMahon of HHS. "We believe that if we ... appropriately target assistance to the most needy, $1.3 billion ... is adequate."

Father Golombek disagreed. So did Anthony J. Maggiore Jr. of the National Community Action Foundation, which represented the nation's 900 community action agencies. If Congress provided only $200 a year to 75 percent of eligible households, the program would still require $3 billion, Maggiore said. Golombek and Maggiore had found some sympathetic ears in Congress. Most Democratic members, as well as many key Republicans from the Northeast and Midwest, favored higher spending levels for energy assistance. With gas prices rising at a rate of more than 20 percent a year and unemployment above 10 percent, they said the need for funds was clear. Those members had already won a victory in the $4.6 billion emergency jobs bill enacted in March 1983, which contained $100 million for the Energy Department's weatherization programs.

Advocates of increased spending also found some unexpected support in the business community. One business group — the Committee for Economic Development — argued that natural gas decontrol must be accompanied by a massive increase in low-income energy aid.

"Society needs to face up to both issues. . . ." the committee said. "For an increase in direct income assistance on the order of $5 billion to $10 billion per year, the country could both protect low-income consumers and eliminate the pervasive economic distortions that flow from our current system of energy price controls."

Given the strong pressures to reduce the deficit, Congress was unlikely to raise funding. Program supporters also would have to fend off conservative attacks. Reps. Carlos J. Moorhead, R-Calif., and Tom Corcoran, R-Ill., charged that the energy assistance program was subject to waste and abuse. A full third of the funds, they claimed, "probably will never be expended for the primary purpose Congress intended."

1983 to give $90 million to states and cities for food, shelter, clothing and minor outpatient care for the homeless. It also would establish a national advisory council to investigate the problem of homelessness.

● Rep. Bruce F. Vento, D-Minn., and Sen. Christopher J. Dodd, D-Conn., introduced two bills to provide $50 million to assist cities in providing emergency shelters. The money would be distributed as grants to non-profit agencies to help them convert buildings into shelters, bring them up to safe conditions and defray the cost of utilities.

Fewer Mental Patients in Hospitals

The number of patients in U.S. mental hospitals dropped to 150,000 in 1978 — the last year for which complete statistics were available — from a peak of about 650,000 in the mid-1950s. Unofficial statistics put the number of persons in mental institutions in October 1982 at 138,000. Many of the deinstitutionalized patients had been placed in nursing homes or community mental health centers. But there were only about 800 local mental health facilities across the country — not nearly enough to accommodate the need. Many former mental patients were therefore either under-served or unserved by community outpatient facilities. Often they wound up on the streets.

The plight of these former patients was worsened, Hopper said, by cuts in social services. Many who lived on Social Security Disability Insurance had been thrown off the rolls because of new review procedures.

"The lack of services for mentally disabled people in the community, particularly for the chronic mentally ill people who have been institutionalized . . . is a contributing factor" in the increasing number of homeless Americans, said Lee Carty, administrator of the Washington-based Mental Health Law Project. "They simply don't connect up with the services in the community."

A 1976 survey of homeless men conducted by the New York City Human Resources Administration found that more of them suffered from psychiatric problems than from alcoholism; 31 percent of those interviewed were former mental patients.

Spread of Problem to Sun Belt States

The homeless also were showing up in large numbers in places where they never made much impact in the past — in the Sun Belt states. Unemployed workers and their families had flocked to cities in the

Southwest and West in search of work. Many ended up broke and homeless. "Austin [Texas] officials cope daily with transients living in cars, looking through garbage cans, hanging around in office buildings," according to the report issued by the U.S. Conference of Mayors. "In Houston, transients are living in their cars on freeways and in their parks. . . . It is estimated that in Tulsa . . . there may be up to 1,000 people living in cars, trailers and tents, in camping grounds or in the woods. . . . There are now between 200 and 300 people living under bridges in the city."

By 1983 the Sun Belt states finally were beginning to feel the effects of the recession firsthand. In Texas, for example, the unemployment rate was 8.4 percent in September 1982, up from 5.5 percent in November 1981. The 8.4 rate was the highest since the state began keeping such figures in 1970. The Texas Department of Human Resources reported a 22 percent increase in the number of applications for food stamps in summer 1982 compared with the previous summer. State welfare officials did not keep tabs on the impact of out-of-state job-seekers on these totals, but they expressed the belief that newcomers were a signficant factor in the increase in persons seeking welfare.

Even though the number of applications for state welfare and food stamps had risen greatly, the number of persons on Texas welfare rolls had not increased significantly. This was due to the state's strict eligibility standards. The state's Aid for Families with Dependent Children program (AFDC), which was funded solely by the Texas Legislature, allowed payments only to children of low-income families without the support of one or both parents due to parent absence or disability. The average monthly payment for families on AFDC in Texas was only $104. The national average was $277.

The state Department of Human Resources (DHR) in February 1983 issued a pamphlet trying to dissuade job seekers from coming to Texas. Entitled "Dead Broke in Texas," it was sent to welfare agencies in other states. "People are pouring into Texas seeking jobs, but here, as in other states, jobs may not be easy to find," the pamphlet warned. "Too often these people's savings run out before work is found. . . . The Texas Department of Human Resources wants to help. . . . But the fact is that DHR doesn't have the money, staff or authority to give all these people all the help they need." The pamphlet pleaded with local communities to help those the department could not reach. "Desperate people are in need of more aid than DHR can furnish," it concluded.

Feeding the Hungry

Closely entwined with the housing problem was the problem of hunger among the poor and unemployed. As with the homeless, it was difficult to pin down the number of hungry people. But city leaders and food program officials said the number of people seeking food assistance was rising — a result of the economic downturn, unemployment and cuts in federal food and nutrition programs.

"All over the country we see people standing in lines in the cold, waiting for a hot meal at a soup kitchen or a handout from a food depot," Detroit's Mayor Coleman Young said. John B. Mattingly, an executive with the Greater Cleveland Interchurch Council, told a housing subcommittee in December 1982 that the number of people coming to church-run hunger centers that year had increased 100 percent from 1981.

To help develop statistical data on hunger, at least four national food groups and the U.S. Conference of Mayors in 1983 tried to document the extent of food needed through surveys of city officials, food groups, religious and charitable groups and labor unions. As of May 1983 there was little research data on the subject.

Congressional panels, however, had heard dozens of witnesses cite anecdotal evidence. For example, the Mayor's Referral Center in New Orleans had experienced a 222 percent increase in calls requesting food aid between 1981 and 1982, according to Ted L. Wilson, mayor of Salt Lake City and spokesman for the U.S. Conference of Mayors. And the Greater Cleveland Interchurch Council's 16 food distribution centers had served 17,000 people in June 1982, 25,000 in October, 35,000 in November and 48,000 in December, according to Mattingly, the council's associate director.

"The worst part is for the people actually working in those soup kitchens," Nancy Amidei, director of the Food Research and Action Center (FRAC) said. "They're doing David Stockman's dirty work. They're the ones who have to turn away people who are actually in need." Stockman headed Reagan's Office of Management and Budget. While many volunteer groups were operating soup kitchens and food banks, officials said they could not keep up with the demand for food.

"We will increase our charity efforts, but the government also has to stop cutting and replace some of those things they have cut to the bone," said Ronald Krietemeyer, director of domestic social development with the U.S. Catholic Conference. "The number of people homeless, hungry and freezing is far too large for anyone to make the case that the private sector can take over and fill the gap," he said.

Effect on Public Health

News of another consequence of inadeqate food availability came from health professionals associated with institutions used by the poor. For example, a research team at Boston City Hospital, measuring weight and height at a children's clinic, found notable departures from the norm in growth rates of children aged five and under.

"We would normally expect to find 5 percent of all children in the lowest 5th percentile of growth. The research team found 14.4 percent, . . . nearly three times the expected rate," said J. Larry Brown of the Harvard School of Public Health.

Nurse-midwife Christine Schenk in 1983 testified that the Cleveland Metropolitan Hospital, which serves about half of the city's low-income population, had experienced a 25 percent increase in demand for nutritional supplements provided by the Women, Infants and Children Feeding Programs (WIC), the federal program for needy pregnant women and children. Eligibility for the program was based on both low income and evidence of health risk such as low birthweight. (Low-birthweight babies face a higher risk of early death or severe physical disability.)

While there were some technical problems in interpreting birthweight statistics, Schenk declared, "One thing is certain: the total number of low-birthweight babies did not decrease, it did not even stay the same. Given the kind of reports [about number] that we receive from reliable people in the field," she added, "there are many good reasons not to endorse a cutback" in WIC.

In January 1983 the FRAC produced a highly publicized report that showed infant mortality rates rising in seven states and in 34 rural and urban areas between 1980 and 1981. The report, which was criticized for methodological problems, was not intended as "a fancy academic study," Amidei said, but simply as an effort "to cause people in public life to take a second look when they consider budget cuts."

Amidei said evidence collected by researchers revealed a mounting infant mortality rate in hard-hit states, like Michigan; growing numbers of infants ill with water intoxication, a result of being fed diluted formula or excessive sugar water; and stories about elderly people who lived on one meal a day because that was the only time the free-meal programs were open in their cities.

Members of Congress See for Themselves

Personal experience was another source of evidence used by those urging more federal food aid. "I have visited feeding programs and eaten with the hungry and needy," Sen. Mark Andrews, R-N.D., told a March 1983 hearing of his Senate Agriculture investigations subcommittee. "Therefore, I am inclined to believe that hunger and malnutrition do exist, to some extent, in this country."

Rep. Leon E. Panetta, D-Calif., who said he was originally skeptical about hunger reports, admitted that his visits to emergency food centers dispelled any notion that they were exploited by people who could afford to eat elsewhere. "My sense is that these are not people sneaking into line to grab a free meal. All you have to do is look at the faces in the lines. That tells you more than anything else about the desperation that is there."

The poor also testified; welfare recipient Dorothy Williams told Panetta's panel about "garbage pickers" at a Cleveland farmers' market. "People go there and take their whole families and go through that garbage to get something to eat. Now that is ridiculous."

Amidei, who traveled continuously to visit food centers and to speak with health professionals, said the situation outside Washington was critical and that social workers, pediatric nurses, volunteer food center workers and others who had to cope with the burgeoning demand were in despair. "They say, 'Doesn't anybody in Washington care?' " Amidei added that in May 1983 there were 44 million Americans living below or just above the poverty level, all of them at risk of malnutrition. Just half that number received food stamps.

Another critic of the Reagan food policies, Robert Greenstein, said the administration ignored the aggregate impact of benefit and eligibility reductions in welfare, Medicaid, subsidized housing, food stamps and other public assistance programs.

While each change by itself seemed negligible to government analysts, their combined effect on families with limited resources was devastating, he said. Greenstein, director of the Washington-based Center on Budget and Policy Priorities, directed the USDA's Food and Nutrition Service during the Carter administration and in 1983 was a food programs consultant for members of Congress. He and Amidei accused advocates of food aid cuts of willful ignorance about the effects of those cuts.

"What will it take for them to increase spending? Are they waiting for children with swollen bellies [from malnutrition]? Do they want bodies in the streets?" Amidei demanded. Richard E. Lyng, deputy secretary of agriculture, said charges that the administration did not want to know about hunger were "politics, just politics."

Reagan Administration Position

Reagan administration officials dismissed suggestions that their policies were causing people to go hungry and babies to die. "Rhetoric is racing miles ahead of the facts," OMB Director David A. Stockman said in a strongly worded speech to the National Press Club in February 1983.

Stockman lashed out at FRAC's infant mortality report, calling it "absolutely, totally and completely untrue." He insisted the reported increases in infant deaths in certain cities and states were "normal statistical variations" that occurred every year.

Dr. Edward N. Brandt, assistant secretary for health at the Department of Health and Human Services (HHS), also attacked the report. He said the findings were unreliable because they were based on relatively small population samples over a relatively short period of time. Brandt maintained that the number of infant deaths continued to decline.

In defending the administration's food policies, officials stressed the enormous size of the feeding programs and the fact that the programs still were growing as of 1983, although not so rapidly as they would have grown without budgeting changes made between 1981 and 1983. "Since this administration [came in], the cost of federal food assistance programs has grown by 34 percent," said John W. Bode, deputy assistant secretary for food and consumer services at the Agriculture Department.

Officials also pointed to the enormous growth in the programs' cost since 1970, the year Congress launched a series of eligibility and benefit expansions whose effects were magnified by inflation in food prices during the following decade.

In 1971, for instance, spending by the USDA's Food and Nutrition Service, which administered the programs, was $2.9 billion. By 1974 it was $4.7 billion, rising to $8.5 billion in 1977, $13.8 billion in 1980 and $18.6 billion in 1983.

For food stamps alone, program costs soared from $8.3 billion to $12 billion between 1980 and 1983, a 45 percent increase, Bode said. The growth rate would have been 75 percent without the budget changes of 1981 and 1982, he added. The increase, in Bode's view, showed that the program was responding to whatever hardships may have been caused by the recession.

Legislation to Feed the Hungry

Prompted by reports that more and more Americans could not afford to eat properly, Congress moved in 1983 to get surplus rice, corn, wheat and other commodities out of storage bins and into churches, soup kitchens, senior citizen centers and other agencies that fed the hungry and jobless.

One major proposal came from Sen. Robert Dole, R-Kan., chairman of the Agriculture Committee's nutrition panel. Dole's bill, which was passed by the Senate Agriculture Committee March 3, 1983, provided for the agriculture secretary to donate federally owned surplus commodities to domestic agencies such as food banks, schools and churches.

The Agriculture Department already had broad discretion to donate commodities that the Commodity Credit Corporation (CCC) acquired in price support programs to feeding programs. However, as of March 1983, it had given only surplus butter and cheese to states for distribution to the needy.

Dole's bill also provided for assisting states in giving away food and for supplying money to food banks and other non-profit organizations to help with the distribution, transportation and storage of food donations. Dole said the bill was expected to move more than $1 billion worth of commodities at an administrative cost of $52 million.

In many cases, soup kitchens and other organizations that operated on a shoestring had been unable to use the dairy products because they could not pay to transport or store them. The proposed bill required the secretary of agriculture to release CCC stocks that he deemed would not be needed for other programs, such as foreign food aid or the domestic payment-in-kind program. The PIK program paid farmers in surplus crops for not farming their land.

The bill also specified as eligible recipients: public and non-profit organizations that provided emergency food aid to the poor, including unemployed individuals; school lunch, summer camp and other child nutrition programs providing food service; nutrition projects for the elderly; charitable institutions serving the needy, and disaster relief programs.

In the House, David R. Obey, D-Wis., introduced two bills similar to Dole's. Also, Panetta was working on a commodity distribution measure as part of the Democratic leadership emergency package. The three bills covered providing funds for transportation, storage, and converting the surplus commodities into forms usable in institutional and home kitchens.

Nancy Amidei, director of the Food Research and Action Center, said the commodities proposal was a useful short-term solution, but it was not a full answer. "Sending around surplus cheese, surplus dried milk, surplus oats only goes so far. It's no substitute for shoring up nutrition programs," she said.

Amidei said another $2 billion to $2.5 billion was needed in fiscal 1984 to improve the food stamp, mother and child nutrition and elderly feeding programs. She also suggested changing the assets test for food stamps, so newly poor families would be eligible. "People, for example, who bought a good car a few years ago and can't sell it, are knocked out of the food stamp program," she said. "These are people affected by rules written for another time."

Congress also included funds in the Emergency Jobs and Recession Relief Bill, signed into law by President Reagan on March 24, 1983, for emergency food distribution. The bill allocated $100 million to the feeding program and appropriated $75 million for surplus food distribution. A separate title of the bill appropriated $50 million to cover administrative, storage and delivery costs associated with food distribution programs approved by the Senate and House Agriculture committees.

The House, in its fiscal 1984 budget resolution, also approved spending levels $900 million above 1983 levels for food stamps and $500 million above 1983 levels for popular feeding programs for infants, children and pregnant women. These changes would increase spending for these programs $2.3 billion above the president's budget request.

In addition, 54 senators and 189 members of the House as of May 1983 had signed on as cosponsors of anti-hunger resolutions opposing any further cuts in food programs.

Hunger Amidst Plenty

The reports of hunger in America occurred at a time when the farm economy was awash in surplus food, and the government not only was paying farmers to stop growing more but also was giving away the surplus. Not since 1967 had the nation faced a similar paradox of hunger, rumored or real, in the midst of plenty.

That was the year a Field Foundation-supported study depicted widespread undernourishment and sickness among the rural poor in the South. Then, as in 1983, reports of hunger met with official skepticism and resistance to more spending. But within a few years, Congress enacted an array of federal food programs.

By 1977 a follow-up Field Foundation study found "far fewer grossly malnourished people in this country than there were 10 years ago." This change could not be credited to better living conditions or employment rates, the report said, since neither had improved materially for the poor. It was federal food programs, the study said, that made the difference.

Whether conditions necessitated still more food aid or whether existing programs could be cut without unduly harming the needy were issues Congress was debating in 1983. The Reagan administration's major fiscal 1984 budget proposals for food stamps were to standardize shelter and earned income deductions, require states to pick partial costs of erroneously issued stamps and make able-bodied recipients work for their stamps. The budget also proposed to replace summer feeding, child care and school breakfast programs with a nutrition block grant to states, at reduced funding levels. WIC and an associated supplemental food program would be funded at fiscal 1983 levels.

While the administration maintained its proposed savings could be made largely by reducing "misexpenditures" in the programs, Panetta and Rep. James M. Jeffords, R-Vt., April 13, 1983, released a Congressional Budget Office (CBO) report contradicting that claim and supporting their contention that Reagan's proposals would make hunger problems worse.

The report showed that nearly half of the proposed $1 billion in food stamp savings "would come directly from the pockets of low-income people," according to Panetta. Nearly 80 percent of households below the poverty level — most with annual incomes of less than $3,800 for a family of three — would lose an average of $100 a year, he said.

Agriculture Secretary John R. Block immediately rejected the CBO conclusions. But Bode acknowledged under questioning by Panetta and subcommittee members that about one-eighth of the eight million households receiving food stamps would lose some benefits in 1984 under the proposals. He also conceded that in 1985 reductions in benefits to individuals would be nearly four times those projected for 1984.

He insisted, however, that the proposals would largely reduce opportunities for error by simplifying deductions and forcing states to go after errors more aggressively. Panetta worried that some budget cuts could slip through Congress in an omnibus budget reconciliation bill, as in 1981 and 1982, even though members individually might not wish to cut aid to the truly needy.

Extending Health Insurance for the Unemployed

Twelve million Americans were unemployed as of February 1983 and, according to CBO statistics, 10.7 million of those jobless people had lost employer-based group health coverage for themselves and their families as of December 1982.

As Senate Finance Committee Chairman Dole told a health conference Jan. 26, 1983, "Their health-care coverage is going down the drain, for the most part in 30 days [after losing their job]. What do we do with somebody with a family? . . . Is there a federal responsibility?"

In 1983 most American workers with health insurance were covered by employment-based group policies, financed in part or entirely by the employer. It was not unusual for such coverage to continue for a while after a worker left a job, but 60 percent of group-insured workers lost coverage within 30 days after their jobs ended. Only 20 percent were covered for three or more months after they were laid off, according to William R. Johnson, senior vice president of the Blue Cross and Blue Shield Associations. For a small minority, benefits may have lasted as long as a year.

Insurance officials told the House committee that many companies — either voluntarily or to comply with state laws — offered unemployed workers a variety of plans to continue health coverage. "The problem is not with the availability of insurance mechanisms; it's with who will finance the premiums, and for how long," said Richard Mellman, a Prudential Insurance Co. executive, testifying for the Health Insurance Association of America.

Dole had thought some medical benefits for the jobless could be financed by placing a new tax on health benefits in the jobs bill that was signed into law in March 1983. The final bill, however, contained no provision for the tax. Financing health benefits for the jobless could cost billions of dollars, and the concept raised difficult issues of fairness. Nevertheless, the interest of influential members such as Dole and Speaker of the House Thomas P. O'Neill Jr., D-Mass., strengthened the possibility for 1983 congressional action.

Dr. Robert J. Rubin, assistant secretary of health and human services, told reporters at a health budget briefing that, given Dole's powerful position as chairman of the Senate Finance Committee, "we would strongly consider any suggestions he might have."

Dole's bill included provisions for new block grants, which would be optional for states. The bill stated that persons currently receiving unemployment benefits and who were covered by group health insurance plans before they lost their jobs would qualify for benefits. But the bill also allowed states considerable discretion to narrow that group by use of a means test that bases eligibility on an individual's financial resources. The program would end after two years.

Health Problems of Jobless

As a group, the unemployed could ill afford to go without health insurance because they were more likely to need medical care than the working population. Unemployed people were especially prone to stress-related illness, such as heart disease, alcoholism and its associated liver problems, Douglas A. Fraser, president of the United Auto Workers union, told the House Energy and Commerce Committee in January 1983.

The Michigan Mental Health Association had experienced a 25 percent increase in calls for help. And, said Fraser, "in Michigan, where some 400,000 workers lost their health insurance as a result of the recession, the state health director. . . reported the first increases in the state infant mortality rate since World War II."

Citing a 1976 congressional report written by Johns Hopkins University Professor Harvey Brenner, Fraser also said that "each 1 percent increase in [the] unemployment [rate] corresponds to a 4.1 percent increase in suicides, a 5.7 percent increase in homicide, and a 1.9 percent increase in deaths from heart disease, cirrhosis of the liver and other stress-related disorders."

Brenner's 1976 work was based on statistics from 1940 to 1974. In February 1983 he was updating the study for Congress' Joint Economic Committee. He said in an interview that he had found the percentages of disease increase were higher and the impact of joblessness on the health of individuals lasted longer than he had reported before. Brenner maintained that an increase in stress-related illness continued for 15 years after a period of high unemployment, rather than for five years, as his earlier study suggested.

Brenner also associated the recession with increases in other diseases not related to stress. Because nutrition, housing and access to medical care were being adversely affected by economic conditions, Brenner said, he expected more cases of infectious diseases such as influenza, tuberculosis and pneumonia. These diseases were associated with crowding, poor sanitation and poor nutrition.

And because impoverished people tended to put off medical care until symptoms became serious, Brenner also expected to see more debilitating illness and death from diseases that responded to early treatment, including cancer and heart disease, especially heart disease related to hypertension.

Brenner found the alleged increase in infant mortality, reported in Michigan and elsewhere, "most extraordinary. It is very rare to see infant mortality increasing. What happens in most recessions is that the rate of decline just slows down."

Problems for Congress

In 1975, when unemployment stood at 8.5 percent, the House Ways and Means and Senate Labor and Human Resources committees approved bills providing extended health insurance coverage for jobless workers. But the legislation went no further, because of disputes over committee jurisdiction, over whether the Treasury or employers should pay benefits, and whether benefits should be provided through private insurers or a federal program. These disputes reflected underlying concerns about setting precedents for national health insurance.

National health insurance was not an issue in 1983, but the precedents and costs of insuring the jobless remained the major obstacles to congressional action. CBO Director Alice M. Rivlin estimated that one relatively generous option — extending Medicare coverage to the jobless — would cost about $6 billion in fiscal 1983.

Another option was a bill introduced by Sen. Donald W. Riegle Jr., D-Mich. It would require employers to provide six months of extended health insurance benefits for workers who were "involuntarily severed" from their jobs. Employers not extending benefits would lose the federal tax deduction for their health insurance costs. The bill also provided for additional coverage through state-based health insurance "pools," financed jointly by employers and local, state and federal governments.

Riegle's bill had a price tag of $1.3 billion to $1.4 billion during the first year for a short-term emergency program, and significantly less

Record Foreclosures Prompt Calls for Aid . . .

In February 1983 you could Dial 461-1800 in McKeesport, Pa., and a hotline volunteer would answer with tips on how to save your home from foreclosure. The advice line was a project of the Mon Valley Unemployed Committee, a self-help group formed by out-of-work steel workers. Volunteers offered information about unemployment benefits, medical care, food stamps and energy assistance — but it was the fear of foreclosure that prompted many calls.

In the Mon Valley near Pittsburgh and in other hard-pressed areas around the country, mortgage defaults in 1983 were becoming a fact of life for the jobless. Some groups like the Mon Valley committee were banding together to protest sheriff's foreclosure sales. Their agitation led a local Pennsylvania judge to order a temporary ban on foreclosure sales of homes whose owners had lost their jobs. But unemployed homeowners said local efforts were not enough, and they were turning to Congress for relief.

Record Defaults

"In 1982, mortgage defaults soared to the highest levels on record," said Sen. Donald W. Riegle Jr., D-Mich., one of several lawmakers who had introduced legislation to help unemployed homeowners. "We are in the midst of a national mortgage default emergency."

A quarterly survey conducted by the Mortgage Bankers Association (MBA) showed that more than six-tenths of 1 percent of all home loans, or about 172,000 mortgages, were in foreclosure proceedings at the end of September 1982. This was the highest level since the MBA began keeping figures in 1953, said Warren J. Dunn, an MBA spokesman.

Not all foreclosure proceedings ended up with a lender taking possession of a house. Dunn estimated that roughly half of the owners involved in foreclosure cases actually were forced to lose their homes.

Legislative Remedies

The foreclosure problem first became an issue in the House and Senate Banking committees in 1982. In its housing authorization bill, which never reached the floor, the House Banking Committee included $760 million to assist homeowners facing foreclosure because of an unanticipated loss of income.

...Congress Responds with Proposals

But another $760 million Democratic plan to help unemployed homeowners make their mortgage payments was narrowly approved by the House May 11, 1983, over the objections of the Reagan administration and GOP lawmakers.

The 216-196 vote to pass the anti-foreclosure bill came after Democrats tightened the eligibility requirements for the temporary loan program to make it more palatable to doubtful members. The administration, House Republicans and conservative Democrats argued that the bill was too expensive and would create an "administrative nightmare" for the Department of Housing and Urban Development (HUD). Instead, they pushed an alternative that would ease federal banking rules so lenders could be more lenient with delinquent borrowers.

A key part of the Democrats' recession relief package, the bill was designed to help about 100,000 of the estimated 200,000 Americans who were more than 90 days late in their mortgage payments and risked losing their homes. Under the first-come, first-served plan, the federal government would cover mortgage costs for out-of-work homeowners for up to three years. Borrowers must contribute 38 percent of their income toward their housing expenses during this period, and they must repay the federal loans. The program would be triggered by high default rates.

"We are not talking about a give-away program or an entitlement program," said sponsor Henry B. Gonzalez, D-Texas. Gonzalez urged members to "respond to Americans in a desperate effort to keep possession of the only thing that identifies them with the country, which is their home."

The bill also encouraged the Agriculture Department to grant a moratorium on payment of home loans insured by the Farmers Home Administration (FmHA) if the owner faced foreclosure.

The bill's fate in the Senate was not promising, where the only chance for mortgage assistance in spring 1983 was contained in an omnibus HUD authorization bill approved in April by the Senate Banking Committee. The Senate panel's plan would provide federal guarantees on private loans to help jobless homeowners pay their mortgages. Up to $750 million in guarantees would be allowed, but the program would have no net cost to the government unless owners defaulted.

thereafter, according to a Riegle aide.

Business representatives did not welcome the additional costs of extending the health coverage of the unemployed. But Riegle's staff said businesses already paid indirectly for much of the hospital care used by uninsured people who could not pay their medical bills. Hospitals added the cost for such uncompensated care onto bills for insured patients, and those charges raised the price of insurance premiums paid by employers.

If the more pessimistic predictions about unemployment were borne out, expenditures for any extended health insurance benefits could continue for as long as five years.

Equity Issues

To act on the problem, Congress had to resolve difficult questions of equity — or live with a partial or unfair solution. If Congress decided to help pay for existing benefit plans, the federal government likely would end up financing very generous coverage of all medical expenses for some families, and far fewer benefits for others.

Another consideration was whether to help only recently laid-off workers, or to include the unknown number of discouraged workers — people who had been jobless for so long that they had given up looking for work and no longer were counted in official unemployment statistics.

The difficulty of these issues and the atmosphere of austerity made helping the uninsured unemployed exceptionally difficult, Henry A. Waxman, D-Calif., chairman of the Energy and Commerce Subcommittee on Health, acknowledged. But, he added, "It's a very serious problem, and we've got to figure out what we can do, if anything." In the meantime, the committee published a list of hospitals required by federal statute to provide charity care.

Waxman also had sponsored a health insurance bill. Waxman's bill would set a single national eligibility standard, specifying that individuals receiving state unemployment insurance or who had exhausted unemployment benefits within two years before the program began could qualify for a specified package of benefits.

Stockman Testimony

Budget Director Stockman gave grudging support to providing federal aid to the uninsured at a April 27, 1983, Senate Finance Committee hearing, but he opposed creating a new program to deliver that aid. He recommended that states use funds from an existing federal program, the social services block grant, to help out in hardship cases.

Stockman also said that if Congress were to approve new taxes to pay for additional aid to the unemployed, the administration would not stand in the way. He recommended changing federal tax law to ease the enrollment of jobless individuals and dependents in a working spouse's health plan and to promote the availability of relatively low-cost insurance plans for the unemployed to purchase.

"We cannot accept, in any way, a new entitlement, especially a non-means tested entitlement for broad segments of the middle class," Stockman told the committee. An entitlement program is one that guarantees benefits to individuals who meet certain criteria.

Legislative Proposals

President Reagan signed a measure March 29, 1983, providing for the stopgap extension of emergency unemployment benefits, set to expire March 31. The bill was approved by the House March 24 and by the Senate March 25 to ensure that the benefits would not run dry before the president signed a Social Security measure that contained a six-month extension of the federal supplemental compensation program. Reagan signed the Social Security extension plan on April 21, 1983, thus ensuring the program's extension.

Background

Only workers covered by unemployment insurance, a state-federal program created in 1935 as part of the original Social Security Act, have been eligible for compensation under the program. The Reagan administration estimated that 10.9 million people received a total of $21.1 billion in such benefits in 1982, at an average rate of $115 a week per person.

The first 26 weeks of unemployment benefits are paid entirely by the states, from funds fed by a tax on employers. The tax rate, and hence the amount of aid available per eligible worker, varied from state to state. Benefits generally were highest in the unionized states of the Northeast and Middle West, and lowest in the South and Southwest, where organized labor was weak.

In states where unemployment was particularly high, jobless workers who had exhausted their regular benefits sometimes were eligible for up to 13 weeks of "extended" benefits under a program established in 1970. The cost of these was borne equally by the state and federal governments.

Additional Benefits

Under a provision of the Omnibus Budget Reconciliation Act of 1981, a state was required to provide extended jobless benefits only when its "insured unemployment rate" rose above 5 percent. This rate showed the number of unemployment claims as a percentage of all employees covered by the insurance program, and thus tended to be lower than the overall jobless rate.

The program allowed an additional 10 weeks of payments in the 36 states (plus Puerto Rico and the Virgin Islands) that were then offering extended benefits, or paid them any time after June 1, 1982. This meant a maximum 49 weeks of benefits in states that were still providing extended benefits and up to 36 weeks of payments in those states that had gone, or would go, off the extended benefit program after June 1.

In August 1982 Congress voted to provide from six to 10 weeks of additional unemployment benefits, at a cost of $1.9 billion, to persons whose eligibility for state aid had run out. The program expired March 31, 1983, so its impact was short-lived. It nevertheless was welcomed by state governments, since it was fully funded by federal tax revenues.

To keep their unemployment-benefit programs from collapsing, a number of states tightened eligibility rules, lowered benefits or increased employer taxes. Illinois, for example, in 1982 required a one-week wait before jobless workers could collect benefits, and it excluded entirely those who quit or were fired.

Provisions in the Social Security extension plan signed in April 1983 extended the emergency jobless benefit program for six months. It would allow those who had exhausted up to 39 weeks of regular and extended unemployment benefits to qualify for a maximum of from eight to 14 additional weeks of payments, depending on their state's unemployment rate.

Individuals who exhausted emergency benefits under the existing program on or before April 1, 1983, would be eligible for up to 6 to 10 additional weeks of slightly lower payments. Those already receiving the emergency benefits, but who would not exhaust them until after April 1, also would be eligible for extra payments. In addition, those who had not exhausted their benefits on Sept. 30, 1983, when the program expired, were to receive up to 50 percent of their remaining benefits.

The bill also allowed states to deduct money from an individual's jobless benefits to pay for health insurance, if the individual elected such coverage.

The stepped-up need to meet U.S. energy demands attracted workers to the the Gulf States, where oil rigs dotted the Louisiana-Texas coastline.

Chapter 6

ECONOMIC PROFILES OF AMERICA'S REGIONS

The different regions of the United States did not fare equally during the economic turbulence of the 1970s and early 1980s. For the "Sun Belt" states of the South and Southwest, those times brought unprecedented economic growth. But for other regions, most notably the Great Lakes states, Middle Atlantic states and parts of the Pacific Northwest, unemployment caused by the failing automobile, steel and timber industries painted a grim picture.

Other regions, struggling through major changes in the industrial capacities of their states, managed to maintain a relatively resilient economy. New England, for example, brought its sagging economy back to life by replacing its once-strong textile industries with more recession-proof high technology and electronics companies. And unemployment caused by the slowed-down timber business in the Pacific Northwest was offset in part by a rejuvenated aeronautics industry.

The South and West not only prospered economically but grew in population as people moved southward. The national census, which provides population and employment trend statistics every 10 years, in 1980 showed that for the first time in U.S. history there were more people living in the South and West than in the North and East. Between 1968 and 1978 two out of three new jobs gained by the country were created in the Sun Belt or Western states. The Rocky Mountain states experienced the nation's largest population growth. Throughout the South and West, population increased rapidly and the development of energy reserves, thriving tourism, booming light manufacturing and rising agricultural output attracted newcomers into the early 1980s.

In 1980 California continued to lead the nation in personal income even though high-technology competition from Japan and a decline in agricultural exports were beginning to plague the state's economy. The

Plains states in 1980 continued to provide as much as one-half of America's corn and wheat production and close to one-third of the soybean production. But market prices for wheat, corn and other important grains had shrunk by one-third between 1981 and 1983. Farm income nationwide had nose-dived along with prices.

The region hardest hit by financial troubles was the Great Lakes states, where sharp declines in the automobile and steel industries sent unemployment soaring and revenues tumbling. The region's annual unemployment rate for 1982 was 12.0 percent, the highest rate of any census region and 3.7 percent higher than the national average of 8.3 percent, according to the U.S. Bureau of Labor Statistics. In 1981, 753,000 workers were employed by the automobile industry. By 1982 the annual average had slipped to 683,000. Michigan had the second highest unemployment rate in the country (17 percent) as of January 1983. By the end of 1981 Ohio, facing a rising deficit in its state budget, had enacted taxes on sales, tobacco, alcohol and utilities and laid off thousands of state employees in an effort to bolster depleted state revenues. Minnesota, in equally dire financial shape, was expected to face a $768 million budget deficit by June 1983. For the Middle Atlantic states, where industries were based on the manufacture of durable goods, the decade also brought high unemployment, low growth in population, employment and income, as well as low rates of capital investment.

As migration to the South and West continued in 1983, the political and economic makeup of the country was in a state of flux. But where regions continued to focus on one industry, rather than diversifying their economic interests, they remained vulnerable to recessions and high unemployment — regardless of their geographical location. As the U.S. economy became more dependent on international trade, competition forced regionally concentrated industries — such as automobile and steel — to look beyond U.S. borders to new markets. Each region's economic success depended on its adapting to worldwide competition and to ongoing technological changes.

Economic Gains in the Sun Belt

States generally included in the Sun Belt classification were California, Arizona, New Mexico, Texas, Oklahoma, Louisiana, Georgia, Mississippi, Alabama, South Carolina, North Carolina, Tennessee, Virginia, Arkansas and Florida. Population in this area increased by 22 percent from 1970 to 1980, nearly triple the rate in the rest of the country,

Annual Unemployment Rate 1982

(By Census Region)

New England	7.2	East South Central	11.6
Middle Atlantic	8.7	West South Central	7.4
East North Central	12.0	Mountain	8.8
West North Central	8.0	Pacific	9.9
South Atlantic	8.1		

New England: Maine, N.H., Vt., Mass., R.I., Conn.; **Middle Atlantic:** N.Y., N.J., Pa.; **East North Central:** Ohio, Ind., Ill., Mich., Wis.; **West North Central:** Iowa, Miss., Neb., Kan., Minn., N.D., S.D.; **South Atlantic:** Del., Md., D.C., Va., W.Va., N.C., S.C., Ga., Fla.; **East South Central:** Ky., Tenn., Ala., Miss.; **West South Central:** Ark., La., Okla., Texas; **Mountain:** Mont.; Wyo.; Colo., Utah, Idaho, Ariz., Nev., N.M.; **Pacific:** Calif., Hawaii, Wash., Ore., Alaska.

Source: U.S. Department of Labor, Bureau of Labor Statistics

according to the Census Bureau. The migration was due to the growth of new companies in the region — a growth encouraged by low wages, low taxes and, in some cases, special business tax incentives.

Per capita income increased most in the Southwest — 167 percent during the 1970s — compared with a 129 percent increase in the Middle Atlantic states and 134 percent in New England. According to figures compiled by the Northeast-Midwest Institute and published in John Naisbitt's 1982 book *Megatrends,* investment in capital equipment increased 74 percent in the South and the West, compared with 23 percent in the Northeast and Midwest.

The Southwest also was blessed with an abundance of energy resources. Oil and gas drilling, especially in Texas and Oklahoma, continued to increase in 1982. Military installations in Texas, Oklahoma, New Mexico and Arizona helped insulate the region from cuts in federal spending. Factories in the region generally were new and efficient, and steady population growth was driving up the value of commercial and residential real estate — promising a boom in the construction industry as interest rates fell in 1983. The diversity of the economy shielded it from failures in any one industry. For example, according to an article published in the Jan. 19, 1982, *Washington Post,* the shutdown of a General Motors plant in Oklahoma City was offset by a boom in oil and gas exploration to the west of the city where twice as many rigs were working in January 1982 as were a year earlier.

But the Sun Belt was beginning to inherit a full measure of social problems that accompanied its economic upsurge. Crime, congestion, pollution and physical decay — problems that long had haunted Northern industrial cities — were beginning to infest the Sun Belt cities. And despite the economic growth, the Sun Belt as of summer 1982 had yet to catch up with the nation as a whole in per capita wealth. A greater percentage of its people continued to live in poverty than in the nation at large. Experts also pointed out that finite natural resources, particularly water in the Southwest, were threatening to limit the growth of many Sun Belt states.

The most vulnerable of those states, according to the census, were those located in the Southeast. Manufacturing employment, in every Southeastern state except Virginia, accounted for at least 22 percent of the total. In North and South Carolina, the percentage was 28 percent — a higher figure than the percentage in Michigan. In no Sun Belt state outside the Southeast did the percentage go as high as the national average of 20.6 percent. The higher the percentage of manufacturing — the sector of the economy most likely to suffer from a recession — the more likelihood of unemployment in that region.

Sun Belt, Snow Belt Controversy

Success stories in the Snow Belt areas — such as New England — helped dispel the theory that the economic gains of the Sun Belt states were made at the expense of the beleaguered Northern states. According to the theory, industries that deserted the industrial North — especially New York, Pennsylvania and New Jersey — were enticed by the South's favorable economic climate, which included low taxes on businesses, a preponderance of "right to work" laws and the overall weakness of organized labor. In short, the Sun Belt region was thought to be "booming in great part because it's pro-business and the Northern cities, by and large, aren't," wrote Gurney Breckenfeld in the June 1977 issue of *Fortune.*

Business Week magazine in 1976 had characterized the situation as a "civil war between the states," with the economic arena as the battlefield in a "struggle for income, jobs, people and capital." That "war," as perceived by a number of business writers and even sociologists, continued throughout the 1970s. There was an outpouring of articles,

Income Variations from the National Average, 1982

(By percent)

Alaska	+18	Kansas	−1
Hawaii	+12	New Hampshire	−1
California	+5	Oregon	−2
Connecticut	+5	Utah	−2
Nevada	+5	Arizona	−3
Illinois	+3	Iowa	−3
Massachusetts	+3	Nebraska	−3
Michigan	+3	Georgia	−4
New York	+3	Kentucky	−4
New Jersey	+2	North Dakota	−4
Washington	+2	South Dakota	−5
District of Columbia	+1	Vermont	−6
Maryland	+1	Alabama	−7
Minnesota	+1	Idaho	−7
Ohio	+1	Oklahoma	−7
Texas	+1	Arkansas	−8
Wisconsin	+1	Louisiana	−8
Delaware	0	North Carolina	−8
Indiana	0	South Carolina	−8
Missouri	0	Florida	−9
Pennsylvania	0	New Mexico	−9
Rhode Island	0	Montana	−9
Virginia	0	Tennessee	−9
Wyoming	0	West Virginia	−9
Colorado	−1	Maine	−10
		Mississippi	−16

Source: Robert Half International Inc.

studies and reports, and at least two books, *Power Shift* by Kirkpatrick Sale (1975) and *The North Will Rise Again* by Jeremy Rifkin and Randy Barber (1978), chronicling a shift of economic power from North to South. Lobbying groups such as the Northeast-Midwest Congressional Coalition and the Council for Northeast Economic Action were set up to advance the economic interests of the North.

By some accounts, the North's economic slippage had been going on for decades and — except for New England — had worsened after the 1974-75 recession. But not everyone accepted the thesis that the Sun Belt's success had come at the expense of the Northern states. James Lothian, a senior consultant with the Fantus Co., an industrial location consulting firm, called it "a myth" that "all the industries in the North are relocating in the South." Although many Northern plants had expanded their capacity in the South, "there have been very few instances where a plant in the North packs up totally and moves to the South."

A U.S. Department of Commerce study reinforced Lothian's view. The study, issued in 1976, found that during a previous three-year period only 1.5 percent of job losses in the North were caused by companies moving; more than half the losses occurred because companies went out of business. According to John Naisbitt in *Megatrends*, the shift from an industrial society to an information society had led inevitably to new industries springing up in the Sun Belt. Manufacturing industries in the North were replaced by new high-technology companies that found the South's "frontierlike" climate attractive.

In addition, the increasing worldwide competition among manufacturers of automobiles and steel encouraged investors to move toward high-technology industries. Outdated factories and businesses, located mostly in the Northeast and Great Lakes states, were abandoned and new companies opened elsewhere. The migration, Naisbitt agreed, was not merely a relocation of manufacturing industries from the North to the South, but a change in the types of industries expected to prevail in the future.

Energy: Regional Weapon of the Future

Politicians from energy-poor states complained that a massive transfer of wealth from their states to energy-producing states would occur later in the 1980s. Rather than a North-South migration of population and capital, future shifts would be from East to West, based upon the availability of energy resources.

In 1982 Eastern states already were complaining about the large revenues generated for Western states by severance taxes levied on exports of oil, gas, coal and other minerals. (Severance taxes are taxes on depletable minerals that are "severed" from the ground.) The energy-rich Western states expected to earn more than $200 billion from severance taxes during the 1980s. In 1980, for example, the 33 states with severance taxes collected $4.2 billion, which amounted to 3 percent of all state tax revenues. In 1981 state revenue from severance taxes grew by 52 percent, to $6.4 billion — 4.3 percent of all tax revenue they collected. Although 33 states had taxes, the bonanza from higher energy prices went to the dozen or so states whose severance taxes were based on energy. *(Severance tax, box, p. 164)*

Eastern states complained that the energy-producing states' increased wealth enabled them to attract industry by favorable tax policies, while their states were losing industries and tax revenues needed to support government services. The Western states maintained the taxes were adequate compensation for the economic and environmental costs of producing the energy.

One visible regional battle erupted over congressional attempts to limit the severance taxes that Montana and Wyoming levied on coal production. Montana levied a 30 percent tax, and Wyoming a 17 percent tax. In July 1981 the Supreme Court upheld the Montana tax, rejecting a suit brought by the coal utilities and supported by the Northeast-Midwest Coalition. However, the court said Congress could set limits on such taxes if it chose, but Congress had passed no legislation as of April 1983.

Regions of the Country

The eight sections that follow examine the American economic mosaic by focusing on the separate regions or, in the case of California, separate pieces of regions, that over the years assumed an importance or uniqueness of their own. Aside from New England, no agreement has existed even among experts as to precisely what constituted each region in the 48 contiguous states. Map makers looked to political affiliations, religious preferences and ethnic origins of the people in an attempt to determine the distinguishing characteristics of the various geographic regions.

Faced with this lack of accord, Congressional Quarterly divided the country as follows: New England, the South, the Rocky Mountain states,

Handful of States Get Most of Revenues

Although 33 states imposed severance taxes on depletable resources in 1981, five energy-rich states collected the bulk — 80 percent — of the $6.4 billion in state severance tax revenues.

Eight energy-producing states got at least one-fifth of all their tax money from severance taxes in 1981. In 1975 only one state got that much of its revenue from severance taxes. The top five states in order of money raised were Texas, Alaska, Louisiana, Oklahoma and New Mexico. Together they took in $5.1 billion in 1981 severance taxes, according to the U.S. Census Bureau. At the bottom end of the scale, Nevada collected just $11,000 on its mining operations.

It is that 30 percent rate that brought the coal-consuming states' wrath down on Montana, as well as Wyoming, which had a coal severance tax rate of about 17 percent, including local taxes. Actually, Wyoming ranked eighth in 1981 in severance tax revenues, collecting $138 million on coal, oil and gas. Montana was 10th, garnering $99 million, mostly on coal.

Texas had much lower severance tax rates but collected far more money than Wyoming, Montana or any other state. It took in $1.1 billion in 1981, almost all of it from a 4.6 percent tax on oil and a 7.5 percent tax on natural gas.

Alaska, flush with oil produced on its North Slope, had the highest tax on oil — 15 percent, although the rate varied with the age of a particular well. The $1.2 billion Alaska got from severance taxes in 1981 came on top of several billion dollars the state received in oil royalty payments. Almost all of Alaska's oil production was on state-owned land.

Only two Eastern states were in the top 10 states in severance tax revenue in 1981. Kentucky ranked sixth, getting $194 million, mostly on coal. Florida was seventh, getting $169 million from its taxes on oil, natural gas and phosphate production.

In addition to energy sources, some states had severance taxes on minerals such as potash, iron ore and uranium. Some, such as Oregon, taxed timber, and — partly in retaliation for the taxes they said their citizens had to pay to energy-producing states — several midwestern states were considering imposing severance taxes on their agricultural products.

the Great Lakes states, the Middle Atlantic states, the Pacific Northwest, California and the Plains states. Many of this chapter's statistics were derived from the 1980 census, yet the regional divisions did not always conform to the standard U.S. Census Bureau divisions. For example, the Census Bureau separated the South into three groupings: the South Atlantic, East South and West South. Where Census Bureau regional data used is for states that differ from regions used in this book, that has been so indicated.

While general trends from North to South, manufacturing to high technology and energy-depleted states to energy-rich states dominated the overall employment picture in the United States, each region continued to maintain its own distinct economic picture. The following portraits are merely thumbnail sketches, with an emphasis on each region's economic picture as a whole.

New England
*(Maine, New Hampshire, Vermont,
Massachusetts, Connecticut, Rhode Island)*

The end of World War I marked the end of a boom for New England's manufacturing and mercantile industries and the beginning of a long period of economic decline. Textile and shoe manufacturers increasingly relocated in the South, and by 1929 over half the textile spindles in the nation were in the South. Employment in the textile and shoe industries dropped from well over 500,000 in the early years of this century to less than 150,000 by the early 1970s.

World War II, like World War I, gave New England's economy a badly needed boost. From the days of the American Revolution, New England had been a major supplier of precision equipment in time of war. Samuel Colt, together with Eli Whitney, did pioneering work in developing mass production techniques at a gun factory they began in Hartford. The Winchester Arms rifle company was started in New Haven during the Revolution. And the Springfield Armory, later turned into a museum, first produced guns for the U.S. military services in 1795. Shipbuilding, above all the submarine construction and repair facilities at Groton, Conn., and Kittery, Maine-Portsmouth, N.H., became a mainstay of the region's economy.

New England's universities also did highly important research and development work for the military, notably on radar. From the end of the war to the present the region's industries built a wide variety of military

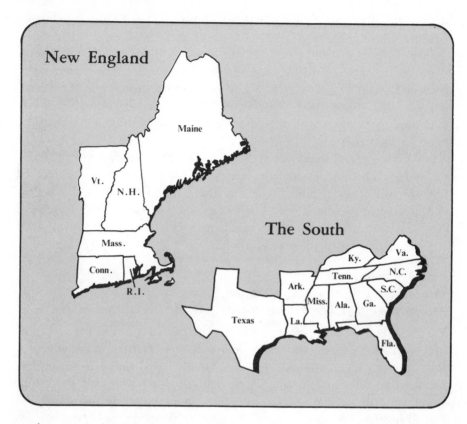

equipment — jet engines, electronic components, and missile and space systems.

In the 1970s, however, U.S. defense budget reductions hurt New England more than any other part of the country. The loss of research and procurement work, together with the closing of many military bases, posed a threat to the regional economy. When energy prices began to rise sharply in late 1973, the long-term outlook for the economy seemed bleak indeed. Exceptionally dependent on energy, and more reliant on fuel oil than any other region of the country, New England seemed to many a place whose day had passed. Both the 1969-70 and 1973-75 recessions hit exceptionally hard. In May 1975, for example, New England's unemployment rate was 11.6 percent, compared with 9.2 percent nationwide; in Rhode Island it stood at 16.2 percent.

Signs of Recovery Since the Middle 1970s. Much to the surprise of the doomsayers, however, New England's economy showed signs of making quite a comeback. After 1975 manufacturing employment in the region kept abreast of the nation as a whole, and signs of vitality appeared in many areas. High-technology industries, many of which had located in abandoned mills around Boston, along the Merrimack into southern New Hampshire, and in Connecticut, continued to prosper. New England also prospered from rapid expansion in business services, health services, finance, insurance and wholesale and retail trade. According to the Bureau of Labor Statistics, the annual unemployment rate for 1981 was 7.2 percent, the lowest of any census region in the country. By September 1982, according to an article in the Nov. 30, 1982, *Washington Post*, Boston's unemployment rate was 6.4 percent — lower than Phoenix's (8.4 percent), Los Angeles' (9.4 percent) and Houston's (8.2 percent).

The fishing industry also revived in the late 1970s after years of suffering from foreign competition in New England's offshore waters. Congress in 1976 declared that national economic interests extended for 200 miles out to sea, giving U.S. fishermen priority in this economic zone. After that, many of New England's coastal towns refurbished their waterfronts, not just as tourist attractions but as commercial centers.

According to Lynn E. Browne, economist for the Federal Reserve Bank of Boston, New Hampshire led the way among the New England states in staying in the same league as the fast-growth Sun Belt states. New Hampshire — with low taxes, low wages and pro-business governmental zest for luring out-of-state businesses — was New England's most evident economic success story. The state gained 381 new firms between 1975 and 1980, most of them involved in making machinery of one type or another. But even in New Hampshire, the rural areas, especially those north of the state's capital of Concord, had not shared fully in the new prosperity.

Rural areas and small towns still were beset by economic stagnation, but the problem also extended to urban workers who lacked job skills that could be used in the new computer and telecommunications fields. High-technology companies were growing and expanding beyond the Boston area, but they nevertheless had not reached the stage where they employed thousands on a mass-production basis.

Job Creation Through Technology and Taxes. New England had prospered once before on technology-based industry. Textiles and shoes, in their New England beginnings, were considered high-technology industries. But the memory of what happened before did not take the edge off of the region's modest economic gains in the late 1970s. New England bankers, who had been downcast, became upbeat. This optimism translated into loans for new business ventures and tended to have a snowball effect. While the region shared the entire country's concerns over economic instability, experts at the Boston Federal Reserve Bank in 1980 pointed out that New England was likely to suffer less than the rest of the country from drops in automobile manufacturing and housing construction.

The High Technology Council, representing 89 fast-growing computer and electronics companies in Massachusetts, complained in the late 1970s that the state's reputation for high taxes ("Taxachusetts") repelled many out-of-state engineers and managers they sought to attract. The council in 1980 entered into a so-called "social contract" with Gov. Edward J. King, promising to create 150,000 new jobs in the state by 1982 if he brought down state taxes to the average for 17 other industrial states. In a move attributed to lobbying by the Associated Industries of Massachusetts, the state Legislature in 1979 cut the state's capital gains tax by 60 percent. And King limited local government spending to a 4 percent yearly increase, bringing about property tax reductions in more than half of the 351 cities and towns.

Most economists agreed that New England would continue to benefit from the same assets that had always enabled it to stay afloat: its early adjustment to problems such as high energy costs, problems that the rest of the country had not fully confronted; its university-based research establishment; its sizable skilled labor force; its experience in precision manufacturing; its possession of numerous cultural assets (including attractive scenery and historic sites) that made New England a pleasant place to live and work; the ready accessibility of capital, both in the Boston banking business and the Connecticut insurance industry; and, not least, its disproportionate political influence at the national level.

The South
(Virginia, North Carolina,
South Carolina, Kentucky, Tennessee, Georgia,
Florida, Alabama, Mississippi, Arkansas, Louisiana, Texas)

In 1938 President Franklin D. Roosevelt took a long, appraising look at the South and declared the region "the nation's No. 1 economic problem." Although various New Deal agencies had pumped large amounts of money into the area during the 1930s, the South, and especially the Deep South, remained mired in poverty. The region's average annual income was only about half that of the country as a whole. The rest of the United States also was suffering from the effects of the Depression, but the South was so much worse off, Roosevelt said, that its poverty produced an "economic unbalance in the nation as a whole."

The South's economic problems antedated the national economic crisis of the 1930s. They originated with the destruction of the Southern economy by the Civil War. A report by the President's National Emergency Council in 1938 attributed the perpetuation of the section's poverty to a high degree of absentee ownership of its resources, high interest rates, disadvantageous freight rates and a protective tariff policy, which, by holding down imports, made it harder to sell abroad agricultural commodities the South had for export. Noting, however, that the region was rich in population and natural resources, the council called it "the nation's greatest untapped market and the market in which American business can expand most easily."

By the early 1980s, the South had come a long way toward fulfilling its economic potential. *Business Week* magazine in 1972 compared the South to a developing country that had reached the "take off" stage of its economic development. From 1972 to 1977, according to John Naisbitt in *Megatrends,* capital investments in manufacturing increased nearly 300 percent in Texas alone. The state replaced Michigan in 1977 as No. 1 in new capital investments in manufacturing. *Business Week* in September 1972 acknowledged some unaddressed and unsolved problems in the region — pollution and congestion and urban sprawl — but on the whole it sketched a glowing profile."The South today means economic growth . . . a still pleasing environment and rich new markets for all sorts of goods and services." The influx of people and industries into the region, it said, was producing social as well as economic benefits.

Businesses Relocate to the South. Southern industrial growth remained strong throughout the 1970s. Non-agricultural employment grew by 27.4 percent in the period 1970-77, compared with a 15.8 percent increase nationwide. As in the rest of the nation, the biggest job gains were in state and local governments and in service industries such as banking, real estate and retail trade. The Southern states were better able than their Northern neighbors to absorb workers leaving the agricultural sector, to provide jobs for the large number of young people entering the work

Texas the Superstate

For many people Texas always would be the quintessential American state — perhaps because the state was too big, too diverse, "too much of a world of its own," as John Gunther wrote in *Inside U.S.A.* in 1947, to be categorized along with any other state.

Texas lies in the center of the "Sun Belt," the southern rim of states running from Virginia to southern California. Like the other Sun Belt states, Texas has experienced an unprecedented influx of people and industry in recent years. Between 1960 and 1980 the state's population grew by approximately 36 percent, to more than 13 million.

Houston, the ultimate boom town, was the fifth largest city in the nation in 1980, with a population in excess of 1.5 million. Of the 500 largest corporations in the United States, as listed by *Fortune* magazine, 18 had headquarters in Houston or Dallas in 1980. Oil and associated service industries contributed greatly to urban growth in the state. Equally important, however, were high-technology industries such as electronics, semiconductors and aerospace.

Even with its large cities and thriving industries, in 1980 Texas still somehow seemed a rural state, with many small farming towns with names like Muleshoe, Kerrville, Sweetwater, Ozona and Levelland.

Texas remained by far the biggest livestock-producing state in the nation. But the character of the beef industry had changed, especially in the Panhandle region.

Since the early 1960s, traditional cow-calf ranches had given way to stocker operations that import yearling calves from other regions — East Texas, Louisiana, Alabama, Florida, Georgia — where more rain falls and grasses grow lusher. Stocker ranches keep the calves through the winter, fattening them by 200 pounds or so, then selling them to feedlots clustered around Amarillo. There they are prepared for market on grain sorghums grown on the High Plains.

The residents of Texas did not share equally in the state's new wealth. About one-sixth of the population lived below the poverty line in 1980. Poverty was especially prevalent among the state's Mexican-Americans, who accounted for at least 18 percent of the population.

force and to accommodate workers migrating from other regions. The South's annual average unemployment rate remained below the U.S. average throughout the 1970s, although the gap gradually narrowed during the latter part of the decade.

According to a report published in 1976 by *U.S. News & World Report*, between 1970 and 1976 corporate or regional headquarters of 55 domestic and foreign companies moved to Georgia, most of them to Atlanta. About 450 companies shifted headquarters or major divisions to Tennessee during the same period, while 180 corporation headquarters, subsidiaries or major divisions relocated in the Houston area.

The South's prosperity in the 1970s was in sharp contrast to the economic decline that plagued many states in the industrial Snow Belt. Accusations surfaced in the mid-1970s that of the billions in public funds that were transferred annually from the federal to state and local governments, a disproportionate amount was going to the Sun Belt states. Others charged that the Southern states were unfairly offering a wide variety of incentives to attract industries from other sections.

Although income growth in the South outpaced the national average in the 1970s, it still remained below national levels. According to the South Growth Policies Board, regional per capita income for the South in 1977 was 89.6 percent of the national average. One reason was that the South remained the least unionized region in the United States. About 29 percent of the nation's workers were members of unions or employee associations, according to the Department of Labor. But in the 12 Southern states the percentages were much lower. They ranged from a high of 29 percent in Kentucky to just 10 percent in North and South Carolina. Between 1963 and 1974 union membership declined in all the Southern states except Georgia, Alabama and South Carolina.

The notion that the Sun Belt prospered mainly by stealing from its neighbors was disputed by a study released in November 1976 by the Commerce Department's Economic Development Administration. During a three-year period of study (1969 to 1972), the report said, only 1.5 percent of the job losses in the North were caused by companies moving, while more than half the losses occurred because companies went out of business. During that same period more than 2.6 million new jobs appeared in the 13 Southern states (The Confederacy, plus Kentucky and West Virginia). Of that number, 35 percent were created by the founding of new companies, 64 percent by the expansion of existing companies and a mere 1 percent by in-migration.

Yet the migration of people and industries to the South appeared to be slowing, according to an economic survey published in *The New York Times* Jan. 6, 1980. "Many states of the Northeast are providing tax benefits and other incentives for companies and their jobs to stay put, and, to a great extent, these incentives have been effective," said Wendell Rawls Jr., author of the survey. As a result, Southern governors had begun courting foreign investors and had been having "considerable success." In Atlanta alone there were nine full-time foreign consulates, four foreign trade and government offices, and honorary consulates representing 23 countries in 1980. Miami, Fla., was a magnet for Latin American trade and investment. About half a million Latin Americans visited Miami in 1978 and spent an average of more than $1,000 each. The city's economy also had been bolstered by the thousands of Cubans who had settled there since Fidel Castro came to power in 1959.

Northern states in the early 1980s had stepped up their efforts to match the South's industrial drawing power. The cost of living in the South was growing in 1983, and wages were expected to follow suit. Freight rates, a primary factor in the location of new plants, were catching up to rates in other parts of the country. Decreased federal funding, spurred by the Reagan administration's "new federalism," drained state and local coffers of needed funds for social welfare programs subsidized by the federal government since the New Deal.

In 1982 many employers in the South were shrinking the size of their industries. According to an article published in *The New York Times* on July 6, 1982, five out of nine Southern states had unemployment rates higher than the national average of 9.5 percent in May of that year and three had unemployment of 10 percent or more. In July 1982 jobs in the textile industry — the top employer in both North and South Carolina — had fallen 11 percent since the summer of 1981.

But unionization remained low in 1983 and relatively low taxes — with special business tax incentives — continued to cushion the region from insurmountable recession. In February 1983 *The New York Times* reported that major cities in the South still appeared to be doing significantly better than large cities in the North in income, employment and racial patterns.

Lingering Poverty in Rural, Black Areas. Amidst the towering office buildings, shiny new factories and other signs of the South's economic boom, many pockets of poverty remained, especially in the black rural sections of the Deep South and the isolated hollows of Appalachia. In

1975 almost 10 million people in 14 Southern states (Oklahoma and West Virginia in addition to Kentucky and The Confederacy) — nearly 16 percent of their total — lived below the officially defined poverty line, according to the Census Bureau. In 1975 the federally defined poverty threshold was $5,500 for a non-farm family of four and $4,695 for a farm family of four. According to the National Commission for Employment and Unemployment Statistics, 60 percent of the nation's rural poor lived in the South in 1977. Another study, published by the Institute for Policy Analysis in 1978, found that 22 percent of the counties in the South had 25 percent or more of their families living below the poverty line. Of the 295 counties, 284 were in rural areas in 1978.

The incidence of poverty among Southern blacks in 1980 was three times as high as that among Southern whites — although in absolute numbers there were more poor whites than poor blacks. In 1978 the median income for black families was just over half (57 percent) as much as for white median families, according to the National Urban League. Some of the South's poorest blacks were found in the unpainted shacks that dotted the Mississippi Delta — the crescent-shaped area of fertile land stretching along the Mississippi River southward from Memphis.

In 1980 about 60 percent of the Delta's population was black and, according to Mississippi's State Department of Public Welfare, 43.5 percent of the area's inhabitants were on some form of welfare. "When the plantation aristocracy decided to mechanize their farms, it wreaked spectacular havoc throughout the whole system," Tony Dunbar wrote in *Our Land Too* published in 1971. "The black tenant farmer and sharecroppers had nothing of their own to fall back on, no alternate sources of employment, no land, no history of diverse occupation." The result, Dunbar said, was "a poverty unparalleled in this country today."

Large pockets of poverty also remained in Appalachia. Congress in 1965 approved an aid and development program for this mountainous region stretching across 13 states, most of them Southern. Some 2.7 million of the 19 million inhabitants lived in poverty, according to the Appalachian Regional Commission. In only six of the region's 397 counties was average per capita income above the national average in 1978. By 1980 evidence suggested, however, that Appalachia was slowly turning itself around. In the late 1970s its poverty population had decreased to about 14 percent, down from 31 percent in 1960. Between 1965 and 1976 per capita income climbed from 78 percent to 85 percent of the national average. Perhaps the most telling indication of an economic turnaround was the reversal of out-migration. In the 1970s there was a net increase of people going — or going back — to the Appalachian region.

Rocky Mountain States
(Montana, Wyoming, Utah,
Colorado, New Mexico, Arizona, Nevada)

In 1980 not only was the West growing rapidly, but in Colorado, Arizona, Utah and Nevada three-fourths of the people were concentrated in metropolitan areas. Between 1950 and 1980, more than 1,250,000 had moved into Colorado's Front Range area stretching south from the Wyoming border through Denver to Colorado Springs and Pueblo. Eighty-one percent of the state's population in 1980 lived in this corridor, roughly 50 miles wide and 200 miles long. Another 1,250,000 were expected to arrive in the next 20 years.

Denver had emerged as the regional center for transportation, communications, trade and high-technology industries. By 1980 more than 2,000 energy-related companies had made the Front Range their headquarters for developing oil, gas, uranium, coal and oil shale resources throughout the Rocky Mountain region. Phoenix had experienced similar growth, mushrooming from a city of 80,000 at the end of World War II into a metropolitan area of more than 1.2 million. In 1980 Tucson, whose population stood at 40,000 in 1945, was the center of an area approaching 500,000. Albuquerque in 35 years had grown from 50,000 to nearly 400,000. And in Utah more than three-quarters of the state's 1.2 million residents lived within 45 miles of Salt Lake City's Mormon Temple Square in a urbanized strip extending from Ogden south to Provo between the Wasatch Mountains and the Great Salt Lake.

Energy-Related Jobs. The development of Western energy reserves was accelerating the growth of Rocky Mountain cities, especially Denver. Gulf, Texaco and Standard Oil Co. of California, among other energy-producing companies, had set up offices in Denver as they prepared to tap oil and gas from Utah and Wyoming's Overthrust Belt, coal from New Mexico's Four Corners area and Wyoming's Powder Basin, oil shale from the Piceance Creek Basin of northwestern Colorado, and uranium from the Four Corners and Wyoming's Red Desert. A Colorado Energy Research Institute study in 1979 calculated that there were 28,000 energy-related jobs in the Denver area.

Important though they were, energy companies in the Denver area provided less than a third of the new employment in 1970-78. Tourism also was important to the local economy, while federal and state government offices, light manufacturing and the region's traditional trade and agricultural businesses together contributed substantially to a growing economic base. Companies such as IBM, Hewlett-Packard, Eastman Kodak, Sunbeam, Frito-Lay, Johns Manville and AMAX opened Denver-area plants and offices, and the Front Range began to rival the San Francisco Bay area's "Silicon Valley" and Boston's Route 128 as a center for high-technology companies. "The technology companies are here probably because of the amenities and general market growth," observed Denver economist David Bramhall in a March 1979 article in *Business Week*. "They're also here for the skilled labor, and because executives and their wives like to live out here."

In Wyoming, weekly wages in the energy industry in the summer of 1982 averaged $447. Towns in the oil and coal zones were booming and a steady incoming stream of workers continued. The expansion was accompanied by growing strains on public services needed to accommodate the burgeoning population. Growth in the region by the early 1980s was outstripping the ability of state and local governments to keep pace with increasing demands on water, sewage, school and public safety services.

In Arizona and New Mexico, service industries and clean, light manufacturing were replacing mining and agriculture as economic mainstays. Arizona drew 15 million tourists a year, six times the state's permanent population, and the Phoenix area was swollen by about 100,000 people who lived there only part of the year. Affluent older people flocked to Arizona to live in posh retirement communities and travel trailer campgrounds. Yet more migrants to Arizona were young, well educated and well paid.

Ranching's Old Values, New Uncertainty. No occupation was more emblematic of the West than that of ranching. The huge 19th-century cattle spreads were long ago broken up, and livestock raising in the late 1970s often was identified with tax shelters for oilmen and other absentee owners. But throughout the Rocky Mountain states, cattle and sheep ranching remained a family occupation, with fathers and sons sharing the work of branding, round-ups and wool shearing.

But traditional Western ranching was a risky venture. Beef, lamb and wool markets were volatile, while the cost of labor, vaccines,

175

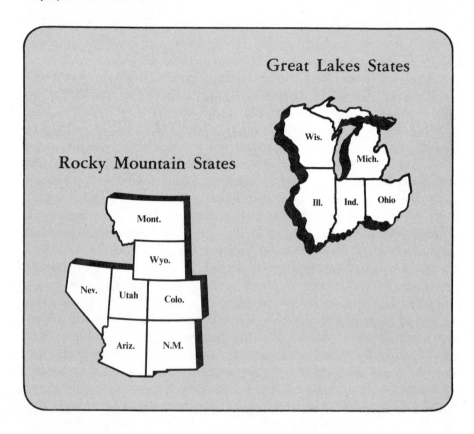

Great Lakes States

Rocky Mountain States

supplemental feed and equipment had climbed upward. By the late 1970s a rancher who ran 150 cows and their calves could clear $20,000 one year and less than half that two years later. In *The Last Cowboy*, a study of Texas Panhandle ranching first published in the *New Yorker* in 1977, Jane Kramer noted that "Ranching lately had less to do with an individual's adventure with a herd of cattle than with that global network of dependencies and contingencies that people had taken to calling 'agribusiness.' "

Rocky Mountain ranchers depended heavily on obtaining grazing rights on national forest and Bureau of Land Management (BLM) public range lands. Much of those lands, overgrazed in the past, had been declining in forage production. But when the BLM tried to reduce grazing, the agency encountered resistance from ranchers. Montana and Wyoming ranchers felt threatened by the strip mining of coal from beneath the grazing lands. Some sold their ranches and left, but others resisted and even formed Sierra Club chapters in the fight to preserve the land. In the long run, however, traditional ranching seemed destined to vanish gradually as older people retired and died.

Western farmers also faced an uncertain future mainly because water was so critical in a region where rainfall was minimal. Western agriculture generally was limited to a relatively few areas where rivers, federally financed reservoirs and underground water aquifers provided a dependable water source for irrigation. In the late 1970s President Jimmy Carter's water policies made it clear to Rocky Mountain farmers that the era of expensive federal dam-building projects to store water for irrigation was coming to an end. In the meantime, ground-water irrigation was ebbing as underground water tables dropped, pumping costs rose and cities expanded onto surrounding farm land.

In central Arizona, where irrigated agriculture accounted for 89 percent of water consumption, the growth of Phoenix and Tucson was increasing competition for limited surface and ground-water supplies. Farther north, "Colorado is rapidly approaching an agricultural crossroads," a Colorado Department of Agriculture study declared in 1979. According to the report, ground-water reserves were declining on the state's eastern plains, and energy projects competed for water on the West Slope, as the western side of the Rocky Mountain range was called.

The Rocky Mountain West states were bracing for continued rapid change in the last two decades of the 20th century. With the spread of big cities, the miseries of boom towns and a troubled outlook for Western agriculture, the region had shifted away from its traditional faith that all-out growth would fulfill its destiny.

Great Lakes States
(Michigan, Ohio,
Indiana, Illinois, Wisconsin)

On Dec. 2, 1942, on the University of Chicago campus, the first self-sustaining nuclear reaction took place under the direction of Enrico Fermi. The atomic age had begun. One side effect would be the birth of a technology that took root outside of the auto-and-steel-centered Industrial Belt.

The great factories that soon were built for the production of atomic bombs were located not in the old industrial heartland but rather in Tennessee, New Mexico, Washington state and South Carolina. As for the planes that would carry these bombs, they were built primarily in the

Southwest and Southeast. Once guided missiles were developed, they were produced mainly in the West, while nuclear submarines and carriers naturally had to be built along the nation's seacoasts.

The high-technology precision instrumentation that was increasingly essential to the operation of advanced weaponry tended, like the planes and the missiles and the ships, to be made mainly in the Southeast, the Southwest and New England. The man who presided over a major shift from reliance on conventional weapons to weapons for mass destruction was, ironically, a former president of General Motors, Charles E. Wilson. Wilson was famous for remarking, as President Dwight D. Eisenhower's secretary of defense, "What's good for the country is good for General Motors and vice versa." What Wilson actually did as defense secretary was not especially good for General Motors or for the industrial Midwest generally.

With the nation's most advanced high-technology industries leading the way in a movement out of the industrial heartland, other industries found plenty of reasons to follow suit. Whereas in the North businesses contended with high taxes, more unionization and a decaying infrastructure, in many sections of the South and West they were able to build from scratch under favorable tax incentives and draw on pools of lower-paid labor. Especially after energy prices began to soar in 1973, businesses had a strong motive to locate in the sunnier regions of the country.

Not only did the Great Lakes states see businesses move funds earned in the industrial heartland into other regions of the country, but they had to put up with the indignity of subsidizing the out-migration. Largely because three-fourths of all federal expenditures for procurement go to the defense industries, and because in a typical year the Great Lakes region receives only about 10 percent of the prime contract awards, it suffers the nation's largest net loss of tax dollars each year. In 1976, according to the congressional Northeast-Midwest Coalition, the Great Lakes States sent the federal government about $20 billion more than they got back, while the South showed a net gain of more than $20 billion and the West of $12 billion.

According to a report entitled "The Pentagon Tilt: Regional Biases in Defense Spending and Strategy," prepared by the Northeast-Midwest Institute and partially published in the *Christian Science Monitor* in January 1983, the Northeast-Midwest regional share of defense spending had dropped from 20 to 15.3 percent between 1981 and 1983, even though the military construction budget had increased 43.4 percent. The region's share of the population at large was 45 percent. The Northeast-Midwest regional share of prime weapons contracts also dropped from 72 percent in 1951 to 39 percent in 1981.

National Policy Effects and Fiscal Strains. After World War II the economic growth of the Great Lakes states was well below the national average. From 1950 to 1975, manufacturing employment in the region grew 4.3 percent, compared with 76 percent in the Southeast, and 141 percent in the Southwest. The national average stood at 20 percent. Although the Great Lakes states were thought to be exceptionally sensitive to recessions, because of their dependence on durable goods industries that were the first to suffer in times of economic downturn, the region — apart from Michigan — generally had not suffered higher-than-average joblessness.

It was no secret that in the late 1970s serious problems afflicted the steel and auto industries, the two industries on which the Great Lakes states depended most heavily. U.S. steel production peaked at 111.4 million net tons in 1973, and by 1978 it had dropped to 97.9 million tons. In 1981 imports accounted for close to 20 percent of steel sold in the United States. By January 1982 imports accounted for 26.3 percent of the U.S. steel market.

American steelworkers were among the best paid of any manufacturing workers. But the United States had lost more than 100,000 steelmaking jobs between 1960 and 1980, and it was quite likely that many more would be lost in the years ahead. In 1980 U.S. Steel closed 15 manufacturing facilities, laid off 10 percent of its work force — some 13,000 steelworkers — and recorded the biggest quarterly loss in American corporate history. According to an April 24, 1983, article in *The Washington Post*, employment in the domestic steel industry fell 36 percent from an annual average of 454,000 workers in 1976 to 289,0900 in 1982. Bethlehem Steel, the nation's second-largest steel producer, decreased its employment roles from 105,000 employees in 1976 to 67,000 employees in 1982.

The auto industry, which purchased about a quarter of the nation's steel production yearly, appeared to be in little better shape. In 1982 imports accounted for 27.9 percent of all cars sold in the United States. The Chrysler Corp.'s 1980 $1.1 billion loss was the largest ever by an American company, sending its management to Congress to plead for aid in an attempt to avert bankruptcy. In January 1981 Congress provided

Chrysler with $1.5 billion in loan guarantees. *(Foreign Trade and U.S. Unemployment, p. 57)*

Federal Intervention vs. Belt-Tightening. In May 1979 the United Auto Workers, the United Steelworkers and the International Association of Machinists joined in publishing a study based on an "intensive study of policies and practices to cope with economic dislocation in three highly industrialized countries, Sweden, West Germany, and the U.K. [Britain]." On the basis of these findings, the three industrial unions recommended the adoption of national planning to ensure full employment, advance notice of industrial layoffs, federal procurement and credit allocations to prevent job dislocations. To stop the flight of capital south and west and the migration of poverty north, they also recommended federalized unemployment insurance and workers' compensation, repeal of right-to-work legislation and abolition of state and local tax abatements to lure industry from one region to another.

In contrast to that position, there were those who argued that regions such as the Great Lakes could solve their problems by tightening their belts and making themselves more attractive to business. That had been Cleveland's goal since its populist mayor, Dennis Kucinich, was defeated in 1979 and replaced by George V. Voinovich. Soon after, the city ran the following ad in several major newspapers: "There's a new frame of mind in Cleveland. This new frame of mind recognizes . . . that the financial community must have confidence and understanding before they can extend the credit necessary for a smoothly running city; and that businessmen, large and small, must have the hope of making a profit before they will venture the money and effort which creates new jobs, wealth and needed tax revenues." Under Voinovich, Cleveland as of April 1983 had paid off its debts, balanced its budget, developed its downtown and won a 1982 "All-American City" award from the National Municipal League.

Jane Byrne, as mayor of Chicago from the late 1970s until April 1983, also appeared eager to restore her city's attractiveness to business. Her efforts to curb the power of the city unions, however, led to bitter confrontations with transit workers, teachers and firefighters. At the same time, the city's poor blacks — for whom the Irish-run city never worked very well — had been increasingly outspoken in demanding more, rather than fewer, services. At a time when urban tax bases were shrinking, while many inner-city neighborhoods remained impoverished ghettos, belt-tightening was a difficult and risky business.

Even though growth trends favored other regions of the country, average per capita income still was higher in most Great Lakes states than in the Southeast and Southwest in 1980. While some areas in the industrial Midwest had experienced serious economic difficulties, and while many neighborhoods had become miserable places to live, many people nonetheless had managed to make a lot of money. These people typically moved to the affluent suburbs. Chicago's suburbs, for example, in 1980 included three of the five richest congressional districts in the United States. The irony was that for those who were working, the average income in Michigan at least was among the highest in the nation.

Middle Atlantic States
(New York, Pennsylvania, District of Columbia,
New Jersey, Delaware, Maryland, West Virginia)

In the early 1980s the economic concerns of the Middle Atlantic states were real, although sometimes overstated. In this region — New York, New Jersey, Pennsylvania, Maryland, Delaware, West Virginia and the District of Columbia — unemployment between the 1974-75 recession and 1980 had averaged about one percentage point above the national average. The Middle Atlantic had lost more manufacturing jobs than any other section of the country as of 1980.

In this region where heavy manufacturing — along with mining — had been dominant since the 19th century, the stagnation was all the more obvious. One problem, possibly the main one, was that many of the industrial facilities were old and could not function efficiently. Competitors using the latest equipment — whether they were in Germany, Japan or the South — had a built-in advantage.

"The best way to appreciate this is to take an Amtrak ride through the once great workshop cities of Pennsylvania, New York, Ohio or Illinois," columnist Nicholas von Hoffman wrote in *The New York Review of Books* in 1980. ". . . [W]hen you see Reading, or Altoona, or Youngstown, or Schenectady you'll think you are touring a museum showing the Birth of the Industrial Revolution. These places look like the English Midlands and the factories are often as old." In western Pennsylvania are "sudsy, sooty montages of the Edwardian era, iron work barns where the old ways of forge and open hearth are passed down from father to son."

Instances of Success in City Revitalization. The overall picture, however, was not one of unrelieved gloom. New York City, for example,

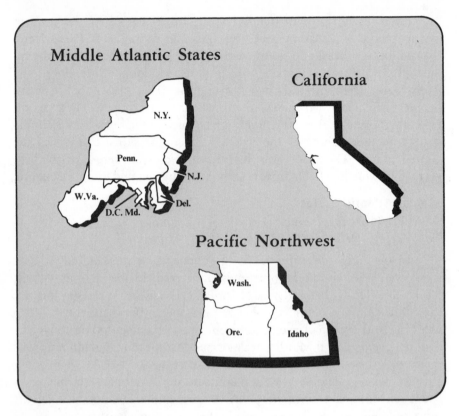

Middle Atlantic States

N.Y.

Penn.

N.J.

W.Va.

D.C. Md.

Del.

California

Pacific Northwest

Wash.

Ore.

Idaho

despite fiscal ills, remained the nation's banking, cultural and communications center. Tourism continued to boom, attracting more visitors (16.9 million) in 1982 than any other U.S. city, according to the city's Convention and Visitors Bureau. In 1981 personal income in New York state grew at a rate above the national average.

While the city's losses of corporation headquarters and manufacturing jobs were well documented, across the Hudson River in New Jersey, especially in semi-rural Morris County, new offices, hotels and convention facilities were springing up. Farther south, Atlantic City was in the midst of a mini-boom, brought on by legalized gambling. State officials were predicting multimillion-dollar annual tax receipts from casinos in Atlantic City, which had been economically depressed.

Despite the economic problems that New Jersey shared with most Northern states, its per capita personal income was one of the nation's highest and was the highest among the Middle Atlantic states in 1980. Only two of these states, Pennsylvania and West Virginia, were below the national average ($7,810) in 1978.

Pennsylvania, the nation's second most populous state for more than a century, in 1980 was fourth in per capita personal income, behind California, New York and Texas. But its two biggest cities, Philadelphia and Pittsburgh, both experienced some degree of revitalization in the late 1970s. Pittsburgh, the "Steel City," advertised itself as the "City of Champions," in recognition of the national attention devoted to its professional baseball and football teams, the Pirates and the Steelers. They played in Three Rivers Stadium at the edge of Pittsburgh's gleaming downtown area, the site of one of the nation's most acclaimed urban renewal areas.

In many cities, downtown urban renewal did not bring new life. But Baltimore, like Pittsburgh, appeared to be one of the success stories. Baltimore's vitality was measured not only by the visual appeal of its new architecture and the restoration of old residential sections but also in reams of statistics on trade and commerce. In nearby Washington, D.C., where federal employment cushioned the shock of recession, a building and restoration boom was also under way. Personal annual income for residents of Washington, D.C., was higher than in any state in 1978. Delaware and Maryland both projected budget surpluses for fiscal 1983. In 1979 Maryland posted a surplus of $300 million. In Delaware, where there was no sales tax, the General Assembly enacted an income tax cut in 1979, only two years after overcoming a budget deficit.

West Virginia's economic future brightened considerably after the rapidly increasing cost of imported oil prompted greater reliance on coal — the state's primary natural resource. The U.S. Geological Survey estimated that at least 1.7 trillion tons of coal lay beneath American soil in 1980. A significant portion was in western Pennsylvania and West Virginia. Bituminous coal, the soft coal used in making steel and other industrial products, long was the economic cornerstone of the two areas. Northeastern Pennsylvania, moreover, was the site of large deposits of anthracite, the hard coal used for home heating.

But coal's heralded comeback had, as of 1980, been disappointing in the Eastern United States. There was fear in the industry that coal remained "the fuel of last resort" because of the soaring costs of mining and shipping it and abiding by anti-pollution rules in burning it. The future of coal was not in the East, analysts also said. According to the brokerage firm of Dean Witter Reynolds, the Eastern states would supply the nation's utilities with 50 percent of their coal in 1985, compared with 78 percent in 1975. The gap would be filled by coal mined, especially strip-mined, in the West where the coal-mining companies were owned primarily by the nation's large oil corporations.

Fiscal Ills of New York and Other Cities. Economic problems were not confined to private enterprise in the Middle Atlantic region. New York City repeatedly faced the specter of municipal bankruptcy in the 1970s. When the city was unable to borrow money to meet and pay debts in 1975, it was bailed out by loan guarantees from New York state and later from the federal government. Moreover, the city was forced to give much of its control over fiscal affairs to a state-created Municipal Assistance Corporation (MAC) as a condition for receiving aid from Albany and Washington.

New York's fiscal problems were not unique. Observers said symptoms of fiscal insolvency — increasing costs of social services, education and city salaries that were unmatched by revenues — were evident in a number of large cities in the nation, including Philadelphia and Washington. In 1980 the city government in the nation's capital faced a budget deficit estimated at some $172 million. In Philadelphia, the city's municipal and school system budgets were expected to run a deficit of $93 million by mid-1981.

Many of the older cities of the industrial North were suffering from wear and tear by the early 1980s. Buildings, streets, sewer and water lines typically were aged and overused. These cities also tended to be the ones that had been hurt most by the departure of the white middle class, leaving behind a lower tax base and a heavier welfare load.

Thus the financial resources to mend physical deterioration and care for the social ills had shrunk as the needs had increased. While there had been success stories here and there, most of the cities continued to be haunted by the same litany of problems they had faced for two decades or more: racial crime, declining revenues and municipal service.

The Pacific Northwest
(Washington, Oregon, Idaho)

There was a time not long ago when the Pacific Northwest might have qualified as one of the country's best-kept secrets. Life in this far corner of the United States was an unpublicized pleasure that residents jealously guarded and people elsewhere usually associated with endless rain. But as of the early 1980s the weather was one of the few things that remained the same. Change in the late 1970s came to the coastal states of

Washington, Oregon and neighboring Idaho, and it was not entirely welcome.

Attracted by the Pacific Northwest's spreading reputation for "livability," outsiders migrated there in growing numbers in the late 1970s. The sharp influx of newcomers and the problems they inevitably brought with them left many natives wondering if the region's best qualities — the unspoiled beauty of its forests and shores, the peace and quiet of its urban areas — could survive its new popularity.

Fluctuating Job Market Destabilizes Economy. In Oregon, where the population rose by 18 percent during the 1960s and 21 percent from 1970 to 1979, coping with the strain of more people became a problem considered by many to be greater than economic concerns. Once considered one of the most liberal states in the nation — in 1971 it decriminalized marijuana and banned throw-away clear containers — Oregon in 1980 began moving gradually toward the right, as a post-Proposition 13 climate began to take hold there. In June 1978 California voters had approved Proposition 13, a ballot initiative that effectively cut the state's property tax revenues in half.

In Washington during the 1970s the main concern was jobs. The economy suffered a severe jolt in the early 1970s when the Boeing Co. began laying off aircraft workers. But the company by 1980 was back on its feet and Washingtonians were turning their attention to what some called "the hazards of good fortune" — finding work for new arrivals and supplying the state with enough energy to meet the demands of a growing population.

Washington also had problems coping with its rapidly increasing population. In a 1981 special session, the Washington Legislature cut spending by $284.6 million, raised sales taxes by 1 percent, and still had to borrow $400 million from New York banks to pay its bills.

Idaho, principally a rural state, escaped many of the woes that accompanied rapid growth. Its largest city, Boise, had tripled in size since 1960 but still had not reached the 100,000-mark by 1980. However, it was beginning to show signs of urbanization, brought on by "platoons of young executives, drawn from the Stanford and Harvard business schools by such corporations as Boise Cascade, Morrison-Knudsen and Hewlett-Packard," according to Wallace and Page Stegner in the April 1978 issue of *The Atlantic*.

Idahoans were troubled less by outside pressure than by internal differences. In a sense the state was split between the growing social and

185

political influence of Mormons in the agricultural southeast, the home of Idaho's much-advertised potatoes, and the "live-and-let-live" outlook in the northern panhandle, where mining and lumbering were the economic mainstays and prostitution, although illegal, was openly tolerated in a number of towns. One indication of Idaho's conservative temper was passage of a Proposition 13-style tax cut in 1979. Unlike similar ballot measures elsewhere, no significant opposition existed in Idaho.

The problems faced by Washington, Oregon and Idaho differed only in degree. Each saw itself threatened by social change and resource shortages. And in each the 1980s were seen as a test, one that could determine whether the region would remain livable and whether it would have enough to live on.

One of the major barriers facing the Northwestern states during the early 1980s was the unprecedented financial disaster caused by an inadequately financed and poorly managed nuclear building program. The Washington Public Power System, responsible for building five huge nuclear plants, as of December 1982 had no money left to pay its creditors. Further construction of two of the plants, which were partially completed at that time, had been canceled. Eighty-eight utilities in three states still owed $7 billion in principal and interest on the defunct plants, even though they would never go into operation. The five unfinished nuclear power plants carried the greatest long-term, tax-exempt bond debt in American history.

Postwar Upsurge in Aircraft and Timber. The Northwestern economy was enhanced during World War II when the aircraft industry began to flourish in western Washington. Boeing, which produced bombers for the war effort, became a prime factor in the upsurge of Washington's economy during the 1950s and 1960s. But building airplanes proved to be anything but a steady business. Prior to 1970, Boeing employed as many as 101,000 people — nearly 8 percent of the state's work force. In 1970, however, its employment rolls dropped to 38,000. One year later, 55,000 people left the state to search for work elsewhere. As a result, the bottom fell out of the real estate markets in Everett, Tacoma and Seattle. Washington's economy took a nose dive.

New military and civilian contracts, including work on the cruise missile, brought Boeing's employment level back near the pre-1970 mark, and Washington's economy improved accordingly in the late 1970s.

Around the time Boeing began building World War II bombers, the Weyerhaeuser Co. started planting the first U.S. tree farm in Grays

Harbor County, Wash. Like Boeing, Weyerhaeuser and other big timber companies — such as Boise Cascade, Georgia-Pacific, Crown-Zellerbach and St. Regis — flourished in the years after the war. The postwar demand for housing created a boom business. Timber prices shot up and the Northwest, where most of the nation's prime housing and construction wood grew, prospered.

As the lumber market expanded, Congress in 1960 enacted the Multiple Use-Sustained Yield Act, declaring that the national forests should be "utilized in the combination [of ways] that will best meet the needs of the American people." The industry in the Northwest benefited, but many environmentalists argued that the legislation was a blanket "license to log." The law, they argued, was too vague. For years, the Sierra Club and other environmental groups petitioned the federal government to tighten restrictions on the timber companies. In 1971 Congress responded by passing the National Forest Management Act. This measure directed the Forest Service to curb timber-cutting abuses on federally owned land. To make up for these curbs, however, companies stepped up harvesting by other methods.

Generally, the states had little to complain about since they received taxes and payments for timber cut on county, state and federal land. The Washington state public school system, for example, received more than $40 million by this means in 1978. But in 1980 the slump in the building and construction industry created the possibility of a serious recession. Oregon officials estimated that 7,000 of the state's 76,000 lumber industry jobs had vanished between November 1979 and June 1980. Authorities in Washington said the state had lost 7 percent of the 52,000 lumber and wood products jobs it had early in 1979.

It appeared likely that many jobs never would reappear. As more Northwestern forests were stripped by logging or declared off-limits by the government, lumber companies were moving their operations to the Southeastern states. Even Weyerhaeuser, the Northwest's biggest private landowner, with 2.8 million acres, had built up its timber holdings in the South to 3.1 million acres.

California

If California were an independent country, its gross national product — estimated at close to $300 billion in 1980 — would be greater than those of all nations save six — the United States, the Soviet Union, West Germany, Japan, France and China. Agriculturally, it would be among the leading nations; it already ranked first in the United States in 1980. California farm goods brought more than $12 billion into the state's economy in 1979. California in 1980 ranked behind Alaska and Texas as the third largest oil-producing state. Its 40,000 wells produced approximately 918,000 barrels of oil a day. According to John Naisbitt in *Megatrends*, capital investments in manufacturing in the state increased 110 percent from 1972 to 1977. In 1981 California created 212,000 new jobs, 27 percent of the U.S. total.

Is was difficult to characterize in a phrase a state with more than a thousand miles of coastline, a variety of landscapes and more than 22 million people. Nevertheless, it often was said that California was not just a state but a state of mind. For some, it represented the final embodiment of America's frontier spirit; for others, it was a version of El Dorado, a place to find fortunes or spend fortunes made elsewhere. California led the nation in fads, fashion and self-indulgence. New religions, new living arrangements, new forms of entertainment, new attitudes toward work, family and education, all were nurtured by California's tolerant social climate.

California's major physiographic regions were the narrow coastal area between the mountains and the sea; the Central Valley walled by the coastal ranges to the west and the Sierra Nevada Mountains to the east; the desert basins of the southern interior; and the rugged mountainous regions to the north. The Tehachapi Range — a short connecting link between the coastal ranges and the Sierra Nevada situated approximately 335 miles south of San Francisco and 115 miles north of Los Angeles — unofficially divided northern and southern California.

The contrasts between northern and southern California extended beyond geographic differences. The Gold Rush, so important to early California history, hardly touched the southern part of the state. It was not until the 1880s that the first significant migration to the southland occurred. As late as 1906, more than a third of the state's population lived within 75 miles of San Francisco. In 1980 more than 60 percent of California's residents lived in the southern third of the state. As the southern section's population grew, so did its political power. "It is becoming increasingly difficult for anyone outside Los Angeles to win a statewide race," California political analyst Ed Salzman wrote in 1979.

Southern California, the third of the state below the Tehachapi Range, had a character and a mood quite different from the northern two-thirds. "This is the California of petroleum, crazy religious cults, the citrus industry, towns based on rich *rentiers* like Santa Barbara and Pasadena, the movies, the weirdest architecture in the United States, refugees from Iowa, a steeply growing Negro population, and devotees of funny money," John Gunther wrote in *Inside U.S.A.* "It is, above all, the world where climate is worshipped as a god." Gunther made his observations in 1947, but, for the most part, they still held true in the 1980s.

The sprawling south, centered in the 6,600-square-mile Los Angeles Basin, was the economic center of the state. The tax revenues from its citizens and companies provided California with much of its income. The Los Angeles area ranked behind New York as the second-largest commercial center in the United States. Southern California's economy was diversified, but four areas dominated: the entertainment business, including films, television and recording studios; aerospace and defense industries; the oil industry, including both production and refining; real estate development and sales.

History of Film, Aerospace and Oil Industries. At first, Angelenos, as citizens of Los Angeles were called, showed a pronounced dislike for members of "the movie colony" — signs on apartment buildings often read "No Dogs or Actors Allowed." But by 1915 the residents had undergone a change of heart. People made a lot of money from the movies, and Hollywood and Los Angeles reaped the benefits. Real estate values soared as actors, producers and movie moguls built residential monuments to their success. Businesses grew up around the industry — fine restaurants, hotels and shops. And there was all that free publicity. Because its name was linked to the world's most publicized industry, Hollywood became one of the best-known cities in the world.

Despite the growing popularity of location shooting, southern California still retained much of the glitter — if not all the gold — of the movies. In 1980 almost 150 films a year were made in the Hollywood-Los Angeles area. Although 60 percent of the 20,000 members of the Screen Actors Guild were unemployed at any given time, the entertainment industry — films, television and records — brought in $13 billion in 1979.

Southern California's aerospace-defense industry dated from World War II, when massive government involvement in the aircraft industry brought thousands of workers and jobs to the southland. In 1980 the list of leading aerospace and defense industries headquartered in southern California included General Dynamics, Hughes Aircraft, Lockheed Missiles and Space Co., McDonnell Douglas and Rockwell International.

In 1892 Edward Doheny, a metals prospector, discovered oil in the

189

form of tar inside the city limits of Los Angeles. Three years later, according to a contemporary account, oil wells in Los Angeles were "as thick as the holes in a pepper box." The new fuel was substituted for coal, and California suddenly found itself with an enviable supply of energy. In the 1920s huge deposits of oil were discovered in Huntington Beach, Long Beach and Whittier. Los Angeles became the oil capital of the world. The dollar value of oil produced in California in the 1920s exceeded the value of gold mined in the state.

One of the byproducts of the oil boom became more associated with southern California than did the huge deposits themselves. Gasoline, initially an unwanted byproduct of petroleum, was found to be the perfect fuel for the horseless carriage. As early as 1925, Los Angeles was heralded as the unabashed leader of the car culture, with one automobile for every three residents.

One outgrowth of Los Angeles' car mania was that it had one of the lowest population densities of any major American city. Scores of small towns developed because of the presence of highways, and access to the city led to the characterization of Los Angeles as "one hundred suburbs in search of a metropolis." In the early 1980s, with one of the best intra- and inter-city road systems in the country, the Los Angeles area remained built around the car. It was one of the few major cities in the world without an extensive mass transit system.

California's High-Tech Leads Nation. California benefited from a burgeoning high technology industry, centered around the Silicon Valley area just south of San Francisco. According to an article in the April 15, 1982, *Christian Science Monitor,* California had posted the largest job growth in the nation during the 1970s — 15.4 percent. The number of jobs in high-technology industries in California grew by 71.6 percent, from 261,000 to 448,900.

"High-tech jobs will account for nearly 50 percent of the growth in basic industry jobs in the 1980s. Computer services is projected to have the highest rate of growth among individual high-technology industries. Jobs will nearly triple to 128,300 in 1990 from 43,300 in 1980," wrote Stephen Levy, senior economist at the Center for Continuing Study of the California Economy in a 1982 report entitled "The California Economy: 1970-1990."

California's electronics industry, however, was in an ambivalent state, mainly due to increasing competition from Japan. In 1983 California was the acknowledged center of the development of low-capacity computer chips, but the higher capacity market — considered to be the more progressive edge of the technology — had been lost to the Japanese who claimed 70 percent of the market. Motorola (in Arizona) and Texas Instruments (in Texas) accounted for the remaining 30 percent.

The Plains States
(North Dakota, South Dakota, Nebraska,
Kansas, Oklahoma, Minnesota, Iowa, Missouri)

Although the Plains states lay in America's "Farm Belt," most of the people who lived in this region were not engaged in agriculture by the early 1980s. Mines and factories accounted for much of the employment. In petroleum production, Oklahoma ranked fifth and Kansas eighth among the 50 states in 1980. A large part of the country's known uranium deposits was in South Dakota, much of it on lands claimed by Indians, and huge lignite coal deposits in North Dakota provided a center for synfuels production. Numerous corporations — Minnesota Mining and Manufacturing ("3M"), Honeywell, and Control Data in Minnesota; Maytag and Winnebago in Iowa; General Dynamics, McDonnell Douglas, Emerson Electric, and Chromalloy American in Missouri; and Boeing, Cessna and Beech aircraft in Kansas — were engaged in activities that had little or nothing to do with farming. Only Michigan manufactured more automobiles than Missouri.

St. Louis, historically a gateway city to the Western plains, in the early 1980s suffered many of the same problems that afflicted most large

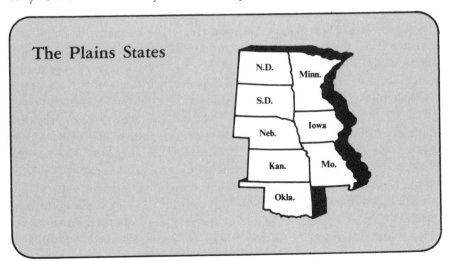

The Plains States

cities: suburban migration, shrinking tax revenues, a stagnant inner-city economy, and — most recently — loss of automobile industry jobs. From 1970 to 1977, the inner-city population dropped nearly 17 percent, and St. Louis in 1980 had the highest murder rate of any major city in the United States — more than double New York's.

Wichita, Kan., on the other hand, resembled a Southwestern boom town. It was the nation's leading producer of small aircraft in 1980; Boeing, Beech and Cessna aircraft companies all had installations there. According to a journalist who visited the city in 1980, the aircraft manufacturers "can't begin to fill the positions they have available."

For every St. Louis or Wichita, however, there were five or 10 medium-sized cities, prosperous but unspectacular, that functioned as banking, insurance, food processing and farm machinery centers for the surrounding agricultural communities. Companies such as John Deere had manufacturing plants and retail outlets throughout the region. And in the larger cities as well, big industries depended heavily on the agrarian hinterland.

In 1980 Kansas City, its downtown rejuvenated by the Hallmark Center and convention site, presented to the world a more cosmopolitan air than in past years when its vast (and now vanished) stockyards filled the nostrils. But agriculture still accounted for much of the city's prosperity. It ranked first in farm equipment and frozen food distribution, and second in grain elevator capacity and wheat flour production in 1980. In Minneapolis, General Mills and Pillsbury vied for leadership in commercial bakery products.

Agribusiness With Wheat, Corn and Hogs. The economy of the Plains states continued to depend heavily on agriculture in the early 1980s, and the monetary value of farm products failed to represent their importance to the country and indeed the world. These states accounted for nearly one-half of America's corn and wheat production, and about one-third of the soybean production in 1980. The United States, in turn, provided about three-quarters of the world's corn exports, nearly half of the wheat exports, and almost nine-tenths of the soybean exports. Kansas and Nebraska, the country's leading wheat states, produced about one-quarter of the total U.S. crop. Iowa and neighboring Illinois harvested roughly two-thirds of the country's corn and one-third of its soybeans. Corn-fattened hogs were another staple of the economy; the two states raised more than a third of the nation's hogs in a typical year.

Midwestern farms, although shrinking in number, had climbed

steadily in size throughout the 1970s. As farm operations became larger, costlier, more complex and in some ways riskier, the successful farmer had to be a person of many talents — the master of diverse manual skills, knowledgeable in agricultural science and economics, and an accountant to boot. Many families hedged their bets with "marginal farming," the standard term for an arrangement in which one or more members of the family work at paying jobs away from the farm.

As farming came to resemble other business operations, standard forms of business ownership became prevalent. Many farms were organized as partnerships, and a partnership was sometimes a stepping-stone toward a corporate structure. The Census Bureau found in its 1974 survey of agriculture that the "1,421 farm partnerships which planned to incorporate had average sales of $172,347, or more than two times the average sales of all partnerships reporting. . . ." Incorporation often led in turn to a takeover by an absentee agribusiness company; in many cases the original farm family stayed on the property to act as employee-overseer for the company.

Closely related to anxiety about the familiy farm was concern about loss of crop land to urban and industrial development, foreign purchases of U.S. farm land and the agribusiness shipping scandals that afflicted the Mississippi River transportation system in the late 1970s.

Pushing Land's Productivity to Its Limits. One important concern in 1980 was the falling level of water in the Ogallala Formation, a vast underground reserve that stretches from South Dakota to Texas. Farmers in the western parts of Kansas and Nebraska, southwestern South Dakota and the Oklahoma Panhandle, along with the Texas Panhandle, depended heavily on this geologic formation for water. It was brought to the surface by heavy pumps fueled with natural gas. With water supplies dropping and natural gas prices rising, more and more farmers were shutting off their wells and putting fields back into dryland cultivation.

Like water, the number of plant varieties also was decreasing, and this too worried some environmentalists. Farmers naturally concentrated production in the crop varieties that gave the highest yields, but if a blight were to hit, uniform varieties might mean uniform disaster. With the country and much of the world dependent on Midwestern agriculture, a crop failure would be disastrous indeed.

SELECTED BIBLIOGRAPHY

Chapter 1 - The U. S. Employment Outlook

Articles

Carey, M.L. "Occupational Employment Growth through 1990." *Monthly Labor Review*, August 1981, pp. 42-55.

"Changing Labor Force." *American Demographics*, July/August 1982, p. 21.

Cox, D. "Inequality in the Lifetime Earnings of Women." *Review of Economics and Statistics*, August 1982, pp. 501-504.

"Employment and Occupation." *American Demographics*, July/August 1982, p. 22.

"Lasting Changes Brought by Women Workers." *Business Week*, March 15, 1982, p. 59.

Personick, V.A. "Outlook for Industry and Employment through 1990." *Monthly Labor Review*, August 1981, pp. 28-41.

Sieling, M.S. "GAO Study Focuses on Problems of Teenagers in Labor Market." *Monthly Labor Review*, October 1982, pp. 33-34.

Thomas, E.G. "Update on Alternative Work Methods." *Management World*, January 1982, pp. 30-32.

"Work Force Trends in the 80's." *Management World*, November 1982, p. 23.

Books

Amsden, Alice. *The Economics of Women and Work*. New York: St. Martin's Press, 1980.

Garraty, John Arthur. *Unemployment in History: Economic Thought and Public Policy*. New York: Harper & Row, 1978.

Freeman, Richard B., and Wise, David A., eds. *The Youth Labor Market Problem: Its Nature, Causes and Consequences*. Chicago: A National Bureau of Economic Research Conference Report, 1982.

Giraldo, Zaida Irene. *Public Policy and the Family: Wives and Mothers in the Labor Force*. Lexington, Mass.: Lexington Books, 1980.

Osterman, Paul. *Getting Started: The Youth Labor Market.* Cambridge, Mass.: MIT Press, 1980.

Sheppard, Stewart C., ed. *Working in the Twenty-first Century.* New York: John Wiley & Sons, 1980.

Wallace, Phyllis A., ed. *Women in the Workplace.* Boston: Auburn House Publishing Co., 1982.

Government Publications

Commerce Department. *1983 U.S. Industrial Outlook.* Washington, D.C.: Government Printing Office, 1983.

Bureau of Labor Statistics, Labor Department. *Occupational Outlook Handbook.* Washington, D.C.: Government Printing Office, issued quarterly and biennially.

U.S. Congress. House. Committee on Public Works and Transportation. *Projected Changes in the Economy, Population, Labor Market, and Work Force, and Their Implications for Economic Development Policy. Hearing, Nov. 18-19, 1981.* Washington, D.C.: Government Printing Office, 1982.

U.S. Congress. House. Select Committee on Aging. *Older Working Americans: A Productive Trend. Hearing, Sept. 8, 1981.* Washington, D.C.: Government Printing Office, 1982.

U.S. Congress. Senate. Special Committee on Aging. *Older Workers: The Federal Role in Promoting Employment Opportunities. Hearing, Oct. 29, 1981.* Washington, D.C.: Government Printing Office, 1982.

Chapter 2 - The Technological Revolution

Articles

Anderson, H. "Jobs Putting America Back to Work (Impact of Hi-Tech)." *Newsweek,* Oct. 18, 1982, pp. 78-82.

Dodd, J. "Robots: The New Steel Collar Workers." *Personnel Journal,* September 1981, pp. 688-695.

Levitan, S.A., and Johnson, C.M. "Future of Work: Does it Belong to Us or the Robots." *Monthly Labor Review,* September 1982, pp. 10-14.

Main, J. "Work Won't Be the Same Again." *Fortune,* June 28, 1982, pp. 58-61.

Reich, R.B. "Why We Are Losing the Hi-tech War." *Resource Management,* May 1982, p. 7.

"Retraining Displaced Workers: Too Little, Too Late?" *Business Week,* July 19, 1982, p. 178.

Riche, R.W. "Impact of New Electronic Technology." *Monthly Labor Review,* March 1982, pp. 37-39.

"Technologies for the 80's." *Business Week,* July 6, 1981, pp. 48-52.

Books

Albus, James S. *Brains, Behavior, and Robotics.* New York: McGraw-Hill Book Co., 1982.

Botkin, James, et al. *Global Stakes: The Future of High Technology in America.* Cambridge, Mass.: Ballinger Publishing Co., 1982.

Collinridge, David. *The Social Control of Technology.* New York: St. Martin's Press, 1981.

Government Publications

U.S. Congress. House. Subcommittee on Science, Research, and Technology. *The Human Factor in Innovation and Productivity. Committee Print, Oct. 1982.* Washington, D.C.: Government Printing Office, 1982.

U.S. Congress. Joint. Office of Technology Assessment. *Robotics and the Economy. Committee Print, March 26, 1982.* Washington, D.C.: Government Printing Office, 1982.

U.S. Congress. Office of Technology Assessment. *Automation in the Work Place: Selected Labor, Education, and Training Issues, March 1983.* Washington, D.C.: Government Printing Office, 1983.

Chapter 3 - Foreign Trade and U. S. Unemployment

Articles

Graham, J.L. "Hidden Cause of America's Trade Deficit with Japan." *Columbia Journal of World Business,* Fall 1981, pp. 5-15.

Grossman, G.M. "Import Competition from Developed and Developing Countries." *Review of Economics and Statistics,* May 1982, pp. 271-281.

Reich, R.B. "Industrial Policy." *New Republic,* March 31, 1982, pp. 28-31.

Uri, N.D., and Mixon, J.W. "Effect of Exports and Imports on the Stability of Employment in Manufacturing Industries in the U.S." *Applied Economics,* June 1981, pp. 193-203.

"Why the U.S. Needs an Industrial Policy." *Harvard Business Review,* January/February 1982, pp. 74-81.

Books

Bluestone, Barry, and Bennett, Harrison. *The Deindustrialization of America: Plant Closings, Community Abandonment, and the Dismantling of Basic Industries.* New York: Basic Books, 1982.

Center for Strategic and International Studies. *The Export Performance of the United States: Political, Strategic, and Economic Implications.* New York: Praeger Publishers, 1981.

Chang, C.S. *The Japanese Auto Industry and the U.S. Market.* New York: Praeger Publishers, 1981.

Destler, I.M., and Hideo, Sato. *Coping with U.S.-Japanese Economic Conflicts.* Lexington, Mass.: Lexington Books, 1982.

Diebold, William. *Industrial Policy as an International Issue.* New York: McGraw-Hill Book Co., 1980.

Gilmore, Richard. *A Poor Harvest: The Clash of Policies and Interests in the Grain Trade.* New York: Longman, 1982.

Hurtland-Thunberg, Penelope. *Government Support of Exports: A Second Best Alternative.* Lexington, Mass.: Lexington Books, 1982.

Zucker, Seymour, et al. *The Reindustrialization of America.* New York: McGraw-Hill Book Co., 1982.

Government Publications

U.S. Congress. House. Committee on Banking, Finance and Urban Affairs. *Revitalization of the U.S. Economy. Hearings, Sept. 15-17, Sept. 22-25, 1981.* Washington, D.C.: Government Printing Office, 1981.

U.S. Congress. Senate. Committee on Banking, Housing, and Urban Affairs. *Foreign Barriers to U.S. Trade, Part One, Service Exports, Hearing, Nov. 9, 1981.* Washington, D.C.: Government Printing Office, 1982.

———. *Foreign Barriers to U.S. Trade, Part Two, Merchandise Exports, Hearing, March 4, 1982.* Washington, D.C.: Government Printing Office, 1982.

U.S. Congress. Senate. Committee on Labor and Human Resources. *Employment and American Automobile Industry. Hearings, Jan. 11-12, 1982.* Washington, D.C.: Government Printing Office, 1982.

Chapter 4 - The Federal Jobs Programs Controversy

Articles

Beck, M. "Can Government Make Jobs?" *Newsweek*, Dec. 13, 1982, p. 31.

"Congress Zeroes in on Jobs." *Business Week*, Nov. 29, 1982, pp. 30-32.

Demaree, A.T. "Infrastructure Chic: How to Judge the Job Bills." *Fortune*, Dec. 13, 1982, pp. 122-124.

"Jobless Benefits: A Vicious Cycle." *Business Week*, Feb. 21, 1983, pp. 123-124.

"Less for More." *Time*, Feb. 8, 1982, p. 124.

Books

Burkhauser, Richard V., et al. *Disability and Work: The Economics of American Policy (Policy Studies in Employment and Welfare Series, No. 38)*, Baltimore, Md.: Johns Hopkins Press, 1982.

Ginzberg, Eli., ed. *Employing the Unemployed*. New York: Basic Books, 1980.

Haveman, J. and Palmer, L. *Jobs For Disadvantaged Workers: The Economics of Employment Subsidies*. Washington, D.C.: The Brookings Institution, 1982.

Schlesinger, Arthur, Jr. *The Coming of the New Deal*. Boston: Houghton Mifflin Co., 1959.

Williams, Walter. *Government by Agency: Lessons from the Social Program Grants-In-Aid Experience*. New York: Academic Press, 1980.

Government Publications

U.S. Congress. Senate. Committee on Labor and Human Resources. *Employment and Training Policy, 1982. Hearings, March 15-16, 1982*. Washington, D.C.: Government Printing Office, 1982.

_____. *Vocational Education and Job Training Programs, 1981. Hearings, Oct. 21 and Nov. 24, 1981*. Washington D.C.: Government Printing Office, 1982.

_____. *Employment and Training Programs in the United States. Hearings, Aug. 25-26, 1981, Indianapolis, Ind*. Washington, D.C.: Government Printing Office, 1981.

Chapter 5 - Problems for the Unemployed

Articles

Chaze, W.L. "Street People: Adrift and Alone in America." *U.S. News & World Report*, March 8, 1982, pp. 60-61.

Hayes, R., and Schoonmaker, M.E. "Hope for the Homeless." *Progressive*, December 1982, pp. 20-21.

Hildreth, J.M. "America's Wandering Jobless." *U.S. News & World Report*, Jan. 17, 1983, pp. 23-25.

Morganthau, T. "Down and Out in America." *Newsweek*, March 15, 1982, pp. 28-29.

"Rescuing Jobless Who Need Health Care." *U.S. News & World Report*, February 7, 1983, p. 6.

Runner, D. "Unemployment Insurance Laws: Legislative Revisions in 1982." *Monthly Labor Review*, January 1983, pp. 57-63.

Ryscavage, P.M. "Employment Problems and Poverty: Examining the Linkages." *Monthly Labor Review*, June 1982, pp. 55-59.

Trafford, A. "A New Health Hazard: Being Out of Work." *U.S. News & World Report*, June 14, 1982, pp. 81-82.

Books

Jahoda, Marie. *Employment and Unemployment: A Social-Psychological Analysis.* Cambridge: Cambridge University Press, 1982.

Kaufman, Harold G. *Professionals in Search of Work: Coping With the Stress of Job Loss and Underemployment.* New York: John Wiley & Sons, 1982.

Mauer, Harry. *Not Working: An Oral History of the Unemployed.* New York: Holt, Rinehart & Winston, 1979.

Chapter 6 - Economic Profiles of America's Regions

Articles

Anderson, H. "Dark Side of the Sun Belt." *Newsweek*, July 19, 1982, pp. 46-47.

Bruce, J.M. "Frostbelt vs. Sunbelt Sites: Avoiding Misconception." *Dun's Business Month*, November 1981, pp. 151-154.

Doan, M. "Cities Where Business Is Bouncing Back," *U.S. News & World Report*, November 8, 1982, pp. 72-75.

Dowd, M. "Tales of Ten Cities." *Time*, January 31, 1982, pp. 30-32.

Matthews, D. "The Future of the Sunbelt." *Society*, July/August 1982, pp. 63-65.

Morrison, A. "America's Changing Population: Demographic Trends.' *U.S.A. Today*, September 1981, pp. 20-24.

Serrin, N. "Collapse of our Industrial Heartland." *New York Times Magazine*, June 6, 1982, pp. 42-46.

Thompson, J.R. "Economic Reconstruction of the Midwest." *Vital Speeches*, October 1, 1981, pp. 741-745.

Weinstein, B.L., and Rees, J. "Reaganomics, Reindustrialization, and Regionalism." *Society*, July/August 1982, pp. 33-38.

Books

Dilger, Robert Jay. *The Sunbelt/Snowbelt Controversy: The War Over Federal Funds*. New York: New York University Press, 1982.

House, Peter Williams. *Modern Federalism: An Analytic Approach*. Lexington, Mass.: Lexington Books, 1982.

Martin, R.L., ed. *Regional Wage Inflation and Unemployment*. New York: Methuen, 1981.

Naisbitt, John. *Megatrends: Ten New Directions Transforming Our Lives*. New York: Warner Books, 1982.

Wheaton, William C., ed. *Interregional Movements and Regional Growth*. Washington, D.C.: The Urban Institute Press, 1979.

Widner, Ralph. "Regional Research and Regional Policy in the United States." *The Case of Regional Policy: A Report on an OECD Seminar*. Paris: Organization for Economic Cooperation and Development, 1982, pp. 83-89.

Government Publications

U.S. Department of Labor. Bureau of Labor Statistics. *Geographic Profile of Employment and Unemployment, 1980*. Washington, D.C.: Government Printing Office, 1981.

U.S. Congress. Joint. Economic Committee. *The Regional and Urban Impacts of the Administration's Budget and Tax Proposals. Committee Print, July 31, 1981*. Washington, D.C.: Government Printing Office, 1981.

INDEX

A

Agribusiness
    Export subsidies - 74-76, 87
    Food giveaways - 144-146
    Jobs - 67-68
    Plains states - 158, 192-193
    Surpluses - 68, 73-74
    Trade - 59, 67-76, 79, 82, 90-91
Aircraft industry - 186
Amidei, Nancy - 140-143, 145
Andrews, Mark, R-N.D. - 142
Appalachian economy - 173-174
Automation. *See* Robotics.
Automobile industry
    Domestic content bill - 58, 61, 111
    GM-Toyota joint production - 62
    Import competition - 59-61, 76
    1980 losses - 60, 179
    Recovery prospects - 10
    Robot use - 42-43

B

Baldrige, Malcolm - 81
Bentsen, Lloyd, D-Texas - 30, 54, 57
Block, John R. - 73-74, 90, 146
Boland, Edward P., D-Mass. - 104
Brock, William E. III - 57, 61, 62, 80-82
Brosseau, George - 40, 45, 52, 54
Byrd, Robert C., D-W.Va. - 57

C

California - 187-191
Carter, Jimmy - 66, 70, 71, 124, 126, 177

China. *See* People's Republic of China.
Civil Works Administration (CWA) - 116-117
Civilian Conservation Corps (CCC) - 115-116, 118 (box)
Clay, William, D-Mo. - 105
Community Renewal Employment Act - 104-105
Comprehensive Employment and Training Act (CETA) - 100, 105, 125-126, 133
Computer industry. (*See also* Robotics; Technological industries.)
    Data processing salaries - 41 (chart)
    Glossary - 33 (box)
    Industry history, advances - 29-35
    Jobs - 14-16
    Training - 16-18, 38-39
    Workplace changes - 20-21
Congress
    Agricultural surpluses - 73-74
    Exports - 72, 87-89
    Fishing rights - 167
    Foreign trade - 57-59, 83, 84
    IMF funding - 91
    Immigration - 112
    Japan, trade with - 76, 78
    Job programs - 14, 96-108
    Protectionism - 58-59, 61, 67, 92-93, 111
    Reciprocity - 80-81
    Science education - 18
    Social welfare - 135-138, 140, 142-144, 173
    Technology - 53-54
    Timber industry - 187
    Unemployment - 25, 95
Construction industry - 8-10
Conyers, John Jr., D-Mich. - 99
Corcoran, Tom, R-Ill. - 137

S

Science education - 16-18
Service industries - 24, 82
Shultz, George P. - 90, 91
Simpson, Alan K., R-Wyo. - 112
Snow Belt/Sun Belt - 160, 162, 171
Social welfare organizations - 131-133, 140, 144
Southern United States
  Economy - 168-174
  Rural poor - 173, 146
Southwest United States - 159-160
Stafford, Robert T., R-Vt. - 102
Steel industry, U.S.
  Import competition - 59, 62-67
  Labor costs - 63-65
  Losses - 65, 179
Steel industry, worldwide - 65-67
Stockman, David A. - 140, 143, 152-153
Structural unemployment - 10-12, 25, 96, 104-107
Sun Belt
  Economic growth - 157-160
  Homeless people - 138-139
  Snow Belt competition - 160, 162, 171

T

Technological industries. (*See also* Computer industry; Robotics.)
  Industry growth - 29-35, 86
  Japan - 36-39, 85-86
  Job changes - 12, 16, 20-21
  Regional economies - 162, 167-168, 170, 175, 178, 190
  Retraining workers - 13-14, 48, 54
  Science teaching - 16-18
Texas - 169, 170 (box)
Textile industry - 90, 165
Third World. *See* Less Developed Countries (LCDs).
Timber industry - 186-187
Transportation Act of 1982 - 97-99
Tsongas, Paul E., D-Mass. - 135

U

Unemployment. (*See also* Job programs, federal.)
  Automation - 30, 48-49, 53-54
  Current - 1-4, 9-10, 11 (chart), 109 (map)
  Foreign trade - 57, 60-64, 66, 84, 88, 91
  Minorities - 1, 103 (chart), 132-133
  Rate, calculation of - 5 (box)
  Recent history - 2, 3 (chart), 103 (chart)
  Regional - 158, 159 (chart), 166, 167, 171, 172, 185-187
  Structural unemployment - 10-12, 25, 96, 104-107
  Youth unemployment - 100-103, 107, 108
Unemployment, social effects
  Energy bills - 136-137 (box)
  Federal budget - 131-133, 143-147
  Foreclosures - 150-151 (box)
  Homelessness - 134-135, 138-139
  Hunger - 140-146
  Psychological impact - 129, 130, 132, 148
  Public health - 141, 147-149, 152-154
Union of Soviet Socialist Republics
  Siberian gas pipeline - 71 (box)
  U.S. trade - 70-73
United States. (*See also* Foreign trade, U.S.; specific regions.)
  Economy - 1-4, 24-26, 57-58, 77, 84
  Industrial policy - 86-87
  Labor force - 4, 6-8
  Population shifts - 157, 159, 171-172, 174-175, 185, 138-139
  Regional economies - 157-158, 161 (chart)

V

Vento, Bruce F., D-Minn. - 138
Video display terminals (VDT) - 20-21
Videocassette recorders, Japanese - 37 (box)